Conversations with Neil Simon

Literary Conversations Series
Monika Gehlawat
General Editor

D1603691

Conversations with
Neil Simon

Edited by Jackson R. Bryer and Ben Siegel

University Press of Mississippi / Jackson

The University Press of Mississippi is the scholarly publishing agency of
the Mississippi Institutions of Higher Learning: Alcorn State University,
Delta State University, Jackson State University, Mississippi State University,
Mississippi University for Women, Mississippi Valley State University,
University of Mississippi, and University of Southern Mississippi.

www.upress.state.ms.us

The University Press of Mississippi is a member
of the Association of University Presses.

First printing 2019
∞

Library of Congress Cataloging-in-Publication Data

Names: Simon, Neil, interviewee. | Bryer, Jackson R., editor. | Siegel,
   Ben, 1925–2010, editor.
Title: Conversations with Neil Simon / Edited by Jackson R. Bryer and Ben Siegel.
Other titles: Literary conversations series.
Description: Jackson : University Press of Mississippi, 2019. | Series:
   Literary conversations series | Includes index.
Identifiers: LCCN 2019035615 (print) | LCCN 2019035616 (ebook) | ISBN
   9781496822895 (hardback) | ISBN 9781496822901 (paperback) | ISBN
   9781496822918 (epub) | ISBN 9781496822925 (epub) | ISBN 9781496822932
   (pdf) | ISBN 9781496822949 (pdf)
Subjects: LCSH: Simon, Neil—Interviews. | Dramatists,
   American—Interviews.
Classification: LCC PS3537.I663 Z46 2019 (print) | LCC PS3537.I663
   (ebook) | DDC 812/.54—dc23
LC record available at https://lccn.loc.gov/2019035615
LC ebook record available at https://lccn.loc.gov/2019035616

British Library Cataloging-in-Publication Data available

Books by Neil Simon

Come Blow Your Horn. Garden City, NY: Doubleday, 1963.

Barefoot in the Park. New York: Random House, 1964.

The Odd Couple. New York: Random House, 1964.

Sweet Charity. Book by Neil Simon. Music by Cy Coleman. Words by Dorothy Fields. New York: Random House, 1966.

The Star-Spangled Girl. New York: Random House, 1967.

Plaza Suite. New York: Random House, 1969.

Promises, Promises. Book by Neil Simon. Music by Burt Bacharach. Lyrics by Hal David. New York: Random House, 1969.

Last of the Red-Hot Lovers. New York: Random House, 1970.

The Comedy of Neil Simon [*Come Blow Your Horn*; *Barefoot in the Park*; *The Odd Couple*; *Plaza Suite*; *The Star-Spangled Girl*; *Promises, Promises*; *Last of the Red-Hot Lovers*]. New York: Random House, 1971.

The Gingerbread Lady. New York: Random House, 1971.

The Prisoner of Second Avenue. New York: Random House, 1972.

The Sunshine Boys. New York: Random House, 1973.

The Good Doctor. New York: Random House, 1974.

God's Favorite. New York: Random House, 1975.

California Suite. New York: Random House, 1979.

Chapter Two. New York: Random House, 1979.

The Collected Plays of Neil Simon: Volume II [*Little Me*; *The Gingerbread Lady*; *The Prisoner of Second Avenue*; *The Sunshine Boys*; *The God Doctor*; *God's Favorite*; *California Suite*; *Chapter Two*]. New York: Random House, 1979.

They're Playing Our Song. Book by Neil Simon. Music by Marvin Hamlisch. Lyrics by Carol Bayer Sager. New York: Random House, 1980.

"I Ought to Be in Pictures." New York: Random House, 1981.

Fools. New York: Random House, 1981.

Brighton Beach Memoirs. New York: Random House, 1981.

The Odd Couple (Female Version). New York: Samuel French, 1986.

Biloxi Blues. New York: Random House, 1986.

Broadway Bound. New York: Random House, 1987.

"Rumors." New York: Random House, 1990.

Lost in Yonkers. New York: Random House, 1991.

The Collected Plays of Neil Simon: Volume III [*Sweet Charity*; *They're Playing Our Song*; *"I Ought to Be in Pictures"*; *Fools*; *The Odd Couple (Female Version)*; *Brighton Beach Memoirs*; *Biloxi Blues*; *Broadway Bound*]. New York: Random House, 1991.

Jake's Women. New York: Random House, 1994.

Laughter on the 23rd Floor. New York: Random House, 1995.

Three from the Stage [*Lost in Yonkers*; *Jake's Women*; *Laughter on the 23rd Floor*]. Franklin Center, PA: Franklin Library, 1995.

Neil Simon Monologues: Speeches from the Works of America's Foremost Playwright. Edited by Roger Karshner. Rancho Mirage, CA: Dramaline, 1996.

London Suite. New York: Samuel French, 1996.

Rewrites: A Memoir. New York: Simon & Schuster, 1996.

The Collected Plays of Neil Simon: Volume IV [*"Rumors"*; *Lost in Yonkers*; *Jake's Women*; *Laughter on the 23rd Floor*; *London Suite*]. New York: Touchstone/Simon & Schuster, 1998.

Proposals. Garden City, NY: Stage & Screen, 1998; New York: Samuel French, 1998.

The Play Goes On: A Memoir. New York: Simon & Schuster, 1999.

The Odd Couple I and II: The Original Screenplays. New York: Touchstone/Simon & Schuster, 2000.

Neil Simon Scenes: Scenes from the Works of America's Foremost Playwright. Edited by Roger Karshner. Rancho Mirage, CA: Dramaline, 2000.

The Dinner Party. Garden City, NY: Stage & Screen, 2001; New York: Samuel French, 2002.

43 Seconds from Broadway. New York: Stage & Screen, 2001; New York: Samuel French, 2001.

Oscar and Felix: A New Look at "The Odd Couple." New York: Samuel French, 2004.

Rose's Dilemma. New York: Samuel French, 2004.

Neil Simon's Musical "Fools." Book and lyrics by Neil Simon. Music & lyrics by Phil Swann and Ron West. Adapted from the play *Fools* by Neil Simon. New York: Samuel French, 2016.

Contents

Introduction   ix

Chronology   xix

On the Square: Simon Says . . .   3
   Frank Gagnard / 1966

Life for Simon—Not That Simple   6
   Joan Barthel / 1968

An Interview with Neil Simon   11
   Glenn Loney / 1969

Neil Simon, Good Humor Man   22
   Gerald Nachman / 1972

Simon Says   25
   Al Morgan / 1972

"Success Has Something to Do with Recognition," Simon Says   30
   Richard L. Coe / 1972

Neil Simon: Broadway's King Moves to Hollywood   34
   David Sterritt / 1976

A Conversation with . . . : Neil Simon Unclenches Fist   40
   Jack Slater / 1977

Make 'Em Laugh   45
   Clive Hirschhorn / 1977

Dialogue on Film: Neil Simon 55
  James Powers / 1977

Simon Says: Gray Days of the Sunshine Playwright 80
  David Richards / 1983

Neil Simon 86
  J. Wynn Rousuck / 1984

Neil Simon: In Conversation with Terrence McNally 93
  Terrence McNally / 1985

Simon Says: A Conversation with Playwright Neil Simon 108
  David Kaufman / 1985

Neil Simon 118
  Jackson R. Bryer / 1991

The Art of Theater X: Neil Simon 141
  James Lipton / 1992

A Life in the Theater 172
  Peter Marks / 1992

Neil Simon 178
  Jackson R. Bryer / 1992

Interview with Neil Simon 198
  Mike Wood / 1997

The Unlikely Couple 226
  Sean Mitchell / 1997

In Conversation with . . . Neil Simon 233
  Joel Hirschhorn / 2003

Neil Simon Keeps On Writing 242
  John Nathan / 2010

Index 247

Introduction

The career of Marvin Neil Simon is filled with paradoxes and ironies. Virtually any article about him will begin with the assertion that he is the most commercially successful playwright in the history of the American theater, or, as J. Wynn Rousuck put it in 1984, "the most successful playwright in the history of, well, history." In December 1996, when his new play *The Star-Spangled Girl* opened, he had four Broadway productions running simultaneously—besides the new play, there were *Barefoot in the Park*, *The Odd Couple*, and *Sweet Charity*, a musical for which he had written the book. On three other occasions, he had three productions running simultaneously on Broadway. By actual count, in the forty-two years between 1961, when his first Broadway play, *Come Blow Your Horn*, opened and 2003, when his last play to open in New York, *Rose's Dilemma*, began its run at Stage 1 of the City Center, he had twenty-eight plays and five musicals produced in New York. Two other plays, *Actors and Actresses* (1983) and *Oscar and Felix: A New Look at "The Odd Couple"* (2002), opened elsewhere and never reached New York. Thirteen of those plays and three of the musicals had runs of more than five hundred performances and three plays and one musical ran for more than a thousand performances. Simon is perhaps even more widely known for his screenplays, some adapted from his plays and others not. Again, the numbers are impressive: he is credited with nine original screenplays for which he is the only writer, two original screenplays which he cowrote, and fourteen screenplays adapted from his plays.

Despite this productivity and the consequent exposure, his work has been undervalued or, in some cases, openly scorned by "serious" drama critics and literary scholars. While several times nominated, he has never received a major award for his movie work; and it was not until 1985 that he won a Tony Award for a play (*Biloxi Blues*; he did win a Tony Award as Best Author of a Play for *The Odd Couple* in 1965 and a special Tony Award for Overall Achievement in 1975). Indicative of the more positive critical reception of his later plays, in 1991 *Lost in Yonkers* received both the Pulitzer Prize for Drama and the Tony Award for Best Play. James Powers accurately summed up Simon's uneven critical fortunes when he observed in the introduction to a 1977 interview, "Sometimes, they complain, a theatergoer can't see the characters for the one-liners in a Simon play. Anyway, they finally ask, why does Simon go on manufacturing skillful fluff when he could be doing something more serious—still funny but more deeply felt?" David Kaufman observed in 1985 that "The critics treated Simon as a contemporary Salieri in the midst of numerous potential Mozarts."

Simon himself, as the interviews collected in this book make clear, was, from early in his career, very aware of the difficulties of being taken seriously when writing plays that are undeniably comic. He acknowledged to Glenn Loney in 1969 that his first two plays, *Come Blow Your Horn* and *Barefoot in the Park*, were not "really serious plays"—they were "plays I had to go through in order to go on to other things"—but his third play, *The Odd Couple*, he described as "basically a serious play." He said much the same about *The Odd Couple* to Joan Barthel in 1968, noting that "the people involved were going through terrible emotional problems, and Felix was really a very sad person—but the situation was so highly comic that the seriousness was overlooked," and to James Lipton in 1992: "I thought it was a grim, dark play about two lonely men."

From early in his career, Simon unapologetically responded to the implication that because he wrote comedies, he was not writing "serious" plays, contending to Loney, "I think any comment that you make about the way people live can be serious" and telling Jackson R. Bryer in 1992 that "I'm always looking for a comic idea that has a dramatic subtext to it. If it's just funny, I'm not really interested." He also offered explanations as to why critics and audiences had difficulty getting beyond the comic surfaces of his plays, frequently citing Lillian Hellman's admonition that a playwright should "never try to mix comedy with drama" because "the critics will never buy it"; he told Terrence McNally in 1985 that her comment had "been a great gripe of mine for years": "Since life is neither all comedy nor all tragedy, why can't it be that way in plays?" That same year, he observed to David Kaufman: "I think the subject matter of many of the plays has been quite serious, and the handling of them was not completely serious. And the problem I was having with the critics was that they don't like you to mix the two." In 1972, he told Richard L. Coe that his idea of "the perfect two-hour play" would be one in which "for 119 minutes the audience would be hysterical with laughter but for the last minute so moved that they leave the theater in a daze."

Like so many writers, Simon has drawn heavily on his own life—his family, his marriages, his professional experiences—although, again like most writers, he stubbornly denies that his writing is autobiographical. "You use people and use your mind like a sieve—and pour people through it. You use characteristics of everyone," he explained to Glenn Loney. "When I say 'autobiographical,'" he protested to J. Wynn Rousuck, "people assume right away that everything in it was true. It isn't. You just use [your life experience] as a stepping stone to a play you wanted to write." Nonetheless, his first play, *Come Blow Your Horn*, was clearly based on his own family; and his second play, *Barefoot in the Park*, was a depiction of the early years of his first marriage. Later plays continued to deal with important moments in his life—*Chapter Two* with the premature death of his first wife and meeting his second wife; *Laughter on the 23rd Floor* with his time as a writer for Sid Caesar; and most prominently, the "BB Trilogy" (*Brighton Beach Memoirs*, *Biloxi Blues*, and *Broadway Bound*), in which he returned to his formative years in a more nuanced and less completely comic tone than in the early plays. He did concede to Joel Hirschhorn in 2003 that "my plays . . . were diaries for me." And he acknowledged to James Lipton in 1992, "Writing plays is a way of working out your life" and that "my greatest weakness is that I can't write outside of my own experience."

In these interviews, Neil Simon talks frequently and candidly about his childhood, and about how his parents' on-again, off-again marriage (they "broke up six or seven times, and they were pretty lengthy stay-aways," as he described it to Mike Wood in 1997) drove him to isolate himself: "I became very protective, very defensive, very insulated," he told Jack Slater in 1977. He sought refuge in books (humorists Stephen Leacock, George S. Kaufman, and Robert Benchley and Mark Twain were his favorites) that he took out of the library every week because, he explained to Wood, "we literally didn't have a book in our house." The movies were his other escape: at the age of "maybe eight," he told J. Wynn Rousuck, watching a Charlie Chaplin film outdoors in a chair he "laughed so hard I went right over in the chair, hit my head and I was unconscious and they took me to the hospital," and when he was about the same age, he described to Joan Barthel how he went to see Chaplin's *Modern Times* "at Loew's 175th Street and [was] laughing so uncontrollably that the usherette made me leave." Humphrey Bogart was his hero in movies, he told Slater, "because of his independence from everybody. Which was what I felt. That nobody was ever going to get close to me. I had been hurt enough."

Through those difficult early years it was his mother who, as he commented to David Richards in 1983, "stood by me and I knew that whatever I did, it was wonderful with her." While he was "always very upset and angry" when his father left home, "when he would come back," Simon confided to Rousuck, "I loved being with him." His older brother Danny served as his role model and early writing partner; he described their relationship to Richards: "I was fourteen, and maybe once in a while, I'd say something amusing around the house. But he picked up on it. He noticed. . . . He paved the way for my entire career. . . . Although I did most of the writing, Danny was the spokesman. He got us through doors, negotiated things, kept the team going, and gave me encouragement and energy." Together they began to write comedy sketches for comedians when Neil was still in high school.

After he graduated from high school and served briefly in the Air Force at the end of World War II, he returned to New York and entered show business in a very conventional way—through the mailroom. Danny was already working in the Warner Bros. publicity department; so when his brother got out of the service, Danny got him a job there as a messenger. This opportunity led to one of their friends sending them to legendary radio funnyman Goodman Ace, who hired them on the basis of a few sentences; and, suddenly, the Simon Brothers were radio writers, Neil at nineteen, Danny at twenty-eight. Eventually, after splitting from Danny, he moved into television, working with, among others, Garry Moore, Jerry Lester, Jackie Gleason, Red Buttons, Phil Silvers, and, most importantly, Sid Caesar on *Your Show of Shows* and *Caesar's Hour*. On *Your Show of Shows*, he was one of a fabled group of writers that included Mel Brooks, Woody Allen, Larry Gelbart, Michael Stewart, Carl Reiner, and Caesar himself. That experience, he explained to Terrence McNally, taught him "to work under pressure," as well as to produce first-rate comic material while, as he told James Powers, "working with people who were very experienced . . . I learned over those years to collaborate." "Having had the opportunity of writing and—week after week—having it performed in front of audiences was invaluable to my work later on," he told Glenn Loney.

Interviewers were often surprised that, in person, Simon was modest, soft-spoken, and unassuming. Joan Barthel found him "amiable rather than jovial, elusively wistful," "even, perhaps, shy"; Jack Slater described him as "a mild-mannered, introspective man . . . sometimes tortured, sometimes nostalgic"; J. Wynn Rousuck observed him to be "reflective, candid, wise—but not a wise guy," and James Lipton focused on "two indelible Simon trademarks: the eyes of an insatiably curious and slightly guarded child, shielded by horn-rimmed glasses, and a faint, constant, enigmatic smile." Interviewers also found him not unwilling to change his attitudes over the years. In early interviews he spoke of why he preferred writing for the stage to writing for television or film, explaining to Al Morgan in 1972 that censorship—"there are certain kinds of words, connotations that sponsors and networks feel hesitant about," because the shows are reaching "twenty or thirty million people . . . and you don't want to offend anybody"—is one of the problems that "drove [him] out of television in the first place." Similarly, he found writing for the stage preferable to screenwriting, because, he explained to Glenn Loney in 1969, "I like the restrictions of theater, because I am more able to concentrate on the characters. I believe in the written word much more than in the visual picture." But after moving from New York to Los Angeles in the mid-1970s, at least partially to be nearer his movie projects, and as he became more experienced at writing films, Simon seemed to change his view, telling David Sterritt in 1976 that he had tired of the "production" part of playwriting and of the same "provincial audience" that showed up every night on Broadway, and that, with films, "because of subject matter and ticket prices," he would be able to write for "a younger crowd" and "a more diverse audience. . . . Describing something that will be visually effective is just as important as writing a terrific line of dialogue." "One of the reasons I'm beginning to like films a little bit more than the theater," he explained to James Powers in 1978, "is that I am less conscious of writing for an audience when I'm writing a film. . . . You cannot perform [a play] without the audience, whereas you can do a film for one person. In a film there are fewer lines directed toward getting a laugh; I find that the dialogue flows more easily than it does in a play. . . . In a film, there's an enormous laugh and the film goes on. In a play, there's an enormous laugh and the actors wait." But by 1991, speaking with Jackson R. Bryer, he again had become more negative about screenwriting, admitting that "I do the films, but I'm not really very happy with them," because the ultimate decisions as to what goes on the screen is the director's rather than the writer's.

Of course, despite his mid-career interest in film, Neil Simon never did abandon the stage; and one reason may be that, as he matured, he began to focus less on "lines directed toward getting a laugh" and more on what he described to David Kaufman as digging "into the truth of the matter." Many of the later interviews here deal with that shift and with the consequent more positive response he received from critics. He admitted to Kaufman that "suddenly everything reversed with" *Brighton Beach Memoirs* and *Biloxi Blues* and that, with those plays, "I've been to that place where I wanted to get to in my search to be a better playwright." But, virtually from the beginning of his career, as these interviews make clear, Simon was restless and questioning his own success. In 1968, having had five plays and two musicals on Broadway in seven years, he confessed to Joan Barthel, "I have much less fun than I used to." He found life in the 1960s "frightening. I live in great anxiety. I'm afraid to read the newspapers or watch television; the bad news is becoming more and more frequent. Comedy writing to me is a defense mechanism; I can't bear to see life as gloomy as it really is. I approach plays and life by laughing at the insanity of it all."

As noted earlier, he felt that critics had overlooked the serious subtext of his most popular play to date, *The Odd Couple*, and, as a result, he told Barthel, he no longer found it satisfying "just to write funny any more," adding "I couldn't write *Barefoot in the Park* again; I can't go back and write a domestic comedy where there is very little at stake." At that relatively early point, he made a very prescient prediction: "I will never become a serious writer and write only serious plays, but I hope that in all the comedies I write there will be a serious theme underneath." One year later, speaking with Glenn Loney, Simon sounded much the same theme, telling him that, like Chekhov, he was "just trying to show people how absurdly they live their lives," but, he added, "I don't do it just to evoke a laugh from an audience. I do it also to show them how absurdly we *all* live our lives." He stressed that "I don't know what the answers are"; at best, a writer "can only present the problems and make people aware," but once the writer starts "choosing sides and putting down the answers to things" he is invariably wrong. By 1977, he was admitting to Clive Hirschhorn, "I no longer laugh at the lines that emerge from my typewriter. The prerequisite for me is that the line must be able to express an old thought with a certain freshness and be seen from a different point of view."

Later, when critics began to see changes in his plays, Simon accounted for those changes in ways that demonstrated his ability acutely and forthrightly to examine his own work. He emphasized that in *Brighton Beach Memoirs* he produced what, to David Kaufman, he called his "first fullbodied play" in that he dealt "with a group of people as individuals and telling all their stories" whereas his earlier plays "had focused, more or less, on two main characters" and the "peripheral people in their lives were more shadowy figures." In *Brighton Beach Memoirs*, "I tried to treat each character as a three-dimensional character that one could possibly write a full play about," he told Terrence McNally. He wrote the first thirty-five pages of *Brighton Beach Memoirs* and then put it away for nine years before returning to it and finishing it in six weeks. "Obviously," he told James Lipton, "what had happened in the ensuing years in my life made clear to me what it should be about. Somewhere in the back of my head I grew up, I matured." He wanted the audience, he told J. Wynn Rousuck, "to remember and to be touched, or to wish for a time like that to be in our lives again, that closeness of a family, where we all can lean on each other and help each other." His next play, *Biloxi Blues*, he told Kaufman, "went even further because I took people who didn't even know each other, so their lives were not yet intertwined by anything except their entering the army." He also acknowledged a deepening of the subject matter in these plays, specifically for the first time dealing with his characters as overtly Jewish in the "BB Trilogy." He had, as he said to Kaufman, "dealt with characters who were Jewish but never specifically called them Jewish"—in *Come Blow Your Horn* and *The Sunshine Boys*—because "their religion or faith had nothing to do, as far as I was concerned, with what was going on in their lives." But in *Brighton Beach Memoirs*, the mother "talking about the Irish across the street and looking down on them" was "one of the things I learned about growing up in New York City—that each ethnic group is always looking down on the other so that they can keep their heads above the water." In *Biloxi Blues*, both anti-Semitism and homophobia became subjects of the play, because "there was a war, a smaller war, going on within the circle of the men even before they went off to fight the big war." What he "began to recognize" with these two plays, he explained to Kaufman, was that "if I'm going to write plays, then I've got to deal with the characters as absolutely truthfully as I possibly can."

This change only intensified and deepened with two of the next three plays he wrote, *Broadway Bound* and *Lost in Yonkers*. Simon acknowledged to Jackson R. Bryer in 1991, "I would not have written *Broadway Bound* if my parents had been alive. I couldn't have put them up on the stage that way." He explained, "I reveal things about [my mother], her inability to be close and emotional," adding, it "was an attempt to try to understand my family and my own origins. It's a play of forgiveness." As he remarked to James Lipton, "I didn't pull any punches with that one." In *Lost in Yonkers*, he told Bryer, "I've written about much darker people than I ever have before. I've written about normal people in dark situations before . . . but in this play I really wrote about dysfunctional people. . . . That's much further than I've gone in any other play, so it's deeper." "I have a feeling," he admitted to Lipton, "that in *Lost in Yonkers* there was a theme within me that was crying to get out, a common denominator that got to everybody," the notion of a dysfunctional family. Simon realized that his parents' "constant breakups" were "like coming from *five* broken families" and "that pain lingers."

Simon is refreshingly open about acknowledging his public failures and his private insecurities. He frequently calls *The Star-Spangled Girl* his least favorite among his plays, despite the fact that it ran for a respectable 206 performances: "I got no fun out of it," he told Joan Barthel; "I hated writing it," he told Clive Hirschhorn; "The typewriter keys all felt as if they were ten pounds each," he told James Powers. He is equally harsh in assessing *The Gingerbread Lady*—"I've come to the conclusion that the situation just wasn't right, that this woman couldn't have been that kind of woman whose background I'd imagined," he acknowledged to Richard L. Coe—and in admitting to several interviewers that he erred by not producing *The Good Doctor*, *God's Favorite*, and *Fools* off-Broadway. He is similarly frank about the limitations he has felt working on musicals, telling Joan Barthel in 1968, when he had already written the books for *Little Me* (1962), *Sweet Charity* (1966), and *Promises, Promises* (1968), "There's no gratification for a playwright in doing a musical book. All the emotional peaks are sung not spoken, so you mostly write lead-ins for songs," and observing to Coe in 1972, "Musicals should have several sets of characters and these, in the time permitted, allow only the most superficial character sketching."

He is also candid about the effect success has had on him personally, both negatively and positively, telling Coe that "the essential thing about all the money the plays have made is that it liberates me from worrying about money. It means I can work on my plays," but acknowledging to Jack Slater that success "isolates you and it affects people around you—your family and friends. They begin to view you differently, as though you were some sort of extraordinary person. You have been to a place they haven't seen, a place they don't know at all." Despite all his success, Simon frequently confesses his own personal insecurities to interviewers, confiding to James Powers that "every time I start a new project I don't know how to do it," to J. Wynn Rousuck, "I think at some point we all think that we're frauds and we're getting away with something," and to Jackson R. Bryer that writing a play is "jumping into this big swimming pool and hoping there's going to be water when you hit."

While these interviews contain much information and many entertaining anecdotes about productions of Simon's plays and about the actors and directors he worked with, they also reveal him to be someone who has thought long and hard about all aspects of writing for the stage and film and about dealing with serious subjects in a humorous fashion. Above all, they reveal a multifaceted human being, willing to deal with and speak about all aspects of his life and work, the difficult and painful as well as the happiest and most rewarding. In many ways, they stand as eloquent rejoinders to the critics who dismiss him and his work as not worthy of attention. In so doing, they compel us to take Neil Simon seriously. As this book went to press, Neil Simon died of complications from pneumonia after a long period of poor health that kept him from public notice for many years; this accounts for the fact that the last interview in the book dates from 2010.

Following the conventions of the Literary Conversations Series, we have, in all but instances where editing has been acknowledged, reprinted the interviews uncut and, wherever possible, arranged them chronologically by the date the interview was conducted rather than by its publication date. We have silently corrected typographical errors, regularized all titles into italics, in Clive Hirschhorn's and John Nathan's interviews converted British spellings to American spellings, and have made other editing changes for consistency.

Finally, a word about Ben Siegel, who died before we could bring this book into print. We conceived of this book together and chose the selections jointly. He wrote a draft of this introduction, which I have altered somewhat but relied on a great deal. Although this was not our intention originally, I offer *Conversations with Neil Simon* as a tribute to Ben, a good friend and a gifted teacher/scholar. For significant assistance, as well as the interviewers and editors who gave us permission to reprint interviews, we wish to thank Mary C. Hartig, Susanna Compton, and Gerard Holmes and Walter Biggins and Seetha Srinivasan, formerly of the University Press of Mississippi, who encouraged this project at its outset, and Mary Heath and Katie Keene, presently of the University Press of Mississippi, who patiently and helpfully brought it to completion.

JRB

Chronology

1927   July 4: Born Marvin Neil Simon in the Bronx, New York City, the second of two male children (brother Danny born December 18, 1918) of Irving Simon, a garment salesman, and Mamie Simon, early in his life, given the nickname "Doc" for his habit of imitating the family doctor.

1942   Writes three comedy sketches with Danny for the annual employees show of Abraham & Straus department store in Brooklyn, where Danny works as assistant manager of the clothing department.

1943–46 Graduates from DeWitt Clinton High School in the Bronx. Enters Army Air Force Reserve training program at New York University; is sent first to Biloxi, Mississippi, and in August 1945, is assigned to Lowry Field in Denver, Colorado, where he is sports editor of base newspaper, the *Rev-Meter*, and takes classes at the University of Denver.

1946   After discharge from the Air Force, works as mailroom clerk for Warner Bros. in New York City; hired with Danny by Goodman Ace to write for radio.

1948–56 With Danny, writes for radio and television shows starring, among others, Robert Q. Lewis, Phil Silvers, and Tallulah Bankhead. In the summer of 1952, while working writing comedy sketches with Danny at Camp Tamiment in the Pocono Mountains of Pennsylvania, meets dancer Joan Baim, a counselor at the nearby children's camp. In September 1953, marries Joan Baim. Soon thereafter, ends his writing partnership with Danny. Writes sketches for Broadway shows *Catch a Star!* in 1955 and for *New Faces of 1956*.

1956–59 Writes for *Your Show of Shows* starring Sid Caesar and Imogene Coca, for *Caesar's Hour*, and for Phil Silvers, Garry Moore, and Jerry Lewis. In 1954, is nominated twice for Emmy Awards for *Caesar's Hour*.

1957	April 25: Daughter Ellen Marie born.
1961	February 22: *Come Blow Your Horn*, Neil Simon's first Broadway play, opens at the Brooks Atkinson Theatre and runs for 677 performances.
1962	November 17: *Little Me*, musical with book by Neil Simon, music by Cy Coleman, and lyrics by Carolyn Leigh, opens at the Lunt-Fontanne Theatre and runs for 257 performances; December 25: daughter Nancy Elizabeth born.
1963	October 23: *Barefoot in the Park* opens at the Biltmore Theatre and runs for 1530 performances.
1965	March 10: *The Odd Couple* opens at the Plymouth Theatre and runs for 964 performances: receives Tony Award for Author of a Play for *The Odd Couple*.
1966	January 29: *Sweet Charity*, musical with book by Neil Simon, music by Cy Coleman, and lyrics by Dorothy Field, opens at the Palace Theatre and runs for 608 performances; cowrites screenplay for *After the Fox*; December 21: *The Star-Spangled Girl* opens at the Plymouth Theatre and runs for 261 performances.
1967	Writes screenplay for *Barefoot in the Park*; receives London Evening Standard Award.
1968	February 14: *Plaza Suite* opens at the Plymouth Theatre and runs for 1097 performances; writes screenplay for *The Odd Couple* (Academy Award nomination); receives Sam S. Shubert Award; December 1: *Promises, Promises*, musical with book by Neil Simon, music by Burt Bacharach, and lyrics by Hal David, opens at the Shubert Theatre and runs for 1281 performances.
1969	December 28: *Last of the Red Hot Lovers* opens at the Eugene O'Neill Theatre and runs for 706 performances.
1970	Writes screenplay for *The Out-of-Towners* (Writers Guild Award); December 13: *The Gingerbread Lady* opens at the Plymouth Theatre and runs for 193 performances.
1971	Writes screenplays for *Plaza Suite* and *The Star-Spangled Girl*; November 11: *The Prisoner of Second Avenue* opens at the Eugene O'Neill Theatre and runs for 780 performances.
1972	Writes screenplays for *Last of the Red Hot Lovers* (Writers Guild Award) and *The Heartbreak Kid*; receives Entertainer of Year Award from *Cue*; December 20: *The Sunshine Boys* opens at the Broadhurst Theatre and runs for 538 performances.

1973   July 11: Joan Baim Simon dies; October 25: marries actress Marsha Mason.

1974   November 27: *The Good Doctor* opens at the Eugene O'Neill Theatre and runs for 208 performances.

1975   Writes screenplays for *The Sunshine Boys* (Academy Award nomination) and *The Prisoner of Second Avenue* (Writers Guild Award); receives special Tony Award for overall contribution to the theater; December 11: *God's Favorite* opens at the Eugene O'Neill Theatre and runs for 119 performances.

1976   Writes screenplay for *Murder by Death*; writes teleplay for *A Quiet War*; April 23: *California Suite* opens at the Ahmanson Theatre, Los Angeles, and runs for 51 performances; June 30: opens at the Eugene O'Neill Theatre and runs for 445 performances.

1977   Writes screenplay for *The Goodbye Girl* (Golden Globe Award, Academy Award nomination); October 7: *Chapter Two* opens at the Ahmanson Theatre, Los Angeles, and closes on November 7; December 4: opens at the Imperial Theatre and runs for 857 performances.

1978   Writes screenplays for *The Cheap Detective* and *California Suite* (Academy Award nomination).

1979   February 11: *They're Playing Our Song*, musical with book by Neil Simon, music by Marvin Hamlisch, and lyrics by Carole Bayer Sager, opens at the Imperial Theatre and runs for 1082 performances; writes screenplay for *Chapter Two*; receives Laurel Award from the Writers Guild of America.

1980   April 3: *"I Ought to Be in the Pictures"* opens at the Eugene O'Neill Theatre and runs for 324 performances; writes screenplay for *Seems Like Old Times*.

1981   April 6: *Fools* opens at the Eugene O'Neill Theatre and runs for 40 performances; cowrites (with Danny Simon) screenplay for *Only When I Laugh*; receives honorary doctorate degree from Hofstra University.

1982   January 21: *Little Me* (revised version), musical with book by Neil Simon, music by Cy Coleman, and lyrics by Carolyn Leigh, opens at the Eugene O'Neill Theatre and runs for 36 performances; writes screenplay for *"I Ought to Be in the Pictures"*; receives PEN Los Angeles Center Award.

1983	*Actors and Actresses* opens in Hartford, Connecticut, but never gets to New York; March 27: *Brighton Beach Memoirs* opens at the Alvin Theatre and runs for 1299 performances; *Brighton Beach Memoirs* receives Drama Critics Circle and Outer Critics Circle Awards; writes screenplay for *Max Dugan Returns*; June 23: Alvin Theatre renamed the Neil Simon Theatre; July 7: divorces Marsha Mason; inducted into the American Theater Hall of Fame.
1984	Cowrites screenplay for *The Lonely Guy*; receives honorary doctorate degree from Williams College.
1985	March 28: *Biloxi Blues* opens at the Neil Simon Theatre and runs for 524 performances; *Biloxi Blues* receives Tony Award and Outer Critics Circle Award; June 11: *The Odd Couple (Female Version)* opens at the Broadhurst Theatre and runs for 295 performances; writes screenplay for *The Slugger's Wife*.
1986	Receives New York State Governor's Award; December 4: *Broadway Bound* opens at the Broadhurst Theatre and runs for 756 performances.
1987	January 13: marries Diane Lander; writes screenplay for *Brighton Beach Memoirs*.
1988	July: divorces Diane Lander; writes screenplay for *Biloxi Blues*; November 17: *"Rumors"* opens at the Broadhurst Theatre and runs for 535 performances.
1989	Receives Lifetime Creative Achievement Award at the American Comedy Awards.
1990	February 10: remarries Diane Lander; adopts Lander's daughter Bryn; writes screenplay for *The Marrying Man*.
1991	February 21: *Lost in Yonkers* opens at the Richard Rodgers Theatre and runs for 780 performances; *Lost in Yonkers* wins the Pulitzer Prize and the Tony Award.
1992	March 24: *Jake's Women* opens at the Neil Simon Theatre and runs for 245 performances.
1993	March 4: *The Goodbye Girl*, musical with book by Neil Simon, music by Marvin Hamlisch, and lyrics by David Zippel, opens at the Marquis Theatre and runs for 188 performances; writes the screenplay for *Lost in Yonkers*; November 22: *Laughter on the 23rd Floor* opens at the Richard Rodgers Theatre and runs for 320 performances.

1995   March 28: *London Suite* opens Off-Broadway at the Union Square Theatre and runs for 169 performances; receives the Kennedy Center Honors.

1996   Receives the Peggy V. Helmerich Distinguished Author Award from the Tulsa Library; publishes *Rewrites*, memoir that ends with death of his first wife.

1997   Receives the William Inge Award for Achievement in the American Theater at the William Inge Theater Festival in Independence, Kansas; November 6: *Proposals* opens at the Broadhurst Theatre and runs for 77 performances.

1998   April 22: divorces Diane Lander; writes the screenplay for *The Odd Couple II.*

1999   Publishes *The Rest of the Story*, memoir that picks up where *Rewrites* ends; September: marries actress Elaine Joyce.

2000   October 19: *The Dinner Party* opens at the Music Box Theatre and runs for 364 performances.

2001   November 11: *45 Seconds from Broadway* opens at the Richard Rodgers Theatre and runs for 73 performances.

2002   June 19: *Oscar and Felix: A New Look at "The Odd Couple"* opens at the Geffen Playhouse in Los Angeles and runs until July 27.

2003   December 18: *Rose's Dilemma* opens at New York City Center Stage I after earlier in the year opening at the Geffen Playhouse in Los Angeles on February 5 under the title *Rose and Walsh*; it closes in New York on February 1, 2004.

2004   March 2: Undergoes kidney transplant, receiving kidney from his longtime friend and publicist Bill Evans.

2005   July 26: Danny Simon dies in Portland, Oregon.

2006   October 15: receives the Mark Twain Prize for American Humor at the Kennedy Center in Washington, DC.

2018   August 26: Dies from complications of pneumonia after many years of poor health.

Conversations with Neil Simon

On the Square: Simon Says . . .

Frank Gagnard / 1966

From the *New Orleans Times-Picayune*, October 23, 1966, sec. 2, p. 12. © 2017 The Times-Picayune Publishing Co. All rights reserved. Reprinted with permission of The Times-Picayune.

If Neil Simon could not write successful stage comedies, he might be a teacher. Or a director. Or a drama critic. But he can and does, and below he writes about writing. The Simon System of playwrighting has produced some of the most profitable shows in Broadway history. One example is *The Odd Couple* which the author mentions below, quite naturally since *The Odd Couple* will play at the Civic Theater November 7–12, its cast headed by Lyle Talbot and Harvey Stone.

Simon's scripts also are the funniest of the day, perhaps the brightest inventions since those laugh machines that George S. Kaufman had a hand in. Simon has no serious challenger today. The closest competition, in mirth and material success, significantly comes from the current revivals of the late Mr. Kaufman's collaborations. In the statements prepared for this newspaper, Neil Simon does not give advice. He tells something about his method, and therefore may be instructive. He is almost as entertaining as an evening with Neil Simon in the theater.

The idea of a prescription for comedy is obviously ridiculous. What works for one playwright rarely works for another, and even the fact that a certain approach succeeded for a writer before does not mean that it will surely produce an amusing play for the same scribe a second time.

The knowledge of this grisly reality gives me a healthy insecurity, which I consider a great asset. Insecurity encourages a writer to criticism by competent professionals; it allows him to face up to the need to revise or rewrite.

Of course, everybody cheerily tells a playwright how to repair his script and it takes cool courage and wondrous manners to endure the amateurs' well-meant advice.

In Boston during the tryout of *The Odd Couple*, I had been up till four o'clock in the morning rewriting the third act—for the fifth time. Exhausted, I finally fell asleep on my typewriter. At 7:00 a.m. a dentist from suburban Salem phoned to tell me he would fix the third act. I thanked him and promised myself I would call him at five the next morning to tell him how I would fix his bridgework.

I happen to like rewriting, a good deal of which is often necessary after one sees how a scene actually plays on stage in rehearsal or tryout. Each chance to fix, polish, and tighten is a glorious reprieve—something I never had in the urgent world of television.

I suppose the greatest problem the writer in the theater has is to face "those ferocious critics." My problem is even greater. I write my own critics' reviews as I write my play. I place Walter Kerr of the *New York Times* just behind my right shoulder holding in his hand a big stick with rusty nails. If I get verbose or careless or stretch for jokes, Mr. Kerr lets me have it right across the knuckles.

The jokes are a special hazard. In the first of 112 versions of my first play, *Come Blow Your Horn*, the opening five minutes of the play were crammed with good jokes—in fact, some of the best I had ever written—and the scene was terrible. The audience, knowing nothing of the characters or the situation, could not have cared less.

Now I know enough to start with the characters. Where do they come from? In the case of *The Odd Couple*, from a party I attended in California. All the men there were divorced, all their dates were their new girlfriends. Most of the men were sharing apartments with other divorced men because alimony payments forced them to save money. In *Barefoot in the Park* and *Come Blow Your Horn*, at least one or two characters in each play resembled, perhaps in speech patterns, mannerisms, or personal outlook, someone I've actually known.

Looking back at what and how I write, I seem to begin a play with two people of completely opposite nature and temperament, put them in an intolerable situation and let the sparks fly. The extra ingredient, and very important, is that they must both emphatically believe that their way of life is the right one. Then it's the playwright's job to support both of those beliefs. As for form, I prefer my comedies in three acts. When I start, I write extensive notes for the first act, a sketchy outline for the second, and nothing for the third. Sometimes I don't find out for certain what's in the third act until a week before we open on Broadway.

If there is anything remotely resembling a key to comedy in theater, I'd guess that it is for the writer, director, and actors to apply one simple rule. Never treat it as a comedy. The actors and characters must treat their predicament as though their lives depended on it. Play it too seriously and the laughs are gone. Play just the comedy and ditto. In casting, my preference is not to go with the "established comic" but with a good actor who understands comedy. Walter Matthau, Robert Redford, Mildred Natwick, Lyle Talbot, and Harvey Stone are among the best.

One question I'm asked quite often is if I consider myself funny. I suppose I apply my own personal humor to life in the same manner as I would in a play. I need a situation. Put me around a table with real funny men like Buddy Hackett or Jonathan Winters or Mel Brooks and I fade like a shrinking violet. No fast repartee for me. I shine trapped in an elevator with six people and a German shepherd licking my ear.

To me, the first ten minutes of a comedy are critical. The writer must (1) set up the rules and the situation, (2) catch the audience almost immediately. Once the rules are announced, farce, satire, straight comedy, or whatever game you are playing, the audience will believe you so long as you stick to those rules and that game. I believe in starting the conflict in the opening minutes (for example, the poker game in *The Odd Couple*) and to be as theatrically arresting as possible. The idea of opening on an empty stage in *Barefoot* intrigued me. Then I begin with some new event in the life of our hero, something that never happened to him before.

My writing routines are actually rather prosaic. No midnight oil burns in my lamp. I type in an office or at home, and put in a ten-to-five day with a short lunch break. I may do a complete draft of a play, use it as an outline, and then set to work on a more finished version. I like to get into the writing quickly to "hear how the characters speak," for once I hear the speech patterns it is easier going. I ought to point out that my insecurity is such that even as I'm writing one play, I'm beginning to think ahead to the next. So if this one doesn't quite pan out, well . . .

Once a play goes into rehearsal, my "normal" routine ceases and the midnight oil begins to burn. There seems to be less time for social obligations, children, and—horror of horrors—I miss Giant football games.

Life for Simon—Not That Simple

Joan Barthel / 1968

From *New York Times*, February 25, 1968, sec. 2, pp. 1, 9. Reprinted with the permission of Anne Barthel. Joan Barthel is the author of *A Death in Canaan* (1976), which was nominated for a Pulitzer Prize and was adapted into an Emmy-nominated television movie; *A Death in California* (1981); *Love or Honor* (1989); and *American Saint: The Life of Elizabeth Seton* (2014).

He did it before, so when he did it again with *Plaza Suite*, it was not exhilarating. The opening night party at the Plaza was elegant and splendid—there were elegant and splendid ice sculptures and aspic things on the buffet table and there were elegant and splendid people like Ingrid Bergman around—but it was not exhilarating. Nobody dashed in waving inky copies of the reviews (although they were raves); nobody cheered wildly (although they applauded); the music was subdued, and nobody got carried away. The next day Neil Simon sat in the elegant and splendid living room of his elegant and splendid townhouse on East 62nd Street and said it was not exhilarating. "I wish I could go back," he said. "I wish I could go back and recapture the exhilaration I felt with *Barefoot in the Park*."

He made "I wish" sound like the two most mournful words in the language, not because he is given to morning-after theatrics, but partly because he is naturally nostalgic, partly because he had a headache and slight hangover, and partly because he is—oh prime time for stocktaking—forty. "I'm really going through a period of saying, 'What's it all about, Alfie?'"

But both those comments came later in the conversation. The first thing he said was "If I say anything pretentious, tell me." And it was, they say, a typical Simon statement, for he is known as a mild man, a moderate man; soft-spoken; even, perhaps, shy, and anyone who expects a comedy writer to be a laugh-a-minute gagster should look up Morey Amsterdam on a *Dick Van Dyke* rerun. Tall and loose, with thinnish dark hair and hornrims, amiable rather than jovial, elusively wistful, Neil Simon does not even look like a comedy writer. He does, of course, write like one.

Maybe the best one; certainly the busiest—no one else in our time has had five plays on Broadway in seven years, while also writing two musical books and three movie screenplays—and, these days, the most brooding. "I just feel like this is the end right now. I have much less fun than I used to. We were such innocent kids, and I keep looking back to that exhilaration, that lost innocence."

Parallels are both too easy and too tempting. In the first one-acter in *Plaza Suite*, George C. Scott, playing a successful middle-aged business-man, says ruefully, "I have it all—marriage, children, more money than I ever dreamed—and I just want to do it all over again. I would like to start the whole damn thing over from the beginning." The audience is moved and silent, until Maureen Stapleton sets off laughter with "Frankly, Sam, I don't think the Navy would take you again."

But nobody comes into Neil Simon's living room with a funny punch line, and he admits that, yes, he likes that play best.

"I like it the best, not only of the evening but of anything I've ever done before. It's something I've seen happen to many, many friends of mine. I feel it's a terrible thing that's happening in our society: when a woman gets to be in her late forties and her husband has gone off in his own way, she is left by herself with no place to go. The tragedy is that her husband still loves her but still is looking for something else, and he doesn't know what it is. I wanted to write about this. I told it with humor because otherwise it would be unbearable, but when people ask me, 'When are you going to write a serious play?' I say, 'I just did.'

"*The Odd Couple* was a serious play too—the people involved were going through terrible emotional problems, and Felix was really a very sad per-son—but the situation was so highly comic that the seriousness was over-looked. People always will misread something that's terribly funny because that's all they'll see. But it's not terribly important because it only has to do with my own ego.

"It isn't satisfying to me just to write funny anymore. I couldn't write *Barefoot in the Park* again; I can't go back and write a domestic comedy where there is very little at stake. I will never become a serious writer and write only serious plays, but I hope that in all the comedies I write there will be a serious theme underneath.

"I have to look forward; I think that's why people in the business after a while look to go on and do other things. Mike Nichols had reached a point with Elaine May where he had to do something else, and now you see Paul Newman and Sidney Poitier directing. It seems that after a while it's too easy to keep doing the things you've done. I know that I could go on for many, many years writing funny and successful comedies"—a wry smile—"not that they would necessarily all be good, because *Star-Spangled Girl* certainly wasn't."

That romantic comedy about a politically right-wing girl and a leftist boy ran eight months, made money, and is being turned into a movie, but it was a failure in relation to previous Simon successes and on the author's own scale. "I got no fun out of it. And I think it was false in that I chose to say that their physical attraction for one another would win out over their intellectual dislike. In real life, I think, they might have had a brief physical relationship, but their intellectual differences would have been dominant. The criterion Mike and I use is whether something seems real to us, whether it resembles life."

Mike Nichols did not direct *Star-Spangled Girl*. Would it have been better if he had?

"Yes. He would have given the actors a different attitude; we would have gone much more for reality than the superficial comedy that came out. That's not to knock George Axelrod; the difference is that Mike would have made me make the play better.

"He couldn't do it because he was busy with *Virginia Woolf*, but it isn't true that he advised me not to do it; as a matter of fact, he came to Philadelphia, and liked it. He gave me some advice on it, which helped.

"I'm not ashamed of that play. I learned more about myself and writing and what's good and what's bad from it. I learn from every play I do, except musicals. I came into *Sweet Charity* only as a favor to Bob Fosse. Now I'm doing the book for the musical version of *The Apartment* because Burt Bacharach and Hal David will do it. They're the best of the contemporary song writers and I'd like to help them introduce a new sound on Broadway. But there's no gratification for a playwright in doing a musical book. All the emotional peaks are sung, not spoken, so you mostly write lead-ins for songs. And it's all so horrible—the rehearsals, going out of town. It's so bad that Larry Gelbart said he hopes Hitler is alive and out of town with a musical."

The Nichols-Simon team was joined when Saint Subber suggested that Nichols, who had never directed before, take on the assignment for *Barefoot*. The collaboration, which continued with *The Odd Couple* and now *Plaza Suite*, has its advantages—"Mike and I have a special chemistry together, a great rapport, almost identical tastes"—and its drawbacks. "People say, 'Here comes another Nichols-Simon play, it better be good.'

"I have such a terrible feeling of responsibility now; I feel they expect so much of me, and I expect so much of myself. The pressures are not financial, it's the pressure of the success syndrome. I'm not above that yet; I still care what people think.

"The really great thing would be if I could write plays and stick them in a drawer, like O'Neill. Or if I could do a play in some subsidized regional theater someplace, just to give myself the pleasure of experimenting. Although, in a way, everything starts out as an experiment; I really thought *The Odd Couple* was going to be a black comedy.

"As much as I want to be successful, it sort of demeans the whole thing when they start saying 'A Big Blooming Hit.' Because certain critics and certain groups tend to look down on things that appeal to so many people. My capsule attitude about critics: I would take ten of the most astute, incisive critics in America and put on a play for them. If only four liked it, and six didn't, it would not be considered very good. If five liked it, and five didn't, it would be controversial. If seven liked it, and three didn't, it would be promising, interesting. If nine liked it, and one didn't, it would be fantastic, brilliant. If all ten liked it, it would be commercial."

Not that the critics have been harsh; even when a review refers to "the laugh machine," it leaves him unruffled. "That doesn't upset me because I don't feel it's true. I felt like a laugh machine when I was writing television comedy. The pattern there is so set; if you died, somebody would come in and take your place and nobody would ever know the difference. And there usually are so many writers on a show; it gets to be, not who is the most talented writer, but who is the loudest."

He worked on the Sid Caesar show and with Phil Silvers, Jerry Lewis, Garry Moore, back in the 1950s. Earlier, he wrote for radio in partnership with his brother Dan; long before that, he was hooked on comedy. "I remember when I was eight, nine years old, going to see *Modern Times* at Loew's 175th Street and laughing so uncontrollably that the usherette made me leave."

He was born in the Bronx, named Marvin Neil and nicknamed "Doc" because he was fond of examining people with a toy stethoscope. He is still called "Doc" by most people, including his wife, and he still feels an almost doomed compulsion to live in New York, even though "I don't really like it here anymore. I have an idea for a film; the idea is terribly funny but also sad and a little scary. Not Alfred Hitchcock scary, but the way in which just living in New York is scary. Here I am living in this lovely townhouse, and when I walk outside I'm right in the middle of all the terrible things going on. But I'd vegetate and rot in the country; if I lived in Hollywood I'd just write about Hollywood parties; and I can't live in Europe because I don't speak Europe. I have to stay here; I'm a fish and I was born in a dirty pond and that's how I breathe, in that pond.

"Life to me these days is frightening. I live in great anxiety. I'm afraid to read the newspapers or watch television; the bad news is becoming more and more frequent. Comedy writing to me is a defense mechanism; I can't bear to see life as gloomy as it really is. I approach plays and life by laughing at the insanity of it all.

"I have a compulsion to write, to keep moving. People say to me, 'You're so successful, why don't you take two years off?' I say, 'What would I do with two years off? My only two functions are my family life and what I can do as a writer.'

"I have an insane passion to keep writing. I'm enormously restless, and I just have to fill every single second of the day. One of the most dominant parts of my personality is this enormous desire I have to do everything myself. I don't trust anybody. Except in finances—in that area I have enormous trust. I'm the owner of the Eugene O'Neill Theater and it's the biggest bore in the whole world; it was just an investment.

"The more money I make doesn't really matter; I've made money for a long time. Money doesn't buy anything special except certain little comforts. Despite the fact that the trappings here are pretty nice, I don't indulge in enormous luxuries. I don't ever want to be in the position of being carried around. You know the joke about the Jewish mother who says to her friend, 'My son the playwright, he has a chauffeur, the chauffeur carries him into the house, out of the house, he carries him into the theater, out of the theater.' 'What's the matter?' asks the friend. 'Can't he walk?' 'Certainly he can walk,' says the mother, 'but thank God he doesn't have to.'"

Those "trappings" in the Simon household include ornate fireplaces in all ten rooms. Creamy lace at a window overlooking a moody, tangled garden. Thick burgundy carpeting on the curving stairway leading to his study, where he writes for six hours a day at an Olympia portable (he used to write elsewhere but started this arrangement to give himself time with his wife, Joan, a pretty brunette whom he married in 1953, and their two girls, Ellen and Nancy). A bumper pool table for gametime. In the living room, ivory carpeting and a big chair covered in bittersweet-chocolate velvet, where he sat, smiling only a little. The portrait of comic artist as an introspective young man is not new, but it is always, when drawn from life, original.

An Interview with Neil Simon

Glenn Loney / 1969

From *Neil Simon: A Casebook*, edited by Gary Konas (New York: Garland, 1997), 205–16. Copyright © 1997. Reproduced by permission of Taylor and Francis Group, LLC, a division of Informa plc. Bracketed insertions are Loney's. Glenn Loney was a professor of Theatre at The Graduate School, CUNY, and the author of *20th Century Theatre* (1983) and *Peter Brook: Oxford to Orghast* (1998).

On Location in Central Park
Shooting *The Out-of-Towners*
14 May 1969

Ed. Note: A one-page condensation of the following interview originally appeared in *Cue* magazine. Except for brief excisions made in order not to conflict with Mr. Simon's autobiography *Rewrites*, the interview appears here in its entirety.

Neil Simon took time out from observing the filming of *The Out-of-Towners* to discuss his work, sitting with Loney on a Central Park bench not far from the famous Dakota Apartments.

Glenn Loney: What have you found to be the chief differences in working in films, as opposed to working on Broadway?
Neil Simon: That is such a broad question that it is rather difficult to answer succinctly. As for the writing itself: I find in the actual physical act of writing—whether you are writing for the films or the stage, or whether you are writing a little poem for yourself—you still have to sit down at a typewriter and write it. First of all, I am not at all that experienced in writing for the films, so I don't yet know all of the pitfalls or the advantages. For me—with all the experience I have had in the theater—I find it is much easier to write for the theater. I like being constricted and restricted: the one-set play. I like the

restrictions of the theater, because I am more able to concentrate on the characters. I believe in the written word much more than in the visual picture.

Loney: Do you think this feeling is peculiar to writers?
Simon: Yes. There is the cliché that the director is king in the films, and the writer is the king in the theater. And this is with good reason, because the film is such a visual medium. When you are sitting down at the typewriter working on a play—at least for me—I visualize what is going to be up there on the stage, and I am rarely surprised when it finally gets up there. I see it sitting up there in my mind's eye. Everyone in the audience pretty much has the same view. There is that proscenium stage, and everything is visible to us at the same time.

But you write the same dialogue for a scene in films, and the director may see fit to have the camera on a completely different thing than you were thinking of. It may be on a character who is not even involved in the scene at that moment. He is bringing out some other kind of point. So you are not always in control of what is going to be up there on the screen, unless you are the director.

Loney: Do you find in working on this film, in working on the set, that you are able to offer advice? Or are you largely here just to check on lines if anything has to be changed? What is your relationship with the director, in this particular case?
Simon: Well, it is for all purposes. For one thing, I consider this period the same as I would for a play that is in production.

Loney: You are still working on it, in other words? The script isn't frozen?
Simon: That's right. On a play, I am there every day during rehearsals, every day during out-of-town tryouts. Nobody is ever surprised that an author is around. But they are very surprised to see a writer around on a movie set. I think that is only because of the precedent that has been set over the years. Writers have always been second-class citizens in films. I refuse to let that happen. I think I can make valuable suggestions.

Loney: Is this in your contract?
Simon: It has nothing to do with contracts.

Loney: You care about what is going to result.
Simon: Yes! And there is no problem. Paramount is delighted that I am

here, and the director [Arthur Hiller] is delighted. I don't interfere with the director's work, but I do make suggestions. Just as I would working with Mike Nichols on the stage. And I find it invaluable to be here. Also, it is good for me to learn about the problems, so that when I am sitting down to write the next film script, I know the limitations that you may have in working on a film.

Loney: When you started writing your first screenplay, *After the Fox*, were you working from a model? You had somebody else's screenplay in hand, so you could see what had to be done? In regard to the mechanics of script-writing?
Simon: No, no . . . I am still an amateur as far as that's concerned. I don't get involved in that. They do that after I have finished with the script—numbering all the scenes and so on.

Loney: You write it, and then they devise the camera angles?
Simon: No, no—I do that now. The more I go along, I have been writing camera angles. When you are writing about two people on a bench, it is kind of pointless to say: "Now cut to his face—now to hers." I only do it when there is some point to be made.

Loney: But, when you are writing for the stage, nothing much is going to happen unless you say to the director: "He should get up and walk to the door."
Simon: Yes. But I do put down whatever stage-directions I possibly can. But it is optional. It is finally the director's choice.

Loney: Do you do this both when you write for the theater and for films?
Simon: Yes. I find that we use about 75–80 percent of it.

Loney: You mean that when Mike Nichols is directing a play, he may say: "Look, Neil, that's no good . . ." And he throws it out. Is this okay, or do you argue about it?
Simon: We hardly ever argue about it, because . . . When you are on the same wavelength with someone, you pretty much agree. There will be discussions and disagreements, but we almost always work it out. But I do put in as many directions as possible.

Loney: When you say that the repetition required of a stage-director bothers you, what about rewriting a play—the endless rewrites that have to be done?

Simon: That is not repetition. Rewrites are something new. I am delighted at getting to rewrites. It keeps me from being bored out-of-town—needing new things, and putting in new things, and seeing them work! It is in a constant state of some sort of action—of being worked on all the time, and I enjoy that thoroughly.

But I think the main reason I don't want to direct is that it is time-consuming, and it takes me away from other projects. I am usually working on two things at one time. For example, we are working on this film, and I am in the midst of working on my new play [*Last of the Red Hot Lovers* (1969)]. I am not writing very much right now, but I am thinking a great deal about it. If I were involved only in the direction of this film, then I couldn't think of anything else. I am primarily a writer, and I really enjoy writing. I don't think I would enjoy directing. It took a long time to say: "No, I don't really want to direct."

Loney: But it is interesting to find out *why* you didn't. You began in television, right?
Simon: Actually in radio. When I was nineteen years old, I got a job in radio, and then in television after about a year. When television was just really coming into its own.

Loney: Who were some of the people you worked for?
Simon: Jackie Gleason and Sid Caesar—for many years, the *Phil Silvers Show*, Red Buttons. Almost every comedian in the business at one time or another I've worked for.

Loney: What do you think are some of the advantages that this experience gave you? Things that you learned, or skills that you mastered?
Simon: Well, anytime you have the ability to write and have it performed in front of an audience is an invaluable experience. I was very fortunate in having that, rather than just writing at home and showing it to somebody. You never know until it gets in front of an audience. A very good example of this is after I had done about four shows—*Come Blow Your Horn* [1961], *Little Me* [1962], then *Barefoot in the Park* [1963], and we were about to go into rehearsal with *The Odd Couple* [1965]. And Mike Nichols had already done *Barefoot* and *Luv* [by Murray Schisgal (1964)], and so we were pretty successful. And we thought we knew what should work and what shouldn't work.

Loney: But while you sit there chuckling, what is funny to you may not be funny to an audience? Or the actors may not be able to make it come alive the way your characters do in your imagination?

Simon: But if he is funny in the first act and second act, and he is not funny in the third act, then it can't be the actor's fault. Then it must be in the material. If the actor is not funny *anywhere*, you have to think about it and say: "This may be the wrong fellow." In the case of *The Odd Couple*, the first and second act read magnificently at the reading, and the third act did not read well. So I couldn't attribute it to any actors. I knew the problem was somewhere in the material.

Going back to television now: having had the opportunity of writing and—week after week—having it performed in front of audiences was invaluable to my work later on. The more you write the more you learn.

Loney: Do you *plan*, let's say, a *grotesquerie*, so that audiences will fall out of their seats—or is this somewhat instinctual?

Simon: I always feel that my writing is all instinctual. I never sit down and plan it. It all happens by accident. But there are all different forms of writing in television. There is the gag-writing. Then I worked in situation comedy, then adapting some of the old musicals—which was a very good experience for me, learning to write for the theater. We worked on shows like *Connecticut Yankee*, *Dearest Enemy*, and *Best Foot Forward*.

I had no experience, prior to that, working on shows that had any length or duration. I always worked on sketches—something with seven or eight minutes duration. The other thing that was very, very helpful, was having to turn it out so rapidly. Doing the *Sergeant Bilko* show, we did thirty shows in about thirty-nine weeks. And so the pressure was there—you had to have it done. If I was a writer who never had that pressure, I guess when I got out-of-town with a play—and in three nights I had to have a new act—I don't know if I would be able to stand up to it. But I've done that in television. So you have to be sort of fearless anyway, when you are sitting down to write. But then you say to yourself: "You are only human, and if it is not going to work, it is not going to work."

Loney: When you were working in TV, didn't you usually have a team—or other people—to help if something wasn't working right?

Simon: Yes, but in a way that was more time-consuming than working alone. And many times, I would say something I thought was very good, and they would say: "I don't know—how about so-and-so?" Sometimes it was a question of ego—because that fellow didn't have anything in—he wanted to get his bit in the show. Sometimes it was just out-and-out lack of agreement on things. About the business of turning it out week after week. [Years later, Simon was to recreate this experience on stage—writing for Sid Caesar—in *Laughter on the 23rd Floor* (1993).]

Loney: Do you find that you do a lot of thinking about a new play before you ever go near the typewriter?

Simon: I am not conscious of it. It just sort of is *there*. It grows and grows and, if it feels right, it just keeps on growing. By the time I am able to get to the typewriter, it has a flow. I have in mind how it is going to take place.

Loney: Was there any particular germ, any experience—let's say, with *The Odd Couple*—that you knew some people like that, who broke up simply because they were mismatched? And the plot all fell into place for you?

Simon: Yes. It is partially specifics. There actually were two people, but then I didn't use those two people, specifically, all the way through. It is not interesting enough to use just two specific people. You use people and use your mind like a sieve—and pour people through it. You use characteristics of everyone. I have found that there is a bit of myself in almost all of the characters that I have written, and they can be the most diversified kinds of characters. There is one character—parts of my brother [writer/director Danny Simon]—for example, that I have used in two plays. He is *not* these people specifically. But I have used him, in a way, as the older brother in *Come Blow Your Horn*, and as a little bit of Felix in *The Odd Couple*.

Now those are completely opposite characters. In *Come Blow Your Horn*, he's a sort of Frank Sinatra type, a swinger. The character in *The Odd Couple*, Felix, is a rather shy, nervous, neurotic type of character—completely different. Yet all of those characteristics are in us—we are all, in a way, Jekyll and Hyde.

Loney: When you are writing, are you actually seeing these characters on a stage—are they actually moving around in your mind?

Simon: Yes. The play is taking place in my mind. I see the theater—hear the audience—always aware of the technical problems in the theater. I know that if I get a character off, and I want to bring him back a few moments later, and there is a costume change, I can't just suddenly have him back there in ten seconds. There has to be some preparation made for his entrance. I am always aware of exits for people: making them on a point, and not just having them drift out of the room—entrances, too.

Loney: Have you always worked with a proscenium stage, or have you also worked with an arena or thrust?

Simon: I have worked with a proscenium, but the plays certainly have worked in an arena. I guess if I were writing specifically for an arena stage, I would think about it while I was doing the play.

Loney: All of your plays have been contemporary. Have you ever thought of doing something that deals with the past? Or is that just not your scene?

Simon: No. It isn't my scene. I would love to write a Chekhovian type comedy. [Later, Simon's *The Good Doctor* (1973) seemed at least an homage to Chekhov.]

I think, in terms of doing farces, they seem to work better in period pieces. If you were writing one today—if you placed it in Paris in 1880, the same situation seems to work much better than using contemporary times. I don't know why that is.

Loney: I once made the mistake of asking Peter Shaffer—whose *Five Finger Exercise* [1958] and *The Royal Hunt of the Sun* [1964] were compelling dramas—why he seemed to prefer writing comedies, rather than serious plays. He was furious with me. He said: "*All* my plays are serious plays." How do you feel about this? So many critics have said: "Well, Shaffer's a very charming, clever writer, but he hasn't given us anything of real substance yet." Do you feel critics expect more "serious" plays from you?

Simon: Some have said that, and some have said: "They *are* of substance." I read all of the reviews. Somehow, it has always been this way—and I don't think it is ever going to change. Certain types of esoteric critics are always going to look down on comedy. For them, it seems too easy—or it doesn't have enough substance. But I don't think so! I won't say all my plays are serious—I haven't written that many yet.

I don't think *Barefoot* or *Come Blow Your Horn* were really serious plays—but they were "beginning" plays. They were plays that I had to go through in order to go on to other things. But I think *The Odd Couple* is basically a serious play. That is a serious situation. I think any comment that you make about the way people live can be serious. I just finished reading this biography on Chekhov, which I loved. He talked about the theme of his life's work. He said it was just trying to show people how absurdly they live their lives. That is what I try to do. I do it through the medium of comedy, but I don't do it just to evoke a laugh from an audience. I do it also to show them how absurdly we *all* live our lives. To me, that is the point that I try to make in all the works.

Loney: The movie that is underway now—*The Out-of-Towners*: is this really a continuation of that?

Simon: If you take out all the humorous aspects, and consider the *points* that I make in the film—well, it is almost a serious film. The people who come to New York: who are mugged or beaten, or who come here in the midst of garbage strikes and turmoil; the Cuban delegation is being bombed and harassed. There are a lot of serious points to be made in this film, but I choose to do it in terms of comedy.

Loney: If, at one point, Jack Lemmon were knifed and he died, it wouldn't be funny.

Simon: Right. Felix threatens suicide in *The Odd Couple*. He could actually commit suicide at some point, and we would say: "Ah, serious!"

Loney: But you feel that this would work against the point you want to make? That people wouldn't get the point quite as well if they are shocked, rather than amused? Or that suddenly making it serious would give it a kind of supercharge?

Simon: I think it is being gratuitous to try and make that serious in order to lend weight to it. The weight is there if you want it. Every one of Chaplin's films have all been, to me, hysterically funny. And yet they have all had great social importance, and they made great points about the same thing: how absurdly we live our lives.

Loney: How did you get the idea for this current film project? Did the film company come to you and say: "Look, we want you to do a film, a Neil Simon film? What have you got in mind?"

Simon: No. But they *are* always doing that. I can't just sit down and say: "Somebody wants me to do something—what can I do?" All the ideas have to come out of something I *want* to do.

Loney: Did this film script start out as an idea for the theater?

Simon: Yes, it did. It was in *Plaza Suite* [1968]. That originally had four acts. The first act was about a man who came from out-of-town and had lost his luggage. He got here in the middle of a transit strike. And it was snowing as well. He checked into the Plaza Hotel, and there was this monologue that

George C. Scott was doing. We put it into rehearsal, and after about the fifth day, Mike Nichols said: "We just have too much show here. If we do that monologue, plus the other three acts, the curtain will be coming down at twelve o'clock!"

In order to cut it, to bring it down to normal, we would have to hurt the other three plays. And the other three seemed to have been the right length. Also—the first play would have been hurt if we opened up the evening with this light little teaser. So we decided to abandon it.

But I liked the idea so much. And I said: "Actually, it is a better film than a play, because all of these things should be seen, rather than talked about." So, like everything else I do . . . I don't make a deal with a movie company and say: "Well, I'm doing the movie. . . ." I just sit down and write it. I do that with all my plays. I just want to see if it is going to work out first. I wrote about half of it, when I thought it would be a perfect vehicle for Jack Lemmon. I discussed it with Jack. He just loved the idea and agreed to do it without even seeing the script. I finished the script and sent it to him, and he said: "Marvelous!"

The thing about using the Waldorf-Astoria in the film—I didn't choose not to do it at the Plaza Hotel because of *Plaza Suite*. There is a scene when he checks into the hotel during the transit strike and he has lost his room. I wanted to show hundreds of people sleeping in the lobby—as they actually did during the transit strike—and the Waldorf has the largest lobby of any hotel in New York.

Loney: I looked at the press summary of the movie. It makes New York look like a *very* unattractive place to live. At the end of the film, he is having strong second thoughts about whether he wants to move here?
Simon: He is!

Loney: Do you feel that way yourself?
Simon: Yes . . . but I do live here, knowing that I am constantly going to be faced by all the terrible problems in New York. But I think life is a constant challenge anyway. I think New York is *worth* the challenge. But to me, it is not a diatribe just against New York. To me, it is against every major city. You run up against this problem everywhere. There just was an enormous garbage strike in Dublin. France, Italy—someone goes out on strike, and the entire country goes out on strike. They say Wednesday there will be no France, and that is it! So I just wanted to make this comment about all the big cities today.

Loney: Well, having done so, do you think there is any solution?

Simon: Yes. I think Mayor [John] Lindsay has done a good job, and I am very much for Mayor Lindsay. He was enormously cooperative with us [in making the film] because he said: "There are ills in the City, and they must be corrected. It is no good just burying the issue." I don't know what the answers are. I don't ever think that is the comic writer's obligation. I think the serious writer should never do it either. I think you can only present the problems and make people aware. Most of the time, people aren't even aware of what the problems are. Once you start choosing sides and putting down the answers to things, you are usually wrong. And they become sort of propaganda plays, and rather uninteresting to see.

Loney: When you are working with comedy—in a film or onstage—are there some formulas that you know will get a laugh? Or don't you ever use that kind of thing?

Simon: No! It is kind of a cheap way to work—using formulas and knowing an audience is going to laugh. I may write something and say: "I know the audience is going to laugh," but it has nothing to do with formulas, or saying that is pure "socko." I put it down because it seems to emanate from the character and the situation. And it makes *me* laugh. Then I say: "Well, my average has been pretty good, and if it makes me laugh, I think the audience will laugh." But the important thing—and the kind of thing I like to do—is that, if the audience doesn't laugh at that moment, that's okay, too. Something else is going on. There is the story that is going on—the characterization—these people are becoming involved.

Mike Nichols would constantly tell this to the actors. He would say: "Forget about them out there! If they don't show up tonight, you still have to do what you are doing up here. The minute you start playing to the audience, you are dead." The same applies to the writer. The minute I start writing for the audience, if you *don't* laugh, it is glaring. So the thing has to have some dramatic import of its own.

Loney: You mean: when a comedian tells a very bad joke, and he is hoping they will laugh—but they don't? Then he has to try something else, to cover up?

Simon: No. I never—well, hardly ever—deal with comedians in my plays. George C. Scott, Maureen Stapleton, Walter Matthau—these are *actors*. They are living flesh-and-blood up on the stage. They are not comedians.

Loney: What is it like, working with a director like Mike Nichols? Has he staged all of your plays?

Simon: No, no. He has only done three. I did *Come Blow Your Horn* and *Star-Spangled Girl* with another director [George Axelrod].

Loney: If a good director invents some fantastic stage-business, when the play is published, is this business included in the stage directions?

Simon: Yes. Why take them out—what is the point of that? Mike has put in certain pieces of business that were invaluable to, say, *The Odd Couple*. When Felix offered the girl a cigarette and he lit it with a cigarette lighter— then he pulled it away, and the cigarette was still stuck in the lighter. That's Mike's business, but there are other pieces of business that I put in there, and it gets kind of petty to say: "Well, I am going to take out your contribution." You are *all* working on the play. Sometimes an actor may say a line differently. He may reword it. And I may say: "That is better than the way I put it. Let us do that." Shall I take that out of the printed version because an actor offered it?

Loney: There is a problem, isn't there, for readers of the acting edition of a play, who want to know how the play was done originally? That certain things can be described—sets, costumes, props, bits of business, stage movement. But the *way* the line was read can't be communicated, other than "rudely" or "languidly." And that really doesn't tell you very much, because each reader will have a different way of interpreting such words.

Simon: Yes. But if the play is good, it will hold up anyway. Who now knows how *Hamlet* was done originally? Where the intonations went? But the play is there, and it is kind of fun for the actor to try various approaches to it.

Neil Simon, Good Humor Man

Gerald Nachman / 1972

From *New York Daily News*, January 13, 1972, p. 97. © Daily News, L.P. (New York). Used with permission.

Despite disquieting asides and offstage whispers that Neil Simon is getting too somber, that his last few comedies were less funny than sad, the playwright promises from now on to be no more serious than necessary.

After a sobriety binge in *The Gingerbread Lady* and a brief tragic relapse in *The Prisoner of Second Avenue*, Broadway's leading—and rather lonely—comic writer is determined to keep audiences laughing in the long face of national gloom.

Should Simon feel unhappy at all, however, he can console himself that he is *Cue*'s "Entertainer of the Year," the first playwright (comic or otherwise) so honored by the magazine in ceremonies tomorrow night at the Americana Hotel in the presence of casts from Simon's first eleven hit shows.

Simon winces at the word "serious," preferring to think of his recent plays as humanly comic as possible with relevant overtones. "People just aren't used to Broadway comedies with darker aspects, though they'll accept it off-Broadway," he said in the rather dimly lit sitting room of his apartment, an unassuming gray townhouse on East 62nd Street.

Explained Simon: "I won't ever write a so-called 'serious' play; I think of 'serious' as negative. I don't like completely 'serious' plays. What interests me are completely good plays, and all the good plays I've seen have elements of humor.

"My favorite play of all, *A Streetcar Named Desire*," he went on, "has whole scenes that are enormously funny. I find humor in Pinter, in an oblique way. I didn't understand half of *Old Times* but kept thinking of funny things."

Simon doesn't consider his latter plays all that serious. "Even when I attempted it slightly, in *Gingerbread Lady*, I got clubbed for it, but they were knocking me more than the play. They didn't want me doing anything serious."

Ideally, says Simon, "I like to write a play in which the audience laughs all night and then, in the final moment, realizes, 'Hey, this is ABOUT something!' I think *Last of the Red Hot Lovers* did that to an extent." He adds, "I'm not averse to doing a farce, though."

Simon, who is pleasant and plain-speaking, smiling rarely and laughing even less, admits, "I think I've been influenced, somewhat, by the times, and I do think plays should be relevant. If I'd written *Barefoot in the Park* today, it would have a harder time being accepted. But that play was relevant in its own time, nine years ago. That's how kids lived then."

What is serious, he points out, is the state of comedy throughout Broadway and, indeed, the country. "I'm very depressed now when I go to theater. I'm one of the few writing comedy, which isn't enough; I'm worried for the welfare of Broadway. Take Chaplin: Why should he have wasted his time, his talent, doing serious films?"

The forty-four-year-old playwright continued: "Our opinion-makers— the press, TV, novelists—tell us anything completely frivolous is a waste of time. It's almost bad taste now to be merely funny. There are few out-and-out comedies on the screen. Even in *Bananas*, much of the humor was political."

Simon says, "Humor has just vanished from this country; I don't understand it. Since the (JFK) assassination, the country's become terribly serious. It's a frightened, militant, crime-infested nation, and there aren't many places of pleasure anymore—with the exception of sports, because it has enough violence to satisfy us.

"It's not just because of the war," he adds, "because there was great humor during World War II. What really worries me is that one country which is totally humorless is Germany. England has always had a sense of humor, and it's still a very civilized, nonviolent country."

Few films, plays, or books today amuse Simon. Woody Allen's work can do it, but comic novels "bore" him (though he just read a new book by Dan Greenburg, *Scoring*, that "knocked me out") and he sees no comic playwrights emerging except George Furth, author of *Twigs*. Comedy writers disappear, he says, "like the guy who wrote *Never Too Late* and hasn't been heard from since."

Simon notes, however, "I'm not unaware that writing a good play is enormously hard. For me, it's not hard once the idea jells." *The Prisoner of Second Avenue*, which took ten years to jell, came easier to Simon than most of his plays.

"The only problem was, again, walking the tightrope over comedy, but I did little rewriting on this play. I was in control most of the way. *Gingerbread Lady* was much harder; alcoholism is more tragic than a breakdown."

Simon's toughest, and least favorite, play was *Star-Spangled Girl*.

"Of those who dislike it," he says, "I head the list. It was all manufactured and my instincts were to quit. I didn't even enjoy going to the typewriter in the morning. All the other plays flowed."

Simon has become "less and less interested" in screenwriting as more and more of his plays are filmed. ("*Odd Couple* was the only good one.") Nonetheless, he just wrote *The Heartbreak Kid*, a movie being directed by Elaine May, and after rehearsals Simon will spend the summer in Spain writing smash hit No. 12 for the spring of 1973.

"I love the theater and there's a real need to contribute. If I have a talent, I can't turn my back on it. That'd be like saying, 'I've got mine, 'bye folks.' Writing plays is the best thing I can do."

Simon Says

Al Morgan / 1972

From *TV Guide* 20 (November 4, 1972): 20–24. Reprinted by permission.

Neil Simon, America's most successful living playwright, has come full circle. In the early days of television comedy, he was one of a covey of gag writers on Sid Caesar's *Your Show of Shows*. He helped turn Phil Silvers's Sergeant Bilko into a national institution, and moved on to Broadway.

After a succession of smash hits that included *The Odd Couple, Barefoot in the Park, Plaza Suite*, and *Last of the Red Hot Lovers*; musicals like *Sweet Charity* and *Promises, Promises*; and currently *The Prisoner of Second Avenue* playing at a theater he owns, Neil Simon is famous, solvent, and in the position of calling his shots.

One of the surprising shots he called turns up on your television screen on Sunday, November 12, on NBC. A special called *The Trouble with People* lists Neil Simon as author and executive producer, with brother Danny Simon as producer and codirector.

In a long, candid conversation with Al Morgan, novelist and former producer of the *Today* show, Simon tells why he's back in TV and his views on comedy, TV censorship, and adaptations of his hits.

It went about like this:

Morgan: Neil, what are you doing back in television?
Simon: It came out of a conversation I had with my brother Danny two years ago. I said, "Gee, I'd love to be able to write a sketch again." I haven't written sketches since I worked in television twelve or thirteen years ago because the revue form is dead in the theater, always has been in films and there just isn't any other outlet for them. Danny thought about it a while and he said to me, "If you'd like, why don't you do a special on television?" The more I thought about it, the more interested I got in doing it and I finally said, "Okay."

Morgan: Were they old sketches, out of your trunk?

Simon: No. I wrote them to order. I needed a theme and I guess I used a theme which is pretty much the theme of all my plays in a way—the frustrations of everyday life.

Morgan: Are these sketches a throwback to the days when you were writing for Caesar or Bilko or is there a difference in sketches these days?

Simon: Most of the television comedy you see today is built around the personality. For example, Flip Wilson will do a sketch, but it will be built around Flip and whoever the guest star is. Sid did a variety of characters. We didn't have to just do a "Sid Caesar" sketch. He adapted to the material instead of the other way around. The new way can be restrictive to the writer. So . . . yes, Al, these are a throwback to the degree that I didn't build any of these sketches around any personality. I did a sketch based on the premise of the show and then cast it, the way I would a show.

Morgan: How *did* you operate back in your Caesar days, as a gag writer?

Simon: Gag writer? There was no such thing as a gag writer. Everybody contributed what they could. One big reason why that show was as good as it was—one of the two, because you have to start with Sid as number one—was that it had the best writing staff ever put together: myself, Larry Gelbart, Mel Brooks (a sometime genius) and Carl Reiner and Sid himself.

Morgan: How did you do it? Can you write comedy by committee?

Simon: We broke up into groups of two. Never one alone. We sort of sparked each other. There was so much material to be written in that hour-and-a-half show every week—approximately seven sketches a week—what we would do was, two or three of us would start a sketch and when it was *almost* completed we would bring it in and read it to the whole group. Sid would sit in with us and we would all edit it, contribute to it, sometimes throw it out and redo it and it would come out as a polished thing. Then, in rehearsal we'd polish it again, and change it.

You had to be young to do it. The amount of work was incredible. As hard as people think I work in doing a play a year or a movie a year, that isn't one-fifth the amount of work I had to do when I worked on the Caesar thing or the Bilko show.

Morgan: Do you think those two shows are better than most of the stuff that's on television now?

Simon: I don't know, Al. I hate to make a general statement. I feel very odd about comedy. I don't read comedy or funny novels. I don't see many comedies I like on the stage. And as far as television is concerned, there'll be an occasional comic who will come on once in a while doing a bit for four or five minutes who will break me up. Occasionally Flip Wilson or Bill Cosby really get to me.

Morgan: Who else do you like?
Simon: I love Art Carney. He's the type of performer I love anyway, the one who is not a comedian but who can do comedy. In that group I'd put all the people I've worked with—George C. Scott, Walter Matthau, Peter Falk, Gene Wilder, Alan Arkin, Jimmy Coco, and Maureen Stapleton and Lee Grant. There's one man I haven't worked with that I'd like to: Dustin Hoffman. There's a man who can do comedy and tragedy.

Morgan: Can I go back to something, Neil, that doesn't quite satisfy me? Why television? It's certainly not the money. And if these five sketches are really first rate, why didn't you put them on a stage and get the smash notices, the road companies, the movie sale, and all the other things that have become your normal pattern? Why television?
Simon: A number of people have asked me that. And they all sound, like you, a little condescending and patronizing toward television. I don't know if this will satisfy you, but I never think of the outcome of what I'm doing. I don't say, "I'm writing for television, I'm writing a thing for the movies or the theater." Of course, in this case, I knew I was writing for this special; but when I sit down and write, I write for the sheer enjoyment of it and then, suddenly in this case, I thought, "My God, I'm writing for television and I'm going to come up against some of the problems that drove me out of television in the first place."

Morgan: What are those?
Simon: For one thing, there's the matter of time. My brother, Danny, came up here one day when the five sketches were finished and said, "Okay, we've got to cut them." It wasn't because we said, "Gee, this isn't funny" or "Gee, this doesn't work." We cut them merely to get them into the time allotted to us on the air. This is not true on the stage. Something runs as long as it's funny and you cut only for quality reasons. I felt very restricted and I felt some misgivings about it all.

Morgan: Fine. Then why do television at all?
Simon: I still thought this was an unusual opportunity.

Morgan: In what way? You've been talking about the restrictions.

Simon: All right . . . then let me tell you one of the advantages and attractions. Suppose I had written these five sketches for the theater? There is no chance in the world that the cast would comprise George C. Scott, Alan Arkin, Jimmy Coco, Gene Wilder, Joe Campanella. Right there is a good reason for doing this show on television.

Morgan: Not to mention the kind of mass audience television can give you.

Simon: Much more of an audience than I've ever had, with my biggest hit play or my biggest hit movie.

Morgan: Let's go back a minute. You were talking about the restrictions that drove you out of television. What are they?

Simon: Well . . . the inevitable one, censorship. Which has been very mild, I must say. The fact that it's there at all disturbs me.

Morgan: Specifically what kind, Neil?

Simon: The things you can't mention—there are certain kinds of words, connotations that sponsors and networks feel hesitant about. I suppose if you are trying to reach twenty or thirty million people and if you have a product to sell them, that comes first and foremost and you don't want to offend anybody. I must say they're better to me than anyone used to be to me when I worked in television earlier. But there are still those restrictions and I have to say, reluctantly, "Okay, I'll take that out." *I* know that I'm not taking it out because I think it's wrong for the material or the show but because they say I should.

Morgan: Be specific, Neil. Give me an example.

Simon: The word "pervert." They objected to the word "pervert." I didn't. It seemed to me to be a rather clinical description of a character. But I took it out. I'm just not used to that anymore . . . taking something out just because somebody says I should and not because I think taking it out improves the material.

Morgan: You watch much television, Neil?

Simon: I don't watch shows much. But I guess I watch a lot of television, certainly almost all the sports events.

Morgan: What do you think the general level of comedy is like on television today?

Simon: I think it's nonexistent with one exception.

Morgan: Which is that?

Simon: *All in the Family.* I do watch that. I think that's good. I know there is a big question about the bigotry in it and which way it really goes but I'm quite sure what the answer to that is. People will take it the way they themselves are. The bigot will cheer it and the liberal will understand it as characterization. Putting that aside, I think as comedy it's the most professional of all the shows. It's really well-written, well-acted, and well-directed.

Morgan: How about *The Odd Couple*?

Simon: I don't watch it. I hear it's very good. People tell me it's good.

Morgan: You *really* don't watch it?

Simon: I really don't. It's very successful and I do know that Jack Klugman and Tony Randall are marvelous. But I always thought it would make a good series. It always had a natural feeling to it. That constant conflict between the two men was a good basis for a continuing thing.

Take another play of mine, *Barefoot in the Park.* I always knew that had problems as a TV series. That was one story, one play, that's all. They made a pilot which was really my play cut down. And then, when it didn't work, they tried to cash in and exploit it by making the couple black. It didn't work.

Morgan: I can't believe, Neil, that idle curiosity, or vested interest, or feelings of responsibility for your baby, wouldn't make you tune in *The Odd Couple* once in a while.

Simon: I'll tell you why. It's like opening up your own family album and you find pictures in it that don't belong to your family. You say, "That's not my cousin, that's not my grandmother. Somebody else has been putting pictures in my family album." I don't feel any proprietary interest in it. You know, I don't get anything out of it financially. There was a very nominal fee paid and it doesn't even go to me anymore.

Morgan: Is this the beginning of a whole new career for you in television? Can we look forward to, say, two or three Neil Simon specials?

Simon: Never. I might do another sometime. Let's leave it at that. I'm doing this because all the people I have are first-rate. I think if we have a good time doing it and that comes over, the show has a chance of being something worth seeing.

"Success Has Something to Do with Recognition," Simon Says

Richard L. Coe / 1972

From *Washington Post*, December 3, 1972, p. E5. © The Washington Post. Reprinted by permission. Richard L. Coe was a theater critic for the *Washington Post* for more than forty years.

"It has something to do with recognition," said Neil Simon on why his plays are so popular. "Take pillows."

On the commercial scales, Simon has been weighed in, probably accurately, as the most successful playwright in world history. While he had four plays running concurrently on Broadway and about a dozen productions playing elsewhere, his weekly income was guessed to be in the neighborhood of $45,000.

At present Simon is at every performance at the National, where his newest play, *The Sunshine Boys*, has another two weeks before Broadway. There his 1971 hit, *The Prisoner of Second Avenue*, healthily continues at the Eugene O'Neill, a theater Simon bought seven years ago. (Shakespeare also ploughed his profits into theater ownership.)

"Yes, little things like pillows," Simon went on. "In the last scene of *Sunshine Boys* the nurse goes over to Willie Clark and ruffles up the pillows behind him on his bed.

"'Damn it,' says Willie, 'it's taken me all day to get these pillows just where I want 'em.' It's a big laugh line. In *Prisoner*, when Lee Grant told Peter Falk he could sleep on the couch, he replied he never has been comfortable with what she's exhibited on that couch. 'You buy a couch for six hundred dollars and then louse it up by adding pillows.' Little things like that get laughs of recognition.

"It's those little things that bug our lives. I sometimes think of how that could be carried to an extreme: say the president of the United States is in the act of declaring war. Someone asks wouldn't he like something to eat or he goes to the john and the door sticks. Here, at this supreme moment, he has to think about ham or tomato or how to keep a door from jamming. It's utter trivia but we're all afflicted with it, understand so well that others are. It keeps us all human.

"The most welcome compliments I've had about *Sunshine Boys* come from recognition, not the recognition that this old vaudeville team could make people think of Smith and Dale and their 'Dr. Kronkheit' sketch, which would be perfectly accurate; but the recognition that Willie or Al are the viewers' own fathers, or uncles, or someone they know well.

"That's the satisfaction I do find, that people do recognize what I'm writing about. When I first began writing plays I used to label people as I watched them walk into theaters. 'There's a non-laugher,' I used to say, or 'There's a real grouch.' I've passed that stage, thank goodness. Now I know that who knows who's really a non-laugher or a grouch or whatever they are? They're all part of the audience and I am sensitive, very sensitive, to audiences.

"Yes, sure I've changed since 1960 and *Come Blow Your Horn*. I'd be pretty much of a vegetable if I hadn't and I have noted that both you and David Richards of the *Star-News* used the word 'mellow' in your reviews of this play. That's probably very true because you go through things and learn from them. Maybe I have been mellowing.

"For instance, thinking in terms of the Oriental philosophies, I've learned that we all have enough real troubles, real problems, not to get upset about matters over which we have no conceivable control. Some critics never have liked what I've written and there's absolutely nothing I can do about that. I do smile, of course, when they write that one work isn't as good as another which, they forget, they didn't like in the first place.

"And when it comes to describing me (as you probably will if only to identify me) as the top money-making playwright of all time, that only makes me think of how wrong we are, in our western civilization, to be labeling certain people by how much they're paid.

"Only yesterday I was reading in the sports pages how an athlete was getting some enormous amount of money for a new contract. That was the pitch of the piece, not how good a player he is. The same is true about the prices paid for a work of art. If people were told to see it because it is beautiful, you'd get a very small crowd. If they're told someone paid millions for it, there'd be a jam. But you seldom read about how much bankers, who deal in money, are paid.

"The essential thing about all this money the plays have made is that it liberates me from worrying about money. It means I can work on my plays. After a certain point, money is just more money."

A New Yorker born on the fourth of July forty-five years ago, Simon would strike Mr. Anonymous American to be as anonymous as himself. He's pleasant looking without being handsome; has dark hair, wears horn-rimmed glasses, and dresses casually. His wife, Joan, a former dancer, is here for the new play's birth pangs and proves to be a tiny, cheerful soul with big brown eyes and a penchant for pantsuits. They live unostentatiously in a town house on New York's East Side and have just bought a country place in Bedford, a Westchester County favorite for writers and players.

The Simons have two daughters, Ellen, fifteen, and Nancy, nine, home at school. Though they keep up with all the latest plays and movies, the Simons aren't conspicuous at the big openings or other social occasions. Because tennis has been pulling his neck muscles a bit uncomfortably lately, Simon is planning to go back to golf so he'll feel more relaxed at his typewriter.

He and his elder brother, Danny, began their writing careers by attracting the attention of radio's then powerful Goodman Ace. He'd liked their description of a Joan Crawford movie: "She's in love with a gangster who is caught and sent to Sing Sing and given the electric chair and she promises to wait for him."

Danny and "Doc" (Neil's nickname stems from his childhood habit of imitating the family doctor and not from requests he's had to "doctor" faltering plays) began to be talked about while writing material for such comics as Phil Silvers, Jerry Lester, Jackie Gleason, and Sid Caesar. "I learned," Simon once said, "that if ever I were to do anything else but write for star comics, I'd have to do it myself. That's when I began to write *Horn*, suggested by my brother's and my relationship with our parents. I must have written that play twenty-three times.

"After twelve plays I've begun to not need that many rewrites. The basic fact about a play, I've learned, is that the basic idea has to be right or else it just won't work. Not ever.

"When I'm asked to look over plays trying out out-of-town, that's what always hits me when it's not right. No amount of fooling around with lines, players, or staging is going to alter the basically false premise.

"I think that's what happened to me on *The Gingerbread Lady*. During the Boston run I softened the ending, but it didn't really rescue the play. I've come to the conclusion that the situation just wasn't right, that this woman couldn't have been that kind of woman whose background I'd imagined.

"Nor was the title right. I'd had to drag that title from the simile she speaks of to her daughters. Some titles come just right. *Horn, Barefoot in the Park, The Odd Couple*. They said it exactly, led the audiences to expect just what they found. The same is true, I think, with *The Sunshine Boys*. That's what they were and this is what happens to them."

It's been a busy month for Simon. November also brought the airing of his TV special with George C. Scott, Alan Arkin (*Sunshine's* director), and James Coco (Barney of *The Last of the Red Hot Lovers*). The newest Simon movie, *The Heartbreak Kid*, starring Elaine May, will be opening in New York on the same day that *Sunshine Boys* reaches the Broadhurst (December 20).

"What next?" I asked.

"Well, I have a play for George C. Scott and he likes it, but, for the first time as a playwright, I felt it's really not ready yet. I had it about finished, a serious play, but I put it away when *Sunshine Boys* occurred to me. I want to let that one sit for a while.

"I have another idea, something in the revue form, lately so neglected. I think I see how I can do it. I want to try.

"As for more musicals," the librettist of *Sweet Charity*, *Little Me*, and *Promises, Promises* continued, "they're really hard to do, to avoid that too-visible gap between the book and the songs. I was very happy working with Burt Bacharach, but so often a musical's book doesn't have the same texture as its songs. *My Fair Lady* was totally seamless thanks to Alan Jay Lerner. That's why it was a triumph.

"Besides, musicals should have several sets of characters and these, in the time permitted, allow only the most superficial character sketching. I much prefer working in a tighter, smaller range. You can probe more deeply that way.

"That's why I'm pleased at the way *Sunshine Boys* is working out. People are seeing beyond the funny lines and, as I have in my last few plays, I'm busy taking out funny lines, big laughs which come in the wrong places. I've been cutting in Act I, not that any but the actors would be that aware of it. I seem to want to get to the point where Sam Levene makes his entrance.

"Isn't it a marvel the way Sam does that, the look on his face, the use of his body, his hands? That moment is a whole comment on a lifetime and it's taken all his years of experience for Levene to be able to do it.

"Again, it's recognition. He gives the audience a man they immediately recognize. Without a word.

"Yes, that's what my plays have been about, recognizable people. I once said that I dream of writing the perfect two-hour play. For 119 minutes the audience would be hysterical with laughter but for the last minute so moved that they leave the theater in a daze. Maybe this one puts me closer to that goal.

"Anyway, I'll never stop trying. That's what the success of the other plays has meant: the luxury of being able to keep trying."

Neil Simon: Broadway's King Moves to Hollywood

David Sterritt / 1976

From the *Christian Science Monitor*, January 15, 1976, p. 14. Reprinted with permission. © 1976 The Christian Science Monitor (www.CSMonitor.com).

New York

He is the king of Broadway. Nobody else has done quite what Neil Simon has done. With a tangy imagination, a way with words, and a typewriter, he has turned out the longest and funniest parade of hits in recent memory. Let a few titles suffice: *The Odd Couple, Plaza Suite, Barefoot in the Park, The Prisoner of Second Avenue, The Last of the Red Hot Lovers*.

And now the king of Broadway has moved to Hollywood. Don't worry— he hasn't left the stage behind altogether. But there are more fertile fields to conquer, out West on the silver screen. The latest Simon smash is a screen farce based on one of his Broadway hits, *The Sunshine Boys*. Since completing it, he has concocted an all-star comedy called *Murder by Death*, now being filmed with a cast that will feature everyone from David Niven and Truman Capote to Peter Falk, Alec Guinness, Peter Sellers, and Nancy Walker. *Bogart Slept Here* is the title of another coming Simon screen extravaganza. Already Broadway's biggest hitsmith, Simon now is reaching out to whole new audiences around the world.

For the writer, who has moved to California from his New York home, the switch to film is part of "a natural progression. . . . I've done fourteen plays in fourteen years and I need some other stimuli now."

Interviewed in New York, just before two big events—release of *The Sunshine Boys* movie and the big move West—Simon showed no signs of slowing down. "I've written three movies back to back, and it looks like

I'm going to do a fourth," he said. Clearly, Hollywood has welcomed Simon with wide-open arms.

Explaining his desire to live near his movie projects, rather than in New York, Simon smiles comfortably and says simply, "I like being around the movies I write. I haven't done it in the past [except for helping out on *Sunshine*] and consequently I haven't always been happy with my works on screen. . . . Being there, I'll be in on the rehearsals and casting and occasionally the shooting. I'll be there to make comments, which is what I do every single day on a play."

You'll be happy to hear that "it won't be the end of playwriting" for Simon. "I'll just do the plays out there first, instead of coming to New Haven or Boston to try them out. . . . I'll have the same life out there in terms of work and career, but I'll have the opportunity to be outside—play some tennis and get some sun, which is what I need."

A modest, plain-looking, and unassuming man, Simon gave up a marvelous midtown Manhattan apartment when he exited the East. But the move had been creeping up on him for a long time. "I don't get the same kick out of writing plays," he muses. "I was sitting in a hotel in New Hampshire and I said, 'It's just not as much fun anymore.' Production isn't fun anyway. I love just the writing part of it."

Simon feels that films will open up new subject matter and new approaches for him. During the past few years he has engaged regularly in audience-watching, and he reports that the same "provincial audience" shows up on Broadway night after night, play after play, season after season. Movies fare differently from place to place, he feels, and he looks forward to seeing his films gather different responses in different cities. He also notes that movies attract a younger crowd "because of subject matter and ticket prices . . . so in films I'll be able to write for a more diverse audience."

The move to movies is not a simple procedure, Simon realizes. "You must remember that you're working in a different medium," he philosophizes. "A lot of things don't have to be said in a film—sometimes just a look into the camera will say five lines. . . . Unlike the theater, in a film everybody sees the same thing."

In screen-scripting though, "you can still keep the language in mind, and remember what writing is. Describing something that will be visually effective is just as important as writing a terrific line of dialogue." Simon nonetheless acknowledges that film is a director's medium. "That's why I will never give up what I have in the theater, which is definitely an author's medium."

With all those hit titles over his name, Simon has become one of the best-known playwrights of our time. Does he enjoy fame? "Sure. It's not bad. But it has its stigma. I constantly get compared to myself. If *God's Favorite*"—a recent Broadway effort—"was the first play I wrote, they would have 'discovered' me. But since it wasn't the first, they say, 'It's not his best.' I have to fight that label all the time. . . . Fame has its difficulties, dealing with it and keeping your individuality."

Speaking of fame, I ask Simon if he expects to be mentioned in future history books. "Yes," he says. "But only because I am very successful. . . . It has nothing to do with the quality of one's work. It remains to be seen whether any of these plays will hold up five, ten, twenty, or fifty years from now. Just in terms of the number of plays and length of runs and number of productions, though—sure, it'll be in the books."

In his own opinion, Simon guesses that two of his plays might prove to be enduring classics: *The Odd Couple* and *The Sunshine Boys*. They share "that basic conflict between the characters . . ." which the playwright values.

Interestingly, Simon thinks of his plays as "entertainments. You have to be crazy to think of your plays as works of art. That would be like writing under the title, 'An important new play by Neil Simon.' That's pretentious. A work of art is qualitative. . . . I haven't the slightest idea if what I'm writing is going to be a hit or a flop, or good or bad. It just feels good as I'm writing it."

Hence Simon has no favorites among his own works. "I only have favorite times. Like when I was writing *Barefoot in the Park*, which was my first big hit. Everything about it was terrific—the atmosphere, the aura. . . ."

Simon does have theories about why he became a writer, however. "It has to do with one's personality," he reveals, after being pressed just a little. "It's like handing your personality through the door, but you don't have to show it. . . . It's on a piece of paper. You say, 'There, that's what I am, but I can't quite face you.'"

According to Simon, a strange "distancing" occurs in a famous playwright's career. To illustrate this idea, he points out that he has been on television shows and received awards, but that his recent reception of a special Tony Award "was the first time when I felt the New York theater audience was applauding me and my work, personally. I've always gotten it from the back of the theater, where you can't tell if they're applauding what the actor did or what I wrote.

"It was a new and interesting experience," he concludes. "It felt terrific, and very warm. It didn't quite hit me until the next night, when I was sort of overwhelmed by it. . . . I could see the audience's faces, and they were all smiling. . . ."

Yet there is a negative side to the fabulous Simon career. He feels that a certain animosity is leveled at him precisely because of his great success. "It happens to me, as in any walk of life. When one is immature, one doesn't deal with it. When one becomes more mature, one becomes more self-confident—not about your work, but about yourself as a person. Things have a way of evening out. In the long run, you get out of life what you put into it. . . ."

Some negative criticism is aimed at Simon's swift writing habits and great productivity. But this sort of jibe doesn't bother him at all. "There is no way in the world that I'll ever be able to write as many plays as Shakespeare did," he sighs with a smile. "If you want to talk about quantity, then Shakespeare has got to be the biggest hack there ever was. . . . If I can be as big a hack, and as slick as Shakespeare—terrific!"

With problems as well as joys to face in his career, Simon lives a busy and complicated life. Some observers say that his plays are getting more serious as the playwright ages and matures. Comments Simon: "I don't seem to think that, but the critics do. . . . So I guess there must be an underlying seriousness in my attitudes toward life that prompts me to write plays with such seriousness in them. But I always *think* I'm writing a comedy."

The darkest of Simon's plays, so far, is probably his tragicomedy about a troubled middle-aged woman, *The Gingerbread Lady*. Simon says, "I knew what I was about. . . . I knew it was going to go back and forth—that there were moments when we were laughing at her and with her, and suddenly she turns into this devastatingly cruel and self-destructive woman, and it makes us uncomfortable. That's the way life is to me. And I try, when writing realistic plays, to get as close to the truth as possible. In a superficial comedy, things are funny all the time. But life isn't that way. And that kind of a play doesn't really interest me. . . ."

Might Simon write a full-fledged tragedy one day? "No way," comes the grinning answer. "I somehow seem to find some humor in everything. That's not to say that I turn everything into something funny, but I do look to find some human element. And all the faults of human characters can—in a way—be funny. . . . There *are* certain kinds of tragedy that I wouldn't deal with . . . that I wouldn't like to jest with. But I think our own human failings—the ones that get us into trouble in our marriages and our work—when you point them up in retrospect, we can laugh at them."

To illustrate, Simon refers to "the lightest of the comedies," his early *Barefoot in the Park*. In it, he recalls, "a husband and wife are having a fight to the death after one week of marriage, and she's asking for a divorce. Well, that happened to me and my wife. When it was happening, it was deadly serious—we both thought the marriage was over—but it was just what young couples go through. Later on we looked back, and saw how silly it was. So in retrospect you can write about that, with humor."

A writer of Simon's experience must inevitably have fantasies of directing his own work, and Simon pleads "no contest" to that charge. "I've thought about it," he admits. "I've thought about directing a comedy murder mystery, after Mike Nichols and I finish *Bogart Slept Here*. But I saw the hours put in by Herbert Ross [director of *The Sunshine Boys* on film]. Getting up at seven in the morning, to the studio at eight, leaving for the location at 8:30. I say life is too short to work that much time.

"I work hard enough as a writer—five, six, seven hours a day for about seven months of the year. And I like making my own hours. If I want to stop for a few hours or a few days, I can do that. But a picture's demands on your personal life are so great that I think it jeopardizes other aspects of your life."

Incidentally, the number of hours put in by Simon includes work on many different projects. He takes about three months to write a play or a screenplay, though a play will sometimes sit untouched for months, between drafts. At one point not long ago Simon had four irons in the fire simultaneously: "*Sunshine Boys* was being shot, and I had the first draft of *Bogart Slept Here* finished, while I was writing this new murder mystery and toying with another idea for a play."

One fantasy Simon doesn't have is of himself onstage or onscreen. Though he once took a cameo role on the *Odd Couple* TV series (which he claims he didn't see when it was aired), he insists that he will never be an actor. "I'm not Mel Brooks," he insists. "I don't have that kind of talent or that kind of desire. I never want to do something, for ego's sake, that somebody else could do better. . . . I don't think a lot of writers can write better than I can—there are some, but it's the one thing I do very well in certain areas. So that's what I would like to stick to."

Not only does he shudder at the idea of finding himself onstage; Simon doesn't even lay claim to being the life of the party in his private life. "I'm not Mel Brooks," he repeats. "But neither is Woody Allen. Woody is a very funny man, to me—he really makes me laugh. But I have played cards with Woody when he has said three words all night: 'raise' and 'I'm out.' . . . Mel has his serious moments too, but he is much more of a performer; he's much closer to being a comic. He's 'on' all the time, he's truly one of the funniest men in the world. . . .

"I've never asked anyone to expect me to be funny. I am funny with my close friends when something amusing happens. But I talk and act the way I write. Sometimes I'm funny, and sometimes I'm sad. Sometimes I'm real, and sometimes I'm not. . . ."

A Conversation with . . . : Neil Simon Unclenches Fist

Jack Slater / 1977

From *Los Angeles Times*, April 22, 1977, Part IV, pp. 2, 6, 7, 8.

Nine years ago, playwright Neil Simon told a reporter, "I'm really going through a period of saying, 'What's it all about, Alfie?'" Today, having traveled through a transformation as a writer and a man and into a more agonizing period in which he, watching his wife die of cancer, suffered a mental breakdown, Simon can say, "I think you have to sink to the depths before you start to come up again."

Question: Do you feel you've lost the exhilaration you surely must have felt when you were writing *Barefoot in the Park* in the early 1960s?
Answer: Not exhilaration. I think maybe innocence is the word. I don't think I'm as innocent a person or a writer as I was then. I don't think I could write *Barefoot in the Park* now. In a way, the new play I've written—*Chapter Two*—could be considered those people in *Barefoot* twenty-four years later. *Barefoot in the Park* was the happiest time in my life—until now. Everything was wonderful. My dreams were coming true. I was finally getting to be a Broadway playwright. And I was young.

One of the most prolific and profit-making playwrights of all time, Neil Simon is sitting in the midst of the Spartan chic of what he calls his office-apartment. The living room is bleakly furnished with a telephone, a desk, a coffee table, a couch, and lots of Beverly Hills sunlight.

"I got this place because it's so close to the Beverly Hills Tennis Club," he says. "I can work from about ten o'clock until lunchtime, play tennis, and feel refreshed enough to want to go back to the typewriter."

Tall and easy-going, with a moonlike face and a receding hairline, Simon, at forty-nine, is a mild-mannered, introspective man, a kind of self-confident Mr. Peepers, sometimes tortured, sometimes nostalgic but always the reliable, likable Next Door Neighbor, who just happens to write sensationally popular comedies for a living.

Q: How much has success as a playwright contributed to your loss of innocence?
A: Success takes you to some very strange places. It isolates you and it affects people around you—your family and friends. They begin to view you differently, as though you were some sort of extraordinary person: You have been to a place they haven't seen, a place they don't know at all. For example, I had relatives who used to call and who stopped calling. Finally, when they did call they would say, "I hate to disturb you." In other words, they were saying that you are now a separate person. Also, it was very difficult for me as a writer to walk along the street and be recognized. One of the joys of being a writer is one's anonymity. I've never enjoyed being stared at or mumbled about. You begin to wonder about being a celebrity. You realize you need not have done anything wonderful. You can assassinate the president and be a celebrity. People will say, "Oh, there goes Lee Harvey Oswald." You begin to wonder what it is people are thinking about you.

More important, Simon began to wonder what to think of himself and how this isolation would affect his work.

"When I was a kid, I used to think I was invisible. I truly believed that. I would go with my parents to visit my grandmother and sit there for hours while they talked. They never noticed me, and I would sit and listen. It would be the same in the subway or on the trolley car: I was absorbing everything, watching, always being a viewer, so that I was able to assimilate all of it and use it eventually in my work." But with success and celebrity, "it becomes more difficult to be a viewer when you're being viewed. That's also part of the isolation."

The plays, curiously, bespeak little isolation on the author's part—or rather, they embrace a special kind of isolation. Simon's world is, for the most part, that softer, warmer, more vulnerable world of marriage and personal relationship, both viewed through the prism of middle-class values. In *Barefoot in the Park*, Simon centered his comedy on young marriage. In *The Odd Couple*, he spoke of divorce and its effect on the relationship of two men rooming together. And in *The Prisoner of Second Avenue*, he analyzes middle-aged marriage interacting with urban despair.

"I've written about marriage a good deal," Simon says, "because I believe in it so much. I know the problems one goes through in marriage. When you work out that relationship, you just keep going to this new and better and more wonderful place with each other. Then you're better able to relate to the rest of the world. If you can't make it with one other person, I don't see how you can make it with a lot of human beings."

Born and reared in New York, he grew up in the thickets of the Jewish lower-middle class and witnessed the "rotten marriage" of his parents for more years than he cares to remember.

"When I think about it," he recalls, "growing up at home was just horrible. My parents were *constantly* fighting and breaking up. I guess they separated ten or fifteen times. My father would leave the house and [we] wouldn't see him for a week, a month, a year, a couple of years. My parents kept getting back together again, but it was always so tentative. I mean, I would come home from school each day and wonder whether or not my father was there. But then when he was coming home, there was great jubilance: 'Dad is coming back and everything is going to be okay!' Then, whamo!" His father, a garment merchant, would leave again. "So after a while you would begin to steel yourself and say, 'Well, I don't care about that anymore, I'll isolate myself. I'll protect myself.' I became very protective, very defensive, very insulated."

He is, as well, controlled, disciplined, calm, considerate.

Like so many children of his generation, he sought release and safety in the fantasies spun on celluloid. "I would go to the movies every time I could. Just sit there alone in that darkened theater, so that there was nothing real coming from the outside." More often than not, Humphrey Bogart was on the screen. "I think he is still my hero in movies . . . because of his independence from everybody. Which is what I felt: That nobody was ever going to get close to me. I had been hurt enough. That's why I felt a rebirth when I met Joan."

In 1963, when he was twenty-six and she twenty-one, Simon married Joan Baim, a dancer, and became wedded to marriage as an institution. They met at a resort in the Pocono Mountains of Pennsylvania. "Often I think that that's when my life really began—which is not true, of course, because pain is as much a part of life as pleasure," he says. "But that's when I really started to feel fulfilled. We were married twenty years, and when the end of that came I felt desolated." (The couple had two children, Ellen, twenty, and Nancy, fourteen.)

Q: You've suggested that you did not particularly like yourself as a young man. How did your self-distaste affect your marriage?
A: Well, I didn't dislike myself in all areas. I think I liked the areas Joan liked. In a way, she had some of the same neurotic problems that I had. She would be very open and gregarious with certain people, and with others she'd be very closed. Our problems were compatible. But her idea was always that if the two of us lived on a little island somewhere, then life would be perfect. And so we did, more or less, live on our own little island.

Even in that relatively happy place, however, his comedies had begun to change from light to dark, from the cotton candy insubstantiality of *Barefoot* to the nameless unfulfillment and restlessness depicted in the first one-acter of *Plaza Suite*. ("I was lucky," a fifty-year-old successful businessman tells his wife in the play. "I got it all . . . marriage, the children . . . more money [than] I ever dreamed of making." But: "I just want to do it all over again. . . . I would like to start the whole damned thing right from the beginning.")

"Inside Neil Simon," a national magazine trumpeted in 1970, "lives a serious playwright struggling to get out. . . . Laughs only count now as echoes of the truth."

But the laughs, even as echoes, soon stopped. Joan Simon became ill with cancer, and her husband's world began to fall apart, even as the control and the discipline in him took over. "Consciously," he says, "my first aim or objective was to stay healthy for my children. Otherwise, I really just felt like curling up and disappearing. . . . I tried working. The work was not much fun in doing it, but I felt it was important to continue doing it."

Finally, however, even the control within him slipped. One day he made a discovery: The distance between his front door and the sidewalk seemed a chasm. He would not leave his house, could not walk out into the street. "Joan and I tried to walk over to Central Park, and it was too far away. It was like going to Asia." At the same time, he realized he was having difficulty breathing, realized that his mind was rushing, roaring. Eventually, he entered a hospital. Then an enormous sense of failure overwhelmed him.

"I could not see it through, and Joan was the one who was really going through it," he says. "I felt pretty ashamed not being able to be strong enough to . . . to . . ."

In the hospital, an acquaintance began talking to him with the utmost urgency. "This person said to me there is no way you can hold onto Joan. He said that the more you try to hold on the more it's going to be impossible for you. He said, 'When you learn to let go, you'll be able to survive it.'"

So Simon tried to let go, succeeded briefly, and a month later "started to fall apart again," as he tried more to hold on. Then, miraculously, he made it over.

His wife's death was an experience he now speaks of with the objectivity of a distant observer and with the fervor of a man in whom hope flourishes. "I'm not the only one who has gone through a tragedy," he notes. "After a while, one doesn't even think of it as a tragedy so much as the next step."

In relinquishing his wife, he says, he let go of other things: his anger, his containment, and certain attitudes in his writing. "I've become more compassionate. It's been mystical, almost. I just changed. I can barely relate to the other person I once was." Illustrating how he views the earlier version of himself, Simon clenches his right hand into a fist. "Now," he says, smiling and spreading his fingers into a fan, "It's an open hand."

Simon married actress Marsha Mason four months after the death of Joan Simon. In meeting her, "I felt there was this gift being handed to me: an opportunity to have continuity to one's life." Together he and his bride began to live in the house on East 62nd Street, where he and Joan had lived for the last ten years of marriage. But Simon soon realized that neither he nor his new wife could continue to live in that house. "It was a different time," he says, "and a different marriage."

And so, because of his growing interest in writing for the screen and her blossoming movie career, the Simons moved to Southern California. That was nearly two years ago, seven years after he had written in another context: "I just want to do it all over again. . . . I would like to start the whole . . . thing right from the beginning."

Make 'Em Laugh

Clive Hirschhorn / 1977

From *Plays and Players* 24 (September 1977): 12–15. Reprinted with the permission of Clive Hirschhorn. Clive Hirschhorn is the theater critic of the *Sunday Express* (London) and the author of *The Films of James Mason* (1975), *The Warner Bros. Story* (1979), and *The Hollywood Musical* (1981).

Clive Hirschhorn: When did you first realize you had the ability to make people laugh?

Neil Simon: They say my mother's obstetrician took one look at me when I was born, began to laugh uncontrollably, and still hasn't stopped, so I guess it started way back then. Actually, I've always had a proclivity towards humor, but then so did my older brother. In fact, he was the *real* humorist in the family, and whose ambition it was to become a comedy writer. And it was he who realized I could also be quite funny when I wanted to be—which was most of the time. This was while I was still in my teens, and I remember at high school I used to write essays very much in the Robert Benchley mold. Benchley was a great influence. So was Mark Twain and George S. Kaufman. But then everyone and everything influenced me during those years. Every film and every play I saw made an impression. That's the way it is when you're young. But I guess if I had to state, categorically, who the *most* influential person in my life was, I'd have to say my brother. It was he who got me started in the business—working on radio, then on TV shows. But once I was on my way, it was life that influenced me. And if that sounds pretentious, it is.

CH: How impressed were you with plays like Kaufman and Hart's *The Man Who Came to Dinner* and *You Can't Take It with You*?

NS: I liked and admired them, of course. They're very funny pieces of theater. But you really want to know what thrilled me more than any theater I saw at the time? The early movies of Chaplin and Laurel and Hardy and

Buster Keaton. They had a compassion that a lot of the American stage comedies lacked. And, of course, they had all those absolutely incredible sight gags—and as my basic training as a writer started in radio where sight gags were, of course, impossible, I found, at the time, I responded more to what the eye saw than the ear heard. But eventually the written word became the most important thing of all to me, and I found myself avidly reading everything I could lay my hands on. For a brief period I wanted to belong to the world of literature rather than radio, TV, the theater, or the movies.

CH: Do you regard yourself as a witty or a humorous writer?

NS: There's a very narrow distinction between the two, you know. After all, the object of both is to make you laugh. Humor, I guess, is something intrinsic to the plot. For example, in *You Can't Take It with You*, a typewriter is delivered by mistake to the house in which the play is set. So one of the characters decides to become a playwright. That's humorous. But in *The Odd Couple*, when Oscar Madison tells Felix Ungar it took him two hours to work out that the initials FU on the note he found on his pillow meant Felix Ungar—that's wit. Most of the plays I've written I'd classify as witty, I guess. Though I have written some humorous ones as well. Like *God's Favorite*, a modern retelling of the Job story. My first play, *Come Blow Your Horn*, is basically humorous. My second play, *Barefoot in the Park*, relies more on its one-liners than on any intrinsic texture the text might have. But these are hair-breadth distinctions, and, if pushed, I could probably say that *Come Blow Your Horn* was witty, and *Barefoot in the Park* was humorous without too many people disagreeing with me. So why don't we just change the subject?

CH: You now live permanently in California, yet, as a writer, your orientation is very much New York. Has your switch of venue affected your choice of subjects?

NS: I'm far too experienced a writer to have to worry about what "vibes" I pick up from whatever place I happen to find myself in. I've written plays all over the world—London, Spain, France, you name it—and most of my New York plays were written on the tip end of Long Island, which, in every respect, is light years away from the center of Manhattan. I've had enough experiences in my life to be able to draw on them regardless of where I, physically, happen to be at the time.

CH: What discipline do you impose on yourself where your writing is concerned?

NS: Well, for a start I don't make it a habit, like some writers do, of writing X number of words a day. I have far too many other things to do with my life— like attend production meetings, auditions, rehearsals, etc. I'm also married (to actress Marsha Mason) and I have obligations in that direction as well. In the last year and seven months, I've written two new stage plays and two screenplays. But I can't tell you how many days I spent on each. Usually, the first draft of a play takes me about three months to write. Then I put it aside for at least a month, and get on with something else. For example, I completed the first draft of my new play, *Chapter Two*, two months ago, put it in a drawer and worked on the screenplays for *The Cheap Detective* and *The Goodbye Girl*. Well, *The Goodbye Girl* has completed shooting, and *The Cheap Detective* has just started. So, with the screenplays out of the way, I'm now working on the second draft of *Chapter Two*. And so it goes.

CH: Everything you say tends to confirm my belief that you're inexhaustible. Do you think of yourself this way? Or, like most writers, do you have a fear of drying up?

NS: I don't really have any fears that I'm going to "dry up," no. I get worried, sometimes, that the ideas I have just aren't good enough. And often they aren't. But with a lot of hard work it's possible to turn a bad idea into a good one simply by playing around with variations on it until you get something that strikes, and is good enough to use. Inspiration counts for very little in this game. It's hard work that's going to get your play to work. Before I had the idea for *Chapter Two*, which is a sort of autobiographical play dealing with the period between the death of my first wife (of cancer) and my marriage to my second wife, I started six plays. I'd only written about ten pages of these plays before I discarded them because none was any good.

CH: How did you know they weren't any good?

NS: Because I just wasn't interested in them. And that's always the main, most crucial test with me. Many times people have begged me to go on with something I've started, and although on a couple of occasions, I have, the general rule is, if it bores me, out it goes. Straight into the trash can. I also have to feel that whatever I'm doing is going in a new direction for me. To you, the plays may appear to be similar in style and content. But if I happen to think, for whatever reason, they're exploring new territory, then I'll carry on with it.

CH: Does it upset you when plays like *God's Favorite* and *The Good Doctor* (a dramatization of some Chekhov stories), which aren't typical Neil Simon comedies, fail to find favor?

NS: Yes, at the time—you know, when the people don't come and we've got to close it. That disturbs and upsets me—after all, no one likes to fail. But right now, sitting here, it doesn't disturb me because it's in the past, I've so much work to do, and I've done so much since *God's Favorite* folded, and I've had so much success with other shows, it would be silly of me to worry about the ones that got away.

CH: But isn't it because you've had so much success with your more recent commercial plays—like *Plaza Suite* and *California Suite*—that you want your more experimental work to get some sort of recognition—both with critics and audiences?

NS: Yes, but to be practical about these things, I don't want to turn my back on the things I know I do well. If people respond to plays of mine like *The Prisoner of Second Avenue*, or *The Odd Couple*, because they can identify with the characters and the situations—as opposed to plays where they simply go and have a moderately good time, but get nothing of value out of them—I'm certainly not going to feel cheated, and I'll go on writing those kind of plays for them. All I want is that the people who've just seen one of my plays will emerge from the theater a little richer than they were when they went in.

CH: At those ticket prices!? Are you, in any way, disillusioned with the average Broadway expense-account audience's interest in musicals and their seeming inability to support quality drama for any length of time?

NS: No. Broadway is Broadway and I don't expect it to change. To succeed on Broadway you've got to know your market, and if I wanted a long run or even a good one with *God's Favorite*, it would have been far more sensible for me to have done it off-Broadway or in a regional theater somewhere. The same applies to *The Good Doctor*. But I was talked into doing them on Broadway because, I was assured, that with my name on them, they'd succeed. It was a mistake and I only have myself to blame. There's just no room for those kinds of plays on Broadway today. It's a fact of life and I must just accept it. *God's Favorite* didn't catch on at all, though *The Good Doctor* might have run a year if it wasn't such a costly show. We had seven musicians, many stage-hands, and generally, the kind of overheads that made it impractical to keep running. So we closed the show when it was grossing $47,000 a week. Unfortunately, we were losing $4,000 a week throughout its run, so there was no point in pushing it further. As for *God's Favorite*, well, there was no way it could have run on Broadway. It was a very controversial play and the notices were bad. A fatal combination. Still, I notice that it's being done throughout the country in colleges and universities and in stock, so, obviously, it still has some life in it. Which is reassuring.

CH: So you would regard *God's Favorite* as the least successful play you've written?

NS: No, the least successful play I've written was *The Star-Spangled Girl* which ran about ten months on Broadway, made a lot of money, went out on tour and made more money, and was also made into a movie—which, incidentally, I never bothered to see. That play, I consider to be *far* less successful than *God's Favorite*. At least *God's Favorite* made a statement. I wasn't very happy with the idea of *The Star-Spangled Girl* right from the start. And I hated writing it. But everyone I voiced my doubts to, said what a fantastic idea it was, and, against my better judgment, I went ahead with it. Actually, the original idea for it was based on an intellectual liberal I knew. He was having a heated argument at a party one night with a woman who was quite bright, but whose opinions were to the right of right. The thing is, she was a very attractive woman, and I noticed how the liberal kept looking at her in a sexual way. And I thought how interesting it was that this man should be so physically attracted to a woman whose ideals he so clearly despises. And I wondered what would happen if they were forced to live with one another. Well, instead of using these two types in the play, I chose two other types completely. I invented a story about a couple of guys living at Berkeley University, and how their lives are disrupted by the arrival of an attractive young girl. Now I'd never ever been to Berkeley so I couldn't even describe the set accurately, or the way the kids dressed. And this is important, because, before I can write convincingly about anyone, I have to know how he or she looks, walks, talks, and dresses, what they have for breakfast and who their favorite movie stars are. With *The Star-Spangled Girl* it was all guess work. And by the time I got well into the first act, I wanted to quit on it. But my producer kept urging me to go on with it. And the only reason I did, was because he had done the same thing with *Barefoot*. I disliked *Barefoot* halfway through and was ready to scrap it, but he persuaded me to finish it and it worked out very well. In fact, I consider it one of my favorite plays.

CH: To change the subject slightly. It seems extraordinary to me that so many of your plays have never been to London.

NS: Ah yes, well. That's quite a sore point. I've deliberately prevented a lot of my plays being done in London, you know. If you go down the list, only *Come Blow Your Horn* which was done at the Prince of Wales, and which ran for fourteen months, was a success. Next came *Little Me*, the musical for which I wrote the book, and which got wonderful reviews but not much of a run at the Cambridge. Then came *Barefoot in the Park*. Sensational reviews again, but no fireworks at the box office. *The Odd Couple* came next, and was only a moderate success.

CH: Possibly because Victor Spinetti was totally miscast as Felix Ungar.
NS: Yes indeed. And that sort of thing happens because I wasn't able to be around to keep an eye on the production. In the past I've also been mis-informed by British producers about the capabilities of certain actors they wish to cast, and about the importance of a well-known British name to draw the crowds. Now, as far as having a good marquee name is concerned, they might be right. I don't know. The strange thing about my plays in London is that the pieces themselves almost always get unanimously rave reviews, but that audiences just don't seem to give a damn. In some instances, it's even turned out that my hotel bill at the Connaught is costing me more than the royalties I was earning! In other words, it was costing *me* money to open a play in London. The only shows of mine that made a substantial profit for me in London were *Promises, Promises* and *Sweet Charity*, both musicals. *The Sunshine Boys*, which my brother came over to direct, got excellent notices, but hardly did any business at all. I guess the humor was just too American. In France and Italy, on the other hand, my plays are very popular—especially Italy. Also Germany and Scandinavia. Somehow, in the adaptation, the gap between the American idiom, and the idiom of whatever European country the play is being given in, is successfully bridged. But how do you bridge the gap between Broadway and the West End? It really strikes me as being pointless to come to London each year and do a play which will probably end up with nice reviews, but with everyone involved losing money. I saw *The Gingerbread Lady*, not in London but in Windsor, and Elaine Stritch was superb in it—as good as anything I'd ever seen. And I thought to myself, if that doesn't run, then England's trying to tell me something. It didn't run.

CH: There have been a couple of exceptions, but generally I don't think your plays have been well-staged, or well-cast in London.
NS: What you see in London is a hybrid form of my work. Often they're neither one thing nor the other. I agree, some of the productions and

performances have been unsatisfactory, but what, I think, is basically to blame for their conspicuous lack of success are the differences between our two cultures in the area of humor. American humor is rooted in people's neuroses, while English humor is more slapstick. There is a slickness about American comedies, and, of course, musicals, that the English are very suspicious of, and which makes them uncomfortable. And these differences make it very difficult for comedy to cross the Atlantic successfully. Your own Alan Ayckbourn has similar problems when his plays go to Broadway. They're quintessentially English, his plays, and American casts and audiences rarely do justice to them. In some cases, like *Absurd Person Singular*, they succeed. But in others, like *The Norman Conquests*, they don't. I saw *Table Manners*, the first of the trilogy, and didn't think it was right at all. All the things you can level against my plays in the West End, could be leveled against that one on Broadway. The cast wasn't right, and the whole "feel" of the production, somehow, was wrong. On the other hand, I recently saw Simon Gray's *Otherwise Engaged* and loved it, even though some of the supporting people on Broadway weren't so hot. But Tom Courtenay was marvelous, and because the play wasn't, essentially, a comedy, it managed to survive its Atlantic crossing. Somehow it's only the comedies which seem to fail. Drama and tragedy usually reach a wider audience. People cry over the same things wherever they are. But the things that make people laugh vary spectacularly from country to country. Even town to town. The reason a play like *Equus* is a hit wherever it's done, is because what it's saying has certain resonances for most Western societies. Drama is much less confining than humor.

CH: How do you answer your critics who complain that your more serious comedies, like *The Gingerbread Lady* and *Prisoner of Second Avenue*, are sabotaged by the witty one-liners you can't seem to avoid incorporating into your work?

NS: I have no answer. When I write something like *God's Favorite*, I'm criticized for *not* writing witty one-liners. So, either way, I can't win.

CH: How do you know when a line is funny? Does it have to make you laugh?

NS: No, I no longer laugh at the lines that emerge from my typewriter. The prerequisite for me is that the line must be able to express an old thought with a certain freshness and be seen from a different point of view. And if I'm convinced it does, the chances are it'll get a laugh from an audience. What, ideally, I want audiences to say is: "My God, I've often thought about that, but I've never heard it expressed quite that way." What audiences are very suspicious of is the easy gag—the obvious "laugh line" that seems manufactured and contrived and which the playwright didn't have the discipline to fling out. I remember I had one such line in *The Odd Couple* and the critic for the *New York Times*, who was then Howard Taubman, pointed the line out in his otherwise favorable review, and asked me not to do such things in [the] future.

CH: Do you remember the line?
NS: Yes. It was concerning the character of Felix Ungar. They were all worrying that he might try to commit suicide, when one of the boys says: "Not Felix, he's not that kind of person. He's the sort of guy that would wear his seat-belts in a drive-in movie."

CH: That's a funny line.
NS: Sure, but it also sounds like a Bob Hope gag. If I had to take the really funny moments out of *The Odd Couple* and quote them to you, out of context they wouldn't seem funny at all.

CH: Mike Nichols claims there is no other writer he knows with your ability to produce page after page of rewrites, each one more funny than the last.
NS: I do seem to have that ability, but that's because of all the years I worked in radio and TV where I had to write a new show every week. So the actual mechanics of writing funny dialogue are really second nature to me, and the prospect of rewriting a scene until it works as well as it possibly can has never intimidated me.

CH: Do you have a sort of "mental filing cabinet" in which you store your jokes?
NS: No. I never think of jokes which are written down then stored away for some future project. My jokes come to me out of whatever situation I happen to be writing about—and only when I'm sitting at the typewriter. I never think of jokes in the bath, for example, which I then rush out and jot down somewhere. And I never know what my next line of dialogue is going to be until it's actually written.

CH: You're considered to be the world's most successful, living playwright. Does this realization impose all sorts of pressures on you?
NS: I'm aware of the pressures, sure—although there was a time when they never bothered me. But a few years ago when I moved from New York to Los

Angeles, there was a definite resentment on the part of some New Yorkers who said "Ah, he's selling out to live the good life in California." Also, I'd just done *God's Favorite* and *The Good Doctor*, and people also began to say that I was slipping and wanted to get out of town fast. I certainly felt pressurized at that point in my life. And it was important for me to prove that I wasn't deserting New York and that I wasn't running away from failure. I'm not complaining about that sort of pressure, understand. If anything, it keeps me on my toes. Just as the failure of *The Star-Spangled Girl* was quite an eye-opener for me. Not so much because the play wasn't any good but because the reviews were so *negative*. I don't mind bad reviews if they're at least bad in a positive kind of way—like the reviews I got in New York for *The Gingerbread Lady*. "A worthy attempt," they said. Now the reviews for *The Star-Spangled Girl* were simply negative-negative. As Walter Kerr said: "Neil Simon didn't have an idea for a play this year, but he wrote it all the same." So I said to myself, I'll never do anything like it again—and I didn't. But what I'm saying is, it needed me to fail, and to feel the pressures of failure, to realize just what not to do with my career in the future. The main thing I've discovered about failure is that other people don't know how to handle it. I'll give you an example. I've gone to the Tony Awards and people have said to me on the way in: "Good luck tonight. It's a cinch you're going to win!" And they're all smiles. Then when you don't win, those same people who saw you on your way in, see you on your way out, and all they can say is, "See you Thursday." They just don't know how to deal with your failure. They think you're so devastated by it, that you, yourself, can't handle it either, and all they want to be is some place else . . . far away from you. It's an unflattering viewpoint of human behavior and I find it very interesting.

CH: Of all the cities in America, Los Angeles, I hear, abhors failure most of all. Is this true?
NS: Oh absolutely. But I'm lucky in the sense that, being a writer, I'm self-sufficient. If I were a director or a producer, though, who'd had two or three flops in a row, costing the studio millions of dollars, it would take ages before I'd be asked to do anything again. And even then I wouldn't be given the good scripts because they'd automatically go to the top man at any given time. So yes, this is one helluva tough town to fail in. But I really try not to let any of that stuff get to me. I turn a blind eye to it all.

CH: Why is it that so many Americans playwrights and novelists burn themselves out at relatively early ages, unlike European writers, who tend to mature as they get older and produce some of their most important work towards the end of their lives?

NS: Probably because of the pressure in America to succeed, and to stay at the top. It's what we were talking about. Failure isn't tolerated kindly, and, in attempting to succeed all the time, writers, who are only human after all, burn themselves out. This is particularly the case with American novelists. For some reason, the literary critics here are the toughest in the world. Now, at least in the theater, the playwright has a second chance. If the critics don't like his work, there's always the possibility that audiences might. It doesn't often happen, admittedly. But such instances are not entirely unknown. Now with novels, because so many of them are published each year, compared with the number of plays produced, they are either ignored totally by the reviewers—in which case there's very little hope for them; or, if they are reviewed at all, they have to be raves in order to get you to go out and buy a copy. More people will see a play like *God's Favorite* than will read the average new novel. I really am glad I'm not a novelist. Quite apart from actually getting someone other than your wife or lover to read your book, unless, of course, you happen to write a best-seller, there is nothing in novel writing, even if you're successful, to compare with standing at the back of a crowded theater and hearing the tidal waves of laughter wafting towards you across the stalls. It's the greatest sound in the world and you never tire of it.

CH: What sort of direction do you see your writing taking in the future?

NS: I don't think my plays will become lighter; but they won't be less funny than they are now either. They might go in a more serious direction, but I won't abandon laughter. Ever.

Dialogue on Film: Neil Simon

James Powers / 1977

From *American Film* 3 (March 1978): 33–48. AFI's Harold Lloyd Master Seminar © 1977, courtesy of American Film Institute.

Most people who call the fifties the Golden Age of Television confuse the glow of memory with the glow on their television sets. But on at least one night of the week and on one program, fifties television lived up to its golden epitaph. That was Saturday night, and the program was *Your Show of Shows*. Talent glittered on the screen, and it glittered especially bright back in the writers' room, where a kind of Algonquin Round Table of wits presided. One of the wits was Marvin Neil Simon.

Two decades later Neil Simon, having leaped from television to Broadway to Hollywood, has become something of a one-man Algonquin table. His latest stage comedy, *Chapter Two*, is a hit. But that's no surprise: He's been turning out a Broadway hit virtually every year since *Come Blow Your Horn*, his first show, opened in 1961. His latest movie, *The Goodbye Girl*, directed by Herbert Ross and starring his wife, Marsha Mason, is a hit, too, and his latest television show would no doubt also be—if he had one.

But even without television, Simon's success has become a show business legend. He is the only playwright in Broadway history to have had four shows running simultaneously. His second play, *Barefoot in the Park*, grossed more than $9 million and was translated into fourteen languages. *Variety*, which keeps an eye on these matters, has reported that Simon is the most financially successful American playwright ever.

But Simon's consistent success has not done him any good with a large number of critics. A little failure, they suggest, might remove the suspicion that Simon is far too slick. Sometimes, they complain, a theatergoer can't see the characters for the one-liners in a Simon play. Anyway, they finally ask, why does Simon go on manufacturing skillful fluff when he could be doing something more serious—still funny but more deeply felt?

Simon has his defenders, and they can be eloquent, like Walter Kerr, who is not soft on fluff: "Simon doesn't exactly write inconsequential light comedies. . . . There is a root, as real as a toothache, beneath the grin of Simon's funniest work, and it is one of the things that anchors the mere playfulness, ties a kite string to the broadest gags."

That root finds its home in domestic life. Simon's plays, or plays-turned-movies, or merely movies are about newlyweds encountering sober reality (*Barefoot in the Park*), the wayward ways of spouses (*Plaza Suite*), new love hampered by the memory of old love (*Chapter Two*), divorced husbands finding no comfort among their own sex (*The Odd Couple*), the mad pursuit of the unattainable (*The Heartbreak Kid*), felicity rescued from unlikely encounters (*The Goodbye Girl*).

Walter Kerr has something more to say about this bright menagerie of misery: "The seriousness, as much as the comedy, is light, deft, not overwhelming, capable of being dealt with in philosophical resignation (followed by a wry grin). What can't be helped is pretty horrible but, still, it can't be helped; have another joke."

Simon's wry grin has been there from childhood. He once climbed a ledge to watch an outdoor movie starring Charlie Chaplin. "I laughed so hard," he recalls, "I fell off, cut my head open, and went to the doctor, bleeding and laughing." The laughing persisted. In his early twenties he started writing comedy material for Goodman Ace and Phil Silvers, later joined *Your Show of Shows*, and then turned to the stage. Movies followed. His early screenplays, he admits, had a stage stiffness; his recent work has more of a cinematic flair. In fact, these days he wonders if he doesn't prefer screenwriting.

In the Dialogue, Simon talks about the differences he's found between screenwriting and playwriting, how much of himself and his family gets into his comedy, those dear old days on *Your Show of Shows*, and how his work improves with a little help from his friends.

Question: You have lived most of your life in New York City, and your plays and movie scripts show it. They have a flavor of the city. Now that you have moved to California are you having trouble adjusting to working here?
Neil Simon: I haven't had any trouble adjusting to California, I just haven't written anything about it yet. I don't know what there is to write about yet. It would have to be about four people in a car. I have had more stimulating conversations with friends at a red light than at a dinner party. I started to write *The Goodbye Girl* about California but it didn't work, because there's something more interesting in the conflicts of living in New York City. My

new play, *Chapter Two*, is about the city. I'm ashamed to say it, but I'm thinking about another play, and it also takes place in New York, around 1940. I spent so many years in New York that I think I write best about New York. Whenever I get away from it I don't do so well. I am working on a screenplay that does take place in California, and interestingly enough a car has a major role.

Question: Either coast, this seems like another Neil Simon year: *Chapter Two* is a hit; *The Goodbye Girl* is doing well; Herbert Ross is shooting *California Suite*. In the midst of this prolific, successful output, does even Neil Simon hit dry patches, moments of self-doubt?

Simon: I need reinforcement quite often. I will show my work to my wife, Marsha Mason, then I'll try my kids, and if I'm desperate I try the dog. I am always prepared for somebody to say, "This is probably the best thing you've ever written," or, "How could you write such junk?" I need the bolstering and encouragement of other people. Once I get that I get another surge of ego, so that I can sit down and say, "I expect people to pay good money to see this." I feel on top of things again, and the work goes well.

The interesting thing is that I've now done sixteen plays and musicals and twelve movies, but every time I start a new project I don't know how to do it. I had an idea for a new movie, and I said, it's a cinch. I've done sixteen plays and twelve movies. I wrote it down and said, that's no good. I wrote it again and said, that's not good; then I began to panic. So I wrote anything, just to try the dialogue and to hear how the characters speak. I started a new movie I'm working on now about seven times. It's finally beginning to take shape for me, I can see the light of day, and I think I'm going to be able to do it. But I must have in my drawer about fifty plays, ten pages long, twenty pages long, one act long. I've never gone further than that. But I don't have any unproduced plays; if I went all the way through, a play would be good enough to at least put on. I've needed all of those attempts to find out what was wrong. Sometimes I've started a play, written one act, hated it, put it aside, gone on to something else, and then returned to it.

Question: For example?

Simon: *The Sunshine Boys* is a good case. I said, "Who's going to want to see these two old men in a dirty old room in Upper West Side New York?" And then I went on to other things that I hated even more. So I took out *The Sunshine Boys* and read it, and after about two months it looked pretty good to me. I showed it to a few good friends, Mike Nichols and others, and they said, "That's terrific, you've got to continue with it." But I've been misled, too. The first producer I had, Saint Subber, read an act and a half of *Barefoot in the Park*. I said, "This is really awful. No one is going to be interested in these two kids in the first week of their honeymoon." He said, "You are so wrong. It's charming and it's sweet and it's loving. And I think you should go on with it." I did, and it turned out to be a major hit that ran for four years. A few years later I was working on *The Star-Spangled Girl*. I got to the same place, and I hated it. He said, "You're wrong, it's even better than *Barefoot in the Park*." Well, I finished it, and it was the worst thing I've ever written. I knew it all along; the typewriter keys all felt as if they were ten pounds each. That was the only time I ever really hated going into a room to work, because I usually don't mind it. I don't have writer's block, or those traumas about looking at the blank page and saying, "What will I put down?" I read the *New York Times* in the morning, I finish it, I put a sheet of paper in the typewriter, and I'm able to click on. I sit and think things out and start to write.

Question: What differences do you find between writing for films and writing for the theater?
Simon: One of the reasons I'm beginning to like films a little bit more than the theater is that I am less conscious of writing for an audience when I'm writing a film. Despite the fact that an audience is in the theater watching a film, they're watching it very privately. Just one person could watch it, and it would still work. But if you went to see any of the plays, and sat all by yourself in the theater, it wouldn't work. It just wouldn't. It's not that the writing is so much geared to an audience, it's that I am aware that there is an audience there, and the audience is very much a part of the play. You cannot perform without the audience, whereas you can do a film for one person. In a film there are fewer lines directed toward getting a laugh; I find that the dialogue comes easier. If you see *The Goodbye Girl*, I think you'll find that the dialogue flows more easily than it does in a play, because an audience disrupts a play. In a film, there's an enormous laugh and the film goes on. In a play, there's an enormous laugh and the actors wait.

Question: Do you have a specific work in mind?
Simon: One of the prime examples is from *The Odd Couple*. It's become almost a classic joke now, and I didn't realize it when I wrote it. It came in a rewrite. Oscar, in the third act, was detailing to Felix all the things that Felix does that drive him crazy; the sounds he makes with his nose in the middle of the night and clearing his ears and the way he cleans up the apartment.

Then I wrote, "And then you leave me little notes on my pillow, 'We are all out of cornflakes.'" I wanted him to sign the note, so I wrote, "Felix." Well, that isn't funny, so I wrote, "Felix Ungar." That isn't funny. So I put down the initials, "F.U." And I said, "Oh God, that's funny." Well, "F.U." got the biggest laugh that I had ever heard in the theater. It was enormous. Mike Nichols staged it so that after Oscar said, "You signed it 'F.U.,' and it took me three hours to figure out that 'F.U.' was 'Felix Ungar,'" he had him move on to the next piece of dialogue. But the laugh was so enormous that Walter Matthau walked into the other room and walked out, and the audience was still laughing. He got himself a glass of water, and they still laughed. He picked up a newspaper and started to read, and they were still laughing. Those are the accommodations that the live theater must make to an audience that one does not make in films.

Question: Do you have more control in any way in one medium than in the other?

Simon: When I write for the theater, what I see in my mind is exactly what the audience sees. It never varies, except maybe the staging. There's the proscenium, and no one can go past it. Herb Ross, in *Chapter Two*, was able to make what I had seen in my mind just a little bit larger. He had the stage extended on the side, and he had turntables, which I did not envision. But still, for the most part, the two apartments that I saw in my mind is exactly what you see. I saw it from the same point of view that the audience does. But for a movie, all I see is the story and the characters in my mind. I have no idea what point of view the director is going to shoot from. I may see a very important moment on the face of the main character. The director may shoot it that way, but he will also shoot this person, and he will also shoot it from here. Once in the editing room, the editor and the director will choose the shot that they feel is the most effective. It's a waste of my time to try to write the specific physical dimension of what's going to be on the screen. Occasionally I do it, and I hope that the director follows it. But I never know where that camera's going to be, I never know what the set is going to look like. I don't know if they're going to be on location. I could pick one place, and they could go to another place. So, I just worry about the overall story.

Question: Are there accommodations you make to the screen—for example, in the dialogue—when you adapt one of your stage comedies?

Simon: On the stage, even though the dialogue may sound natural, it's bigger than life, because the actors are talking loudly for fifteen hundred or two thousand people in a theater. But when that movie camera moves in so close, someone just saying, "Uh-huh," can be the most telling and important thing. I have been learning in the last few years to cut some of the dialogue—I don't want it too talky. I am a person who writes with words rather than pictures, so I don't lose the words entirely. But I do try to diminish them somewhat if I can.

Question: What are your thoughts about "opening up" a play for the screen?
Simon: I remember Alfred Hitchcock talking about *Dial M for Murder*. People said, "Why didn't you open it up? It all took place in one room." But he said the very reason it was a success was that the play itself all took place in that room. The confinement of that particular place makes the pressures very, very important. You cannot get out, you cannot go someplace else; the girl is screaming for help, and there is nobody there to help her. I have found, invariably, that the best scenes in some of my films are the ones from the plays. When I open up scenes they sort of mark time. In *The Odd Couple*, all the best things took place in Oscar's apartment. When I went outside it was just for the sake of trying to be cinematic. I learned to be a little more skillful in *The Sunshine Boys*, but there, fortunately, a lot of the offstage dialogue took place elsewhere. Two of the best scenes in the movie were not in the play. They were at the house of Al Lewis—George Burns—in New Jersey.

In the play *Barefoot in the Park*, the best scene was the confrontation between the boy and girl when they've come home from an evening out on Staten Island with the mother and the man who lives upstairs. It was a twelve-minute fight that was, as far as I was concerned, the best piece of writing I had done in any twelve-minute section. It just built beautifully to a big climax at the end. When we got to the film, the producer, Hal Wallis, said, "No, you can't go in a film for twelve minutes in one room." The scene was cut in half, and it just fell off, there was no climax. But Herb Ross will say, "Don't worry about it. You can be in a room as long as you want, as long as it's interesting. If it's not interesting, then let's get it out of there." So I no longer worry about how long I'm going to be in a stationary place; I just try to get it out only because it's better outside. But I really don't like adapting the plays. I would much rather write original screenplays, because it just seems like a fresher thing to do. It's also more fun."

Question: Of all your plays adapted to the screen, I would say *Plaza Suite* is your least successful. Do you agree?

Simon: Yes, I didn't like *Plaza Suite* at all. But there are a number of movies I didn't like that were adaptations from the plays. *The Odd Couple* worked mostly because that play is almost indestructible. It's such a funny concept that even though I thought the film was done just fairly well, it still works. In *Barefoot in the Park*, I didn't know too much about screenwriting, and that was okay. But *The Prisoner of Second Avenue* I was not happy with, *The Last of the Red Hot Lovers* I was not happy with, and *Plaza Suite* I was not happy with—as films. They were practically photographed plays. I really didn't have an interest in films then. I was mainly interested in continuing writing for the theater, and I thought I would have some permanent record of a play by putting it on film. The plays never became cinematic. But I just finished the second draft of *California Suite*, and I think it is definitely more cinematic. One thing was wrong about *Plaza Suite* that, incidentally, was not my fault. I never thought that Walter Matthau should have played all three parts. But he insisted on playing all three parts, and the studio said, "Well, that's the only way we can get Walter." They gave it to him, and he was wrong. I think the only one he really should have played was the last one, with the girl locked in the bathroom. He's great at farce, and not very good at the other pieces. Although *California Suite* was on the stage with four people playing in the four one-act plays, in the film we will have ten stars playing the various roles. It will be done more or less like *Grand Hotel*, cutting back and forth and going outside the various rooms. It won't be one hotel room, it will be a bungalow and a cottage and a suite and a single room. I'm quite sure it will be better, because Herb Ross is going to direct it. And Herb did *The Sunshine Boys*, which up until now I consider the best adaptation of any of the plays into film.

Question: The question of opening up a play for the screen has interesting results in *Barefoot in the Park*. In the play, the laughs build every time someone staggers into the apartment, because you've established that the apartment is at the top of several flights of stairs. In the movie, the camera follows some of the characters up the stairs, and the laughs are diffused.
Simon: We found that out afterward. But if you just had them all come in the door, someone would say, "I don't understand why you didn't shoot on the stairs. It's a movie, and you can go anywhere with it." So, it was a choice that one makes, and in that case probably a wrong choice. Some critics of the play said, "Well, I think they milked the gag a little too much." Do they mean that after the third time we've seen them do it, they shouldn't breathe hard after walking up five flights of stairs? But that's where translating from

stage to screen does not always work very well. If I had conceived it as a film play originally without having gone through the stage process, it probably would have been written from a different point of view.

Question: *The Heartbreak Kid* was unusual—an adaptation not of one of your plays but of a short story by Bruce Jay Friedman. How did you become involved in that project?

Simon: I rarely like to adapt. I've only done it with, as I recall, three musicals that I did for Broadway. One was *The Apartment*, which became *Promises, Promises*. But I love Bruce Jay Friedman's writing—I thought his *A Mother's Kisses* was a wonderful book. His writing doesn't adapt very well to other media, and I thought that was unfortunate. I read his short story "A Change of Plan," which was a very short, short story—and quite different from the movie. The only similar event was that the husband does see another girl on his honeymoon and leaves his wife. He does not have that scene at the dinner table, but he does go off to Minnesota after the girl, and very easily wins her and marries her. At the end of the short story he's walking off into the garden with the mother, on the make for her—put that on the screen and we'd have been in big trouble, I think. I just fell in love with the story, and I tried to buy the rights to it to do it as a film. I found out that it was owned by Palomar Productions. Ed Scherick was the producer at Palomar, and had it in the works. He was going to make a three-part film of various love stories, and this was going to be one of them. He asked me to write it. I said, "No, I don't want to write that. I want to write a feature film." And we made a deal.

Question: Do you see *The Heartbreak Kid* as an original screenplay?

Simon: It was an original, in one way, as far as I was concerned. I was using almost none of the events, there was no dialogue whatsoever in the story, and very few of the other characters were in it. But what I did—and I've never done it at any other time—I wrote it as though I were Bruce Jay Friedman. I didn't write it as Neil Simon. The writing is quite different from the style of writing I'd done in other pieces. Friedman has a very oblique and unique sense of humor, and I tried to write it like him. When I got halfway through, I got nervous. It seemed very bizarre, and very heavy to me—not heavy-handed, but heavy. I had no idea how audiences would accept it. The character is a hero, but he's an anti-hero. You like him one minute, and you hate him the next minute. It's exactly what happened with audiences. When he was with Jeannie Berlin in that restaurant, and she had the egg salad all over her face—now, that's an interesting point about directing. In my own directions in the script, I wrote, "She takes a bite of her egg salad sandwich, and a small piece of egg salad is left on her face, and he says, 'You, uh, you have . . . '" He doesn't quite know how to deal with it. But in the movie, she ducks her head into her sandwich, and there's egg salad all over, so it becomes not quite what I intended. I thought that was a little heavy.

Question: Some of the scenes in *The Heartbreak Kid* seem improvised. How much leeway did you give?
Simon: There was almost no leeway. I had it in the contract: no words changed until you discuss it with me. Otherwise, if I was not on the set, they could suddenly do something else. I'm not wedded to the words, in that you have to do my words. I just want to be in on the conversations that are going to change a scene, because it can go off in a different direction. Suddenly, the actors or the director or the producer become my coauthors, and I don't want coauthors unless I am there to coauthor it with them. The reason it seems improvised is that that's the way Elaine May directs, and that's what was so wonderful about it. She would rehearse the words, then throw out the words, then just have them do the scene the way they wanted to, and then put back the words. It's her style of directing, and I found it wonderful.

For example, there's the scene where the husband tells his wife that he cannot go on with the marriage, that he's going to dump her for another girl he met two days ago. Every word that I had written was on the screen, but for a number of days during shooting Elaine threw the words out and said to the actors, "Just play those attitudes, make up your own words." They did, and so they knew what the attitudes were. Then when they put these words back in, it seemed as though they were still improvising. Not all actors can do that. There are some actors, even gifted actors, to whom you will say, "Improvise something," and they go, "I, uh, I, uh." A lot of them have great difficulty revealing themselves.

Question: Are you often on the set during the shooting of one of your movies?
Simon: Yes, that's one thing I think is terribly important on a film. I'm on a set the same as I would be on a play. That's why some of the early film adaptations of the plays were not so good, because I was rarely, if ever, there. On a play, I'm there constantly, and I can see if something is not playing. I will rewrite it, I'll fix it up, or talk it over with the actors or the director. I did not do that on any of the first plays into films. But on the last few, on *Murder by Death*, on *The Heartbreak Kid*, on *The Sunshine Boys*, on *The Goodbye Girl*, I was there every day, rewriting. Sometimes I would be very

satisfied, and Herb Ross, for example, would say, "This is not going to play on film. You have to trust me. I think we need something else." I would just go back and rewrite it.

I was amazed at the attitude of some writers I met at the Writers Guild about being on the set. First, some of them feel that directors do not want them on the set because they interfere. If the writer is any good, a director who doesn't want him on the set has got to be crazy. Second, a lot of the writers feel—a rather petty point of view, I thought—that they should be paid extra for being on the set. I couldn't quite understand. Their argument was they were giving up their time when they could be working on something else. My point of view is, if you're on the set and you're making it better, you'll have a better film, which means you'll get more money the next time, which means you'll get more to say the next time. You'll be getting everything you want eventually if you make what you're doing the best possible product.

Question: Are you aware of different audiences when you write for the stage or the screen? Do you find yourself thinking, "Now, what's going to make these people laugh?"
Simon: No—what's going to make me laugh, first of all. I don't always know what's going to make people laugh, but I do know what I think is going to be funny for me.

Question: Would you agree that the interests of a New York theater audience are narrower than a movie audience's?
Simon: Granted. That's why, in many instances, I prefer writing for films.

Question: The movies let you stretch boundaries, take chances, don't you think? Your play, *God's Favorite*, tried to do so, but it was short-lived on stage.
Simon: *God's Favorite* is interesting. It's one of the reasons I'm somewhat ambivalent about the theater. *God's Favorite* played best with younger audiences, because it is obviously irreverent. It deals with the Book of Job, but to me it was not putting down the Book of Job. Based on my own experiences in life, both tragic and otherwise, life sometimes becomes so grim and so terrible it becomes absurd. We don't know why these terrible things are happening to us. I once saw a television newsreel about Detroit during the riots. A black man was talking. His home had been burned, and he had spent the night in his car. He got out of his car, went back to the ruins of his house, and his car was stolen and his two kids were beaten up. It just got

worse and worse. As he was telling it, it almost seemed funny to me. It was so absolutely absurd that one tragedy on top of another could happen in life. That's how I looked at the Book of Job. A few months ago I read in the *Los Angeles Times* religion section that a group of theologians had got together and said that they thought the Book of Job was a comic piece. The attitude was comic. One of them cited *God's Favorite* as being more of an accurate point of view of the Book of Job than *J.B.* by Archibald MacLeish.

A play now is anywhere from ten to fifteen dollars for the orchestra. *The Act* with Liza Minnelli is playing for twenty dollars. That eliminates practically everyone under thirty from the audience, except upstairs in the last few rows. Only those who can afford to go to the theater, go to the theater, for the most part, and those are older people. When a play gets too far out and bizarre, they will not accept it. For years I had been doing my plays in New York, and after the play people would come back to me. They were able to associate their own lives with the plays—*The Odd Couple, Plaza Suite*—and they would say, "Oh, Mr. Simon, wonderful, terrific, I just loved it." I was coming out of one performance of *God's Favorite*, and there was a little old lady there. She looked at me, and she said, "Mr. Simon, come here." I walked over expecting my terrific compliment, and she said, "Shame on you!" Yet when we did the play during the Christmas holidays, when we were able to get a younger audience, the play went infinitely better. I would look at the lines on Third Avenue, outside Cinema I and Cinema II, and the Baronet and the Coronet, and I would see almost only younger people. I said, I want to write for that audience. I don't want to keep writing for an older, middle-class audience that can pay twelve dollars and fifteen dollars for their seats. I would never attempt something like *The Heartbreak Kid* for the theater, because the audience just wouldn't buy it. I do get somewhat disenchanted with the theater, though I think *Chapter Two* can bridge the gap. To me it is a play for and about young people, middle-aged people, and older people.

Question: There's a difference in taste between movie and theater audiences.
Simon: Sure. I don't think the people who spend sixteen dollars to see *Annie* are the same audiences who would go and laugh at *Blazing Saddles*.

Question: Does the difference affect your own taste when you write?
Simon: My taste is constant. I always try to write in the best possible taste, even though it is stretched sometimes. Some people would not agree that it's the best possible taste, but I try to write with a certain amount of quality all the time. I never say, "Well, for this audience you don't have to give

them so much." You always have to give them the best, although in television that's not true.

Question: A pretty disparaging remark about television. Obviously, you're not planning anything for television.
Simon: Well, I have been asked to. But I picture an audience in my mind when I'm writing. When I'm writing for the theater, I see about nine hundred or one thousand people in front of me. For a film, I see either one person, or a few million people. But the few million are the one person multiplied over and over. I know that's strange. If I write for television, I have no idea who's out there—it's forty million people. My early beginnings in television meant working with the mentalities of some of the network heads and the sponsors, who say, "No, no, no, we don't want this for our audience, you can't do this, you can't do that." *Hallmark Hall of Fame* wanted to put *The Gingerbread Lady* on television as a two-hour special. I was told, "But, of course, we'll have to eliminate this and eliminate that." I said, "Well, why do it? Why do I want to eliminate all that when I can do it the way I want in film?" There's no point in writing for television. It's going to take us three months to make a film of the play, and another three or four months to edit it. I don't think one spends six or seven months in television. It's just economically not feasible. So, there goes television.

Question: You started in television in the fifties, as a writer on *Your Show of Shows*—you and Mel Brooks and others. What were those writing sessions like? There must be nothing like it today.
Simon: Possibly not. Maybe *The Carol Burnett Show* works the same way. I watch that list of credits when the show is over, and it just goes on and on. That's the way it was with us on *Your Show of Shows*. We had seven writers, among them myself and Mel Brooks and Larry Gelbart, and a number of other first-class writers. In the room, not as writers, were Carl Reiner and Howard Morris and the producer of the show, Max Liebman. There were ten or eleven of us, each Monday morning, sitting around on sofas and chairs. If you didn't get there early, you didn't get a seat. It was very crowded, and it was pretty difficult to write under those conditions.

Here's what we would do. Michael Stewart, who later wrote *Hello, Dolly!* and *Carnival* and a number of other Broadway successes, sat behind a typewriter. Sid Caesar would sit opposite Michael. He was about the best comic editor that I had ever known. In other words, he knew better what was right for him than almost any other comedian I had ever worked for until then. To get things going, sometimes we would all start to write a sketch. Everybody would be throwing ideas out, and Sid very mysteriously would nod to Michael every once in a while. Michael would type away. We never knew what he was typing, because we were all throwing out terrific ideas and laughing. After about an hour and a half Sid would say, "All right, Michael, read it back." And there would be a sketch that we had written. We didn't even realize that we had written it.

After that, we would generally break up and go off in groups of twos and threes to our offices. One week Mel Brooks and I would work on the German professor, and Larry Gelbart and Shelley Keller would work on the Imogene Coca domestic sketch. Then we would all come back into the first room with the material, and we would tear it apart. We became ruthless. We would all pitch in and work on it. That's how the show got written. We would all be there up until the dress rehearsal, still editing and doing some rewriting. Then we would go home to watch the show, which was live. I would sit there laughing, because I'd forgotten what had been written. My wife would say, "That's your joke. I know that sounds like your joke." I would say, "I can't really remember," because everybody had been pitching in so hard on the show.

Question: Where did you go from *Your Show of Shows*?

Simon: From there I went to *The Phil Silvers Show*, and I worked on that for about two years. That was a completely different kind of writing. It was not group writing; there were just two of us in the room. The show had two teams of writers. At that time, one team, Billy Friedberg and myself, would write one week's show, while the next team, Coleman Jacoby and Arnie Rosen, would write the other week's show. That was a much more difficult show to write, even though it was a half-hour situation comedy. The pace was so rapid, and Phil Silvers as Sergeant Bilko spoke faster than any other comic—there were five or six more pages than for your average show. The plot twists and turns were so complicated that we spent infinitely more time plotting the show than dialoguing it. We would spend about four days plotting the show, then spend about three days putting in the dialogue. But I learned more about the technique of writing for films from that than I did from writing for *Your Show of Shows*. I also worked on a series called *Max Liebman Presents*, which was an offshoot of *Your Show of Shows*. It consisted of adaptations of Broadway musicals done for television. It was my first experience working with book shows. I updated *Dearest Enemy*, which was a Rodgers and Hart show, and *Best Foot Forward*, and countless other

Broadway musicals. Sometimes we put new songs into the shows, and I got to learn about doing Broadway musicals.

Question: How would you compare television then and now?
Simon: I think some of the shows then were better than any of the shows today. I think specifically *Phil Silvers* was, not because I worked on it, but because it was such a well-conceived show by Nat Hiken. I think *Your Show of Shows* was terrific; I think *The Ernie Kovacs Show* was terrific, which I never worked on. I'm not crazy about most of the television situation comedy shows of today. I just don't think it's possible, week in and week out, to do quality work, no matter who it is. Let's say Shakespeare made a series out of *Hamlet*. In the fourth week it's going to be pretty awful. I think one can go just so far in television, and that's pretty much the reason I got out. I came to Los Angeles and worked on *The Jerry Lewis Show*. I did another show with somebody else, and then I started to do a show by myself. But I thought, I don't think I want to spend the rest of my life doing this, I've got to branch out. That's when I started to write my first play, *Come Blow Your Horn*. Someone said, if you're going to write a play, at least write about something you know about, and I knew a lot about *Come Blow Your Horn*, because it was my life. It propelled me out of writing for television situation comedy.

I think that anyone who aspires to write quality should get out of television. After a while it does you in. I think it does most good actors in. I see so many quality actors I knew in New York who go into television. They're quite good in what they do in the situation comedies, they're better than anyone around, but they find it a hard adjustment to go back to acting in films or in the theater. The demands of television, I think, aren't nearly as high as they are in film, though God knows there are a lot of dreadful films and bad plays. I spend up to a year on a play, not in the initial writing, but all in all. The same thing with a movie; I get to do it over and over. You don't get all of those shots in working on a television show. It's a great place to begin and learn, and a good place to get out of.

Question: What influence did those years of collaborating on television scripts have on you?
Simon: They influenced me by being my education. When I came into the business, I was nineteen years old and working on a radio show. I was working with people who were very experienced, and so I learned over those years to collaborate. I did it up until that period when I wrote *The Jerry Lewis Show*. I realized that not only did I not want to write *The Jerry Lewis*

Show for the rest of my life, but that I had things that I wanted to say, personal statements, and I find them almost impossible to make in collaboration with someone else. For example, I've written a number of plays about my family life and, particularly, about my brother. He appears in *Come Blow Your Horn*, in *The Odd Couple*, in *Plaza Suite*, and in *Chapter Two*. Danny has a completely different viewpoint of all of our experiences. He's seven years older than I am. His attitude toward all of those things that happened to us is opposite, or at least different, from mine. Had we written any of those plays together, in order to have a common meeting ground, we would have had to water down our attitudes.

When you write things not out of your own experience or out of your own personal feelings, it's just a story, let us say an Alfred Hitchcock type of story. He deals more often with situation and plot than with character. That kind of thing I think collaborators can work on, that can be argued and discussed. But you cannot discuss my viewpoint of life. Even if it's wrong, it's my viewpoint, and I have to put it down. I sometimes have to laugh bitterly at some critics who write about my plays, "That's ridiculous, that can never happen," when I'm talking about specific incidents that have happened in my life. They have just never happened in their lives.

I learned a great deal from some very talented people in the beginning. But I would find it impossible now to work with anybody again. After I wrote *Come Blow Your Horn*, which was my first experience writing alone, I really got to like the experience of being alone in a room writing. There's no one who can say, "That's no good. That's terrible." I once had to write a television show with another writer, and he got to sit behind the typewriter. We were working, and I said, "The character says, 'I won't see you Tuesday, because Tuesday I have to see my mother.'" He just sat there. I said, "That's good, put it down." He said, "No." I just hated the idea that he had the power of the typewriter. I said to myself, I want my own typewriter from now on.

Question: You have your own typewriter now and a solid reputation from the theater. That gives you something of an immunity from having your movie scripts butchered or rewritten. Would you call your relationship with the producer Ray Stark, who did *The Goodbye Girl* and *The Sunshine Boys*, atypical for a screenwriter?

Simon: Granted it's unique, because I have come from the theater and have established myself as a theater writer. I know that a young writer is going to have his work butchered, but we all do in the beginning. I did, too, in television and in films. Other writers weren't brought in, but it was butchered in other ways, butchered even by myself, by my own ineptitude at the time. I think that's part of the price you pay, and one has got to go through that bitter learning relationship. It's almost impossible for any young writer to have it in his contract that no one is going to change anything. If there is a good working relationship with a director, and the writer is talented, I think they'll be able to work it out correctly. But it's all hit-or-miss in the beginning until you're able to know so well that what you do is right that it becomes known in the business that what you do is right. But I don't know what is right all the time. Sometimes I do and sometimes I don't.

Question: Has a director—either in a film or play—helped you find out what was right or wrong in a work?

Simon: Yes, there was on incident in *Prisoner of Second Avenue*. We had a run-through of it in New Haven, the night before we were going to open. The run-through seemed very good, the ending seemed okay to me, but I wasn't quite positive. Mike Nichols, the director, came to me and said, "The ending is not going to work." I said, "We'll find out tomorrow night." He said, "Why wait until tomorrow night?" I said, "Well, because I'm not sure. It's liable to work. I'm not positive about it." He said, "I know it's not going to work. Let's go and just talk about it." We went back and sat in the lobby of the hotel, and neither one of us said a word for four hours. I can work very well that way, quietly, and Mike can, too. I started to search my mind. I remembered planting early on in the play that there was a snowfall headed for New York. I said, "Ah, I've got it. At the end of the play, snow starts to come down, and the main character goes in and gets the shovel. He sits there like *American Gothic*, because he's ready to take the shovelful of snow and throw it on his hated enemy at the end of the play." Mike said, "Good night," and he sent to New York for the snow. It worked, it was a wonderful ending. Had Mike not pushed me to it, I would not have thought of it then.

I do have a knack for hearing very early on what is wrong. But I only know it by hearing it. The day before we went into rehearsal with *The Odd Couple*, Mike Nichols had a party. We felt very good about the play. We had Walter Matthau and Art Carney and a wonderful cast, and we knew the story was good. I said to Mike, "Are you very happy with the play at this point?" He said, "Very happy." I said, "Is there anything you want me to rewrite that you think I have not done?" He said, "No, it seems right to me. You're getting me nervous. Is there anything that you think is wrong with it?" I said, "No, it all seems right to me. Yet I know that at noon tomorrow after the first reading we're going to be in big trouble someplace in the play.

We don't know it right now—and we're professionals." The next day, at ten a.m., we brought out the scripts, the cast sat around, and we started to read the play. The first act was dynamite, it just was sensational. We read the second act, and it was better than the first act. The producer got up and said, "You don't even need me. It's a smash hit, and I'm going home." He went home and didn't listen to the third act. We read the third act, and it was in the toilet. It was terrible. None of us knew this until we read it. None of the actors knew it, nobody had said a word. But suddenly those words start to come to life, and they lose their life, and it is not working. In some instances other people are not as aware of it as I am. In that case, we all were. We knew it didn't work. I had to go home and in three days write a new third act that had taken me two months to write previously. I brought it in, thinking I was a genius. When we read it, it was worse than the first third act. I had to write it over and over.

These readings have saved my life a couple of times, specifically in *The Goodbye Girl*. I wrote the script specifically for Marsha Mason and Richard Dreyfuss. It was sort of a spin-off from the aborted *Bogart Slept Here*, another screenplay that we just didn't get to do. Six months before we went into production with *The Goodbye Girl*, I had Marsha and Dreyfuss sit down and read the screenplay, with another actress reading various other roles. About 50 percent of it sounded good to me; the other 50 percent was terrible. I went home and rewrote it. Three months later they came together again, we reread it, and about 75 percent of it seemed right to me. By the time we had a reading on the first day of rehearsal of the film, the picture was structurally right, and there was only minor work to be done. Had we waited until that first day of rehearsal, as most films do, we would have found ourselves in desperate trouble. The majority of films never really get the work that should be put into them.

Question: When you show your work to others, how much attention do you pay to their comments?
Simon: I generally go to people I respect, and they can be wrong, but I get feedback from them. Sometimes they will say, "Gee, I love it. But I don't like this scene at all, I don't think that scene works." In my heart, I say, "Gee, I really do like it. I think it works. Let's wait until we get up there and start to read it." I use them as sounding boards. Even when I get compliments from then, I can tell when it's not effusive. I show everything I write to Marsha. I understand the problems that she may have, thinking, "I'm not a writer. Who am I to say to him, 'Gee, it's not very good.'" She assumes

what I do is good. But because there's something very truthful and honest about her, and her instincts are wonderful, she will tell me it's good in not a truthful way. She will say, "Yes, I like that. I think that works." I know right away what the reading is. I can tell. But if she comes out with tears in her eyes or laughing and says, "Oh my God, that's wonderful," then it's a very positive feedback.

Question: Do you show your work to other writers?
Simon: I never show it to a writer. I don't have that kind of relationship with other writers. It gets back to that collaborative thing I talked about before. They would see it from their own point of view. I am the worst judge of other people's material. If they asked me to come in and fix someone else's movie script, I would be petrified. Being a writer, I would have such a sense of obligation to their work. Producers and editors have a much more objective point of view, and so they can deal with it a lot better. Some writers are able to deal with it; I am just not able to.

Question: Have you ever thought about directing a film or play yourself?
Simon: Yes, for about three minutes. I have no affinity for it. I have no liking for it. I don't like talking to the actors. If I say, "You know, I think you ought to move over there," and they say, "Why?" then I say, "Leave me alone, will you." I just know it's better if they go over there. So I have the best of both worlds. As long as I can get top directors like Mike Nichols and Robert Moore and Herbert Ross, then I can stand over their shoulders. They think of so many more things; they embellish it. It's better to have two good minds than one cluttered mind directing the film. I toyed with the idea, but fortunately for me and the world, I've given up on it.

Question: Let me read you something Clive Barnes recently wrote: "Mr. Simon once left us with a memory primarily of giggles; now, probably more than ever before, we are left with a memory of people." He was writing about *Chapter Two* and referring, of course, to your reputation for one-liners at the expense of the character. How do you react to that reputation?
Simon: I think the early plays have one-liners, plus lines emanating from character. I think as the plays go on there are fewer one-liners and more and more lines coming out of character. In New York, the critics really catch you for it. I think in *The Odd Couple* there was only one one-liner. My description of a one-liner is something that you could take out, that has nothing really to do with the character, that almost any other character

or a stand-up comedian like Bob Hope can say. There was a specific line in *The Odd Couple*, and the *New York Times* critic Howard Taubman picked up on it. That was constructive to me. I said, "Ah, I must be careful of that in the future." I think now there are fewer and fewer one-liners. Sometimes, though, it's a misnomer. Somebody says something, and the other person answers it. If you answer it in twenty-seven lines, it's very hard to get a laugh. So you just have a one-line answer. It's a term that I really take umbrage at when it's not fairly given. I don't think, for example, there are any one-liners in *The Heartbreak Kid*.

Question: Your work has often dealt with two persons in conflict with each other. Do you worry that introducing more characters dilutes what has been a successful formula?

Simon: No, I don't. As a matter of fact, I think I've been changing the last few years, certainly in the movies. *Chapter Two* is four characters. *The Odd Couple* is eight characters, granted that the main characters are just two people. I think it comes from my beginnings, of working in television, and being able to focus only on two persons. It just seems to be a formula I hit on, of getting people of opposite interests and putting them in a state of conflict, just stripping them to a room or a house or some untenable position. It has served me well for a number of years, in some instances not so well. I'm working on a new play now that is eight characters, and not just eight characters supporting the two main characters, but eight individual stories, eight individual lives, more in the vein of *You Can't Take It with You*. *The Goodbye Girl* is about three characters, but a new film that I'm also working on—my God, I'm busy—is about five or six characters. It served me well for a long time, but I'm looking to get out of that formula.

Question: Do you sometimes write a character's part with an actor in mind?
Simon: It rarely happens. It happened partly in *The Odd Couple*. I had finished an act and a half when I met Walter Matthau at a party, and I thought, he's the perfect actor. "Walter," I said, "I'm writing a play for you. Don't do anything next year." So I had him in mind. But one doesn't like to write for an actor specifically because chances are you won't get him. Then you have to rewrite the part for somebody else to fit his characteristics. That's with a film. With a play, you write the character essentially, so that no matter who plays it, he can play that character. For *California Suite*, I wrote the first draft of the screenplay just for the characters. We then sent it to the actors we wanted, and we got six or eight of the actors that we were after,

which meant I had to do some rewriting. One of the stories in *California Suite* is about two couples on vacation, who start off in Chicago, go to San Francisco, go to Hawaii, come back to Los Angeles, and after two weeks hate each other and want to kill each other. On the stage the couples were played by Jack Weston, Barbara Barrie, Tammy Grimes, and George Grizzard. In the film, Richard Pryor and Bill Cosby appear. Knowing that I had them, I was able to rewrite for their characters. In *The Goodbye Girl* I knew it was Marsha and Richard all along. I'm working on a screenplay now, and in my mind I say it's Marsha and Dustin Hoffman and Walter Matthau. If I don't get them it's okay, but it's good sometimes to keep somebody in mind for a film. In films it matters a great deal more who plays than it does on the stage. On the stage a name is not important at all, just a good actor. Unfortunately, in films, for the most part, you need what the studio calls "bankable names."

Question: Have you ever considered acting yourself?

Simon: No. It surprised me when I saw two of my good friends, Mel Brooks, whom I always thought was a frustrated actor, and Woody Allen, on the screen. They've become two of our major box-office stars. It doesn't amaze me now when I see them, because I think they're sensational, but I never thought it would happen. Everything has changed over the years; writers are beginning to be able to express their own point of view. Mel, instead of putting the words in somebody else's mouth, is now doing it for himself, just as Woody is doing. I just don't think I have that kind of ability to get up in front of an audience. I'm much more introverted than they are.

Question: Have you ever been on stage?

Simon: Yes, when I was younger. I liked it then. But now I like the anonymity of being a writer, being in the back of the house in the dark watching the play. If it's no good, you can always run out. The actors have to stay there. My heart goes out to the actors an opening night when that curtain goes up. How they get that first word out, I just don't know. It's incredible.

Question: How do you see your work compared to that of Mel Brooks and Woody Allen?

Simon: It's hard for me to be completely objective about my own work. I feel that Mel specifically works in one genre. I don't know what label one should put on—it's madcap, I guess. *The Producers*, *Blazing Saddles*, *Young Frankenstein*—for the most part I find it hilarious comedy, and I enjoy it. But he never goes off into other directions; he doesn't seem to want to. He's quite happy in what he's doing, and he does it about the best that anyone could do it. Woody Allen is peculiar in that, up until now, he has only written for himself. Every movie stars Woody Allen. He is writing for one specific character, and we see that character in all of his adventures. He varies slightly, but he is always the small, urban, put-upon, neurotic man, who is again, to me, hysterically funny. I write sometimes about myself, and sometimes out of myself, and I write in all different genres. *Murder by Death* and *The Cheap Detective* are spoofs, parts of my plays are farces, and some of my plays, like *The Gingerbread Lady*, *God's Favorite*, and *Chapter Two*, are serious works. I can't categorize myself, so it's very hard to compare my work with their work.

Question: Let's turn to your method of work. Do you have a particular routine you follow when you write?
Simon: I work when I can. For the most part I work normal hours; after breakfast I'll go and write. If I'm working at a studio on a picture, I will spend the morning there, and then I will get bored. After the master shot is done and the angles of the same scene start, it's no longer necessary for me to be there. They're not going to change anything in content. So I can go back to my office and work. I don't like to work at night, because it makes it hard to sleep. I only work at night if I'm out of town with a play, and I need to do drastic rewriting. But I can work anywhere at almost any time.

Question: Do you keep an office?
Simon: For a number of years I worked at home. But it's becoming increasingly difficult because of the kids and the household noise. So I found a little office, and it's quiet.

Question: Do you work every day?
Simon: I work not every day, but I do work about five days a week.

Question: On several projects at once?
Simon: I haven't been doing that. I will write a draft of something and then put it away. I might show it to the producer, the director, or the people involved if it's a play or a film. But I know that it's not nearly ready to see the light of day. It's not going to get into production for at least six months anyway, because one has to assemble a cast and get a starting date for a film or a play. So, during that six months, rather than just sit around and keep working on that project when I'm too close to it, I will work on something

else. Then, after about three months, I start the second draft. Sometimes I may have the opportunity to put it aside again, and have a third draft before we even get to that first reading. It's an old adage in the theater, and it's absolutely true, that plays are not written, they're rewritten. It's the rewriting that does it all. As far as I'm concerned, any first work is a blueprint for me. I can't rewrite a blank page. I can only rewrite the things that don't seem to me to work, and so I have to read it over and over again.

Question: When you have several characters or a situation in your mind, what leads you to decide to write a stage play or a screenplay?
Simon: First, it's what I want to write. Do I want to write a play or do I want to write a film? *The Goodbye Girl* could easily have been a play, but I wanted to write a film that way. It all has to do with the original concept that comes into mind. It's hard work, just sitting down and thinking, What is it that I want to do? You start to dig into your past and your experiences. But once some inspiration presents itself, it is as a piece, as a play or a film. The concept of *The Sunshine Boys*, I guess, could have been a film, too. I'm never aware of that moment when something presents itself.

Question: What's your procedure in writing? Do you assemble notes? Do you prepare a careful outline?
Simon: If I need notes, it means I don't know it well enough. If you wake me up in the middle of the night, I should be able to tell you how the characters speak and what the story is about. I really have to get it firmly in my mind. In the very beginning, when I first started, I had no idea how to write a play. I read all the books on playwriting, and I went to some courses on playwriting. Most of them said you have to make a very detailed outline of what the play is about. So, I made a very, very detailed outline of what *Come Blow Your Horn* should be about, and then I started to write it. I found during the writing that the characters started to move off in their own directions. I used to force them back into the outline. I would say, "No, no, you can't go there. You have to go where I already planned for you to go." I found that the play was becoming very stilted and forced. Gradually, I let them go where they wanted, and I found out that my notes and outline didn't mean very much. What I try to do now is to make a general outline in my head.

Sometimes I'm lucky, and the whole play will come to me in a piece. *The Odd Couple* is an example. It wasn't really my idea, it was my brother's idea, because he literally had that existence. He got divorced, moved in with his best friend to save money on the alimony, and got into terrible fights because my brother was cooking the pot roast, and the girls were coming late. My brother was going to write the play, but he could not write by himself because he was so used to working in collaboration. So I wrote the play instead. It presented itself in its three acts to me—at that time I was writing three-act plays, which you don't see much anymore. I knew I had to do the exposition, which is always the most difficult thing in a play, to tell what is going on with the characters, who they are, where they came from, and what the situation is. You must tell the exposition entertainingly. It must not seem like exposition. I felt the best way to do it was through a poker game. The concept that I had the first day, just sitting and thinking about it, was to open up the first act with a poker game, in which we find out what Oscar and Felix are like. The second act will start with the poker game, but because of the changes in their lives, Felix has now moved into Oscar's apartment and wreaked havoc on their lives. I said, the play will end on the poker game, when we see all the changes. That is enough of an outline for me. Then I just start to write. Sometimes I will make notes about a character, where he comes from, what his background is, who he's married to, how he dresses.

Question: Does the humor sometimes come out of overheard conversations? Do you jot down what strikes you as funny?
Simon: No. I would never listen to somebody else and say that's very good. If somebody said the funniest thing in the world, it's not going to fit the play I'm writing. Nor would I try to base a play on some overheard conversation. How much would I know about those people? I will never make notes about humorous things or lines, because it would mean that I'm going to work the play to get to that funny line. When I write one line for a character, I haven't the vaguest idea what the next line is going to be. I want to be as surprised as the audience is going to be. Sometimes I find myself laughing, because I don't think that I thought of it. I think he thought of it. It only then seems organically right.

Question: If you are not jotting down what you hear or see, certainly you're absorbing everything around you. As you said earlier, your own life and the lives of those around you give you the material you need.
Simon: You have to eventually become some sort of litmus paper, where you absorb. The things that you absorb will stay with you. There's a genesis, a period, that can sometimes take years. I've found this is not unique with me. I've read that many playwrights have worked this way. For example, in

the film I've been working on now, there are fragments of ideas I had seven or eight years ago that I tried to work on then and discarded. But for this film, they simply fell into it. As for the characters, I have written about people I have known specifically in life—me, my wife, my family, my brother, my friends. Then it starts to branch out, and they start to become people that I have observed. Some are observed through some sort of osmosis. You aren't even really aware you are observing them. You're certainly not doing it with the intention of writing a play. When you are called upon to do work about such a person, you find out that you know a great deal about him. I know that for me and a great many writers, writing is not inspiration. You don't just walk around and wait until this wonderful idea comes. You sit down and it's work. You say, "What will I write?"

One of the things I've felt most proud about was the third act of *California Suite*. It is about a British couple. She is up for an Academy Award, and she is coming with her husband, who is an antiques dealer in London and a former actor. As the play unfolds, we find out that he is bisexual. She obviously has known for years that he is bisexual. But through the process of the telling of the story, their conflict and their problems in working out their relationship also come out. They are quite close, and they know and like each other enormously, and they want to continue their relationship in spite of their sexual problems. I thought it was one of the best pieces of writing that I had ever done. I can't tell you the names of the real people because they are not any two people. They are a composite of dozens of people: British actors that I know, people who are up for awards, people who are bisexual, people who have just normal sexual problems. They all seemed to come into my mind, and I was able to put them into that weird process and make it come out the way that I thought was right. But, you have to have not sensitive ears so much as sensitive antennae. It's not just listening to the words. It's what stays in your mind. The other stuff falls out anyway, it's not important. The good stuff manages to stay there, and you will draw upon it on the day you need it, even if it's years later.

Question: Are you often a character in your own works?
Simon: Did you see *Chapter Two*? That's me. About as honest as I've ever written about myself. I've written about myself in many instances. *Come Blow Your Horn* was about me leaving home at the age of twenty-one. *Barefoot in the Park* was literally about myself and my first wife living in a Greenwich Village apartment, but only about one facet. It was a very light-hearted comedy, and I didn't really get into any depth. There have been

facets of my own personality in other characters that I have written about, in *Last of the Red Hot Lovers*, in *Plaza Suite*, in all the plays. In *Prisoner of Second Avenue*, there are attitudes I had about living in New York City, although the circumstances did not happen to me. I was not a forty-eight-year-old businessman who'd lost his job and was petrified about what he was going to do with the rest of his life. But I identified with him, so I was able to think of myself as him in certain instances.

But *Chapter Two* is specifically autobiographical. It has to do with the death of my first wife, and meeting Marsha, and learning what it is to let go of the past in order to start a new relationship. It was the most difficult period of my life. I knew I couldn't be lighthearted about that, even though there's a great deal of comedy in the play. There were certain comic aspects in the arrangements for the dates and the meeting with Marsha. I really dealt with myself as honestly and objectively as I could. I made myself not always very attractive, showing the neurotic behavior that I went through at certain times. It was the most cathartic form of writing. Having dealt with the situation is one thing, but having written about it, I find it's now gone out of my life. I'm past it for the most part. One never loses all the memories, but I have dealt with the situation.

I think writing is one of the best ways of dealing with certain situations even if you're not a writer. A girl who works for us who is going through some bad times said, "I didn't know what to do about it, so I thought I'd write a play." She's not a writer. She wrote an act and a half of it, and she said, "I felt I didn't have to write any more. I got it out of my system." It's yelling at the world, or telling off all those people. You can't really stand on a rooftop and scream. But you can get it on paper, and it's a terrific thing.

Simon Says: Gray Days of the Sunshine Playwright

David Richards / 1983

From *Washington Post*, April 10, 1983, pp. L1, L5. © The Washington Post. Reprinted by permission. David Richards was a theater critic for the *Washington Star*, the *Washington Post*, and the *New York Times*; he is the author of *Played Out: The Jean Seberg Story* (1981).

NEW YORK—Neil Simon—the playwright who has tickled America's funny bone more consistently in the past twenty years than anyone else—sits on a plush couch thirty-five floors above Park Avenue and contemplates his fate.

"Here I am at the highest peak in my career," he says, "and I'm at the lowest point in my personal life. And they're both going on simultaneously. There's some odd joke in that."

But for the moment, damned if he can find it.

First, the silver lining. The King Midas of humor, Simon has converted odd couples, red hot lovers, sunshine boys, and husbands who go barefoot in the park into an emperor's fortune. His newest film, *Max Dugan Returns*, is shaping up as a box-office smash (its first weekend out, it grossed more than $2.7 million in 790 movie houses across the country). Meanwhile, his latest play, *Brighton Beach Memoirs*, has won him his best reviews from the New York critics in years and is settling in for a long and lucrative Broadway run. What's more, the critics, who have sometimes begrudged the playwright his ability to coin more funny lines per minute than seems humanly possible, have now decided that he has a very warm heart. Neil Simon, who arrived a long time ago, has in a manner of speaking, well, *arrived*!

Now the cloud. After ten years of marriage, Simon is splitting from Marsha Mason, his actress wife and the costar (with Jason Robards) of *Max Dugan*. Simon makes no bones about being a family man, needing that warmth, the support, the routine. Between his two wives, he's had twenty-eight years of marriage behind him and can't conceive of life in any other terms.

It took him only four months, after the traumatic death from cancer of his first wife, Joan, to fall in love with Mason and marry her. Their whirlwind courtship formed the basis of *Chapter Two*, his most overtly autobiographical play until *Brighton Beach*. When Mason wanted to go West to get a film career going, Simon willingly followed. He even wrote most of her films (among them: *The Goodbye Girl, Only When I Laugh, The Cheap Detective*).

"I've never felt alone writing in a room," he says, "because I've always had a family to go to at the end of the day. Without that family, writing is the loneliest life in the world. I don't want to go into late middle age saying, 'I've got to have another play, I've got to have another play.' I don't need another play now. I need a life. I'm fifty-five. I have a lot of years left. I don't want to waste them over a typewriter. I'd rather find my sustenance somewhere else. The joy of writing has stopped, because the joy in my life has stopped."

He pauses—a vaguely overweight, tanned, middle-aged man with thinning black hair, owlish glasses, and expensive tennis shoes. This morning he awoke with a firm resolve in mind: He's put all of his projects on hold for a minimum of a year. Maybe two, before tackling the film version of *Brighton Beach Memoirs*. He's going back to his Bel Air home, because that's where he feels his roots are—not the Park Avenue apartment he views primarily as a pied-a-terre, even though its dimensions render the term slightly ludicrous. Perhaps he'll do a little traveling. But mostly, he wants to think this mid-life crisis through.

"Maybe this split is the best thing that could have happened to me," he says, wanting to believe it.

There's more cloud. He's spent most of the morning on the phone, learning that he's lost "a great deal of money" on some bad investments. The grim details have furrowed his brow. But even that he's trying to put behind him. "It doesn't mean that much," he tells himself, "even though it means about eight years of work in terms of money gone down the drain. But I would rather have my life together than think about that money. I've got enough. If I watch it, take it easy, there's no need to worry. I'm never going to be broke. The royalties will come in for the next fifty-four years. I want to be able to leave something to my two children, but not so much that it's going to screw up their lives. Mostly, I want to get over this period of being suspended."

If Simon feels he can abandon the theater for a while, it's because *Brighton Beach* represents a personal apotheosis, not simply another fat, commercial hit. Some critics have even gone so far as to say that it is his *Ah, Wilderness!*, an observation that puts him in the company, if only for comparative purposes, of Eugene O'Neill. For the first time in his career, Simon has begun to think of the legacy he will leave behind. "I feel that if I had died without writing my *Brighton Beach Memoirs*, well, I would have had a nice legacy as a writer of light comedies," he explains. "But it would have been incomplete. This play has satisfied me so much that if it were all over right now and I never wrote another play, I'd be quite content."

In it, Simon is writing for the first time about his youth, growing up poor and Jewish during the Depression. He's writing about his mother and the way she would pack him off to the corner grocery sixteen times a day for a stick of butter or a quart of milk—never a pound of butter or a gallon of milk, because who knew what the following morning would bring and there was no sense in wasting money on food you might never consume. He's writing about her bark ("Stop that yelling. I have a cake in the oven") that was far worse than her bite. And her stern bigotry that was really just her manner of putting her imperiled family first.

"She left such a deep mark on my personal life," Simon reflects, "that I have both gained and suffered from having this bizarre, close relationship. I say bizarre, because it seemed so at the time. And yet she nurtured me so much that women and a domestic life are terribly important to me, despite the fact that I lived in broken homes all through my childhood. My mother was the one who stood by me and I knew that whatever I did, it was wonderful with her. When you grow up being loved like that, you gain a great deal of security and confidence in yourself. On the other hand, you grow up wanting and needing so much that when it's not there, the loss is enormous. For all those opening nights, all the plays and movies I did over the years, I never had an ulcer until my mother died. That's when the acid starting flowing."

He's writing about his father, or, more accurately, the principled father he always wanted, since his real father was constantly disappearing for months, while the remaining Simons, with mother at the helm, were shunted from relative to relative, trying to keep up a semblance of home life.

He's writing about his big brother, Danny, who told him, prophetically, "You're going to be the best comedy writer in America." Simon still marvels at that. "I was fourteen, and maybe once in a while, I'd say something amusing around the house. But he picked up on it. He noticed. I idealized him. I realize now that he bore the brunt of the terror that came down to the children. I was spared a lot by his being in the way. He paved the path for my whole career. We used to go out for writing jobs on radio and early TV shows and I never could have lasted without him. Although I did most of the writing, Danny was the spokesman. He got us through doors, negotiated things, kept the team going, and gave me encouragement and energy."

Mostly, though, Simon is writing about himself in the guise of fifteen-year-old Eugene, who serves as the play's narrator and whose cockeyed slant on the family's tribulations keeps the play in comic perspective. As played by Matthew Broderick, Eugene is the most immediately appealing character in *Brighton Beach Memoirs*. At curtain call, audiences cheer.

"He's a lot cuter than I was," admits Simon. "But that's the way I remember it. I decided that Eugene would be the only character in the play who's funny. Take him out and you have a straight play. But his perspective on life is my perspective. It's not that I try to make things funny. It just happens.

"There've been a lot of tears in my life in the last ten years. Before that it was all joy. The career was going upwards, the kids growing up, it was terrific. Then my first wife died. That was so devastating to me I literally thought I wouldn't live through it. Then your children move away. Your parents die. I had to adjust to change. But I still try to maintain the humor. That's what makes whatever I do unique and different. In the deepest, darkest hours of my despair, I say something funny as a life-saving device, I guess. Whether I do it consciously or unconsciously, I'm putting things in perspective. Really, it's the luckiest thing about me.

"I think it's what attracts people to my work. It says to them, 'Look, he can laugh at some of the same problems we're going through.' Some of them, not all of them. We're certainly not going to laugh at death. But I think audiences feel if my characters can get through problems without that deadly seriousness, well, maybe they can, too."

Even as Simon is trying earnestly to plumb his current pain, the old life-saving mechanism clicks on. "I began to find out that life is filled with disillusions early," he says. "As a kid, all I wanted was enough money to go to the Polo Grounds anytime I wanted to. And when I did, the Giants picked up and moved to San Francisco."

Lighthearted as it is, the fantasy that is *Max Dugan Returns* is also rooted in Simon's remembrances of his fractured upbringing. The story is contemporary Cinderella. An attractive widow (Mason) in Venice, California, is struggling with heroic good spirits to raise her teenage son (Broderick again) on a paltry teacher's salary. But it's tough going. The kitchen appliances are on their last legs and her ramshackle Volvo is stolen out from under her nose. Then her charming wastrel of a father, Max Dugan, shows up. He had abandoned her when she was nine, has served time in the clinker, and informs her he's got six months to live. He also has $687,000 in neatly packaged bills in an attaché case and promptly sets out to buy her and his grandson every gift their hearts could desire.

"I was afraid to write it at first," Simon acknowledges, "because it came right after '*I Ought to Be in the Pictures*,' which was also about the reunion of a father and his daughter. I think it was me still trying to resolve the relationship with my own father. Growing up, we always seemed to be going through reunions. Partings and reunions. The partings were painful and the reunions were terrific.

"But the story just popped into my mind and it seemed so timely. Then I got nervous about the movie. It's such a simple story about simple people. I think audiences are looking for warmth, but someone out there—the producers, the critics—are pushing away from it. It seems to me the grimmer the piece, the more the critics like it. But we all need our fantasies. They're what get us through. We deal with reality enough."

The current round of huzzahs notwithstanding, Simon nurtures a certain skepticism toward the critics. "They accepted the lesser plays much more vigorously than the later plays, which were better," he says. "Certainly, *Prisoner of Second Avenue* is a better play than *Barefoot in the Park*, but the hats went into the air with *Barefoot*. They said, 'Here's a new, young playwright who's going to give us a lot of wonderful light comedies.' But you give them enough light comedies and they say, 'We want something deeper.' So you go to something deeper and they say, 'Where are the light comedies we liked so much?' You realize that they want you to write what they want to see. And they all want to see something different!"

In Simon's estimation, the one that counts with him, *Brighton Beach Memoirs*, "is about as high as I've gone so far." But it's also been consuming. He used to write a play, then go off on vacation and enjoy the fruits of his labor. "Something's been driving me these last few years. I don't know what. If I did, I'd have the answer to my problems. In one sense, I'm glad because I came up with my *Brighton Beach Memoirs*. But I'm also sorry, because I've spent so much of myself."

His tone is without self-pity. There's even a kind of professorial sobriety about him as he sorts through the glory and the wreckage of his life. "I hear I'm the most eligible bachelor in town right now," he says a bit ruefully. "People tell me, 'You can have any girl you want.' But any girl you want isn't the right girl. It's like writing any play you want. That doesn't mean anything unless it has quality. It was almost easier for me to fall in love quickly with Marsha, the way I did just four months after Joan's death, because Joan was gone. And when someone dies, you know you have to let go. But I can't let go of Marsha yet, because she's still there. And she hasn't let go completely either.

"We've parted. We're getting a divorce. But I don't consider that the end. There's no law that says you can't get remarried again. We still talk to one another on the phone every day. From the conversations you'd think it was Romeo and Juliet. But I want to change my life and that takes more courage than anything else in the world. I've got to make the move. Go out and seek it, whatever it is, and not wait for the doorbell to ring and someone to say, 'Hi, I'm the beautiful girl next door.'"

So Simon is heading back to California. No slow fade-out and swelling music this time. Where the sunset usually is, there's a big question mark.

Seemingly, he's had it all—acclaim, success, wealth beyond most mortals' daydreams—while the rest of the world fights merely to keep up with the mortgage payments. He must be a nice guy. Because when he says he just wants to find out what his life is all about, you suddenly find yourself wishing him—this, the most successful playwright of his generation—good luck and Godspeed.

Neil Simon

J. Wynn Rousuck / 1984

From *Baltimore Sun*, September 23, 1984, *Sun Magazine*, pp. 10, 11, 19, 23, 24. Permission from The Baltimore Sun. J. Wynn Rousuck was, for twenty-three years, the theater critic of the *Baltimore Sun*.

New York

This is the boyhood home of playwright Neil Simon: there are twin beds and a Yankees pennant on the wall in the second-floor bedroom Neil shares with his older brother. Downstairs, there's an old-fashioned sink with draining boards in the kitchen, a dusty hutch jammed with crockery in the dining room, and a bulky radio in a walnut cabinet in the living room. Inside the house, the carpet is worn. Outside there is sand, and the sound of not-so-distant gulls.

Nothing too peculiar in any of that, except that this is a house without exterior walls. Eight times a week more than a thousand people sit outside the living room and stare in. You see, this isn't really Neil Simon's childhood home. It is Neil Simon's memory of his childhood home—the stage set of his most recent Broadway hit, *Brighton Beach Memoirs*.

It is the most fragile and transparent of glass houses.

In this house, Neil Simon the child is represented by an actor. Neil Simon the adult is sitting in a suite in a Park Avenue hotel.

He's not what you'd expect.

You'd expect Neil Simon to be funny, right? I mean, being funny is what this guy does for a living.

Right now, though, he's off duty. Neil Simon is paid to be funny on paper. In person he's reflective, candid, wise—but not a wise guy.

He does *look* funny—which is not to say he's funny looking. No, it's just that this egg-shaped head with its horn-rimmed glasses somehow looks the way you figured Neil Simon would look: not laughable by any means, but like someone who, instead of headaches, has little laughs breaking out in his head—laughaches, you might call them.

Neil Simon is someone who finds the world he is living in "slightly absurd."

He's also someone who's had twenty plays produced on Broadway in twenty-two years. Those plays are said to have been seen by more people than have seen Shakespeare. (Two of them will be playing at the Mechanic this year. *Brighton Beach Memoirs* opens the season Tuesday night, and in November the distaff version of *The Odd Couple*, perhaps his most popular play, will have a pre-Broadway tryout at the Mechanic.)

Last year Mr. Simon became the only living playwright to have a Broadway theater named after him (". . . try to keep the carpets clean. This is my theater now," he said at the dedication).

Fourteen years ago he was reported to be taking home $45,000 a week. That was before the big bucks starting rolling in from Hollywood.

It's probably not an exaggeration to call Neil Simon the most successful playwright in the history of, well, history.

That is to say, he's got this playwriting business beat. To use the sports metaphors he likes to use himself, he knows the playwriting score, if anyone does. So, the one thing you would not expect him to be is insecure.

"I think at some point we all think that we're frauds and we're getting away with something," he says, "and any minute somebody says that in print, I'll say that he's an idiot."

Rest assured, Mr. Simon, no one's throwing stones. Come to think of it, if you study that face again, there is something in that sheepish, boyish grin that seems to be seeking reassurance, a pat on the head, perhaps.

"I am always surprised when I write something and I give it to somebody and they say, 'This is wonderful.' I'm always shocked by it," he says.

Well, few other people are. True, right before *Brighton Beach* Neil Simon did have a show—*Actors and Actresses*—that didn't make it to Broadway. But it's also true that there was a time when he had four shows running on Broadway simultaneously.

He is the Sunshine Boy, the Last of the Red-Hot Playwrights. So could it be that the man who broke into Broadway with *Come Blow Your Horn* refuses to toot his own horn? Apparently it could.

The prolific Mr. Simon was once quoted as saying he begins four plays for every one he completes. Hearing that again today, he says, "Maybe nine."

"I have a greater sense of what's wrong than what's right," he insists. "I pretty much know when what I'm doing is wrong, and I'll stop it because the typewriter keys feel like they're ten pounds each. You say, 'Oh, God, this is dragging a dead horse up hill. I've got to stop it.' But when it's going along well, it feels good, but it is not necessarily a sure sign that what you're doing is really right."

Then there's the sand test: "There is this mysterious process that when you build a foundation right, the building's not going to topple over," he says. "When the foundation is not right, it's like sand, and you start to sink into it and you get fooled—spend a lot of time working on it and then find out you don't have anything there."

He's just as humble talking about success. He tries to evade the subject for a while. This is a game of Simon Says we're playing, and what Simon eventually says is that there are people who have a will to succeed, and evidently he is one of them.

"I must have asked for success," he admits. "I mean, you could win the lottery, but if you win it twenty times, you're really trying."

The subject of success may make him uncomfortable, but he finds the pursuit of it fascinating. Last month he became an Olympics groupie.

He watched because he wanted "to see the attitude of the people who want to win," he explains. "It's not the winning that's so important, because winning doesn't last very long. When I see some of the commentators who say, 'This moment will live in his memory the rest of his life—these two minutes that he won the gold medal will last him forever.' It doesn't last me forever.

"The success of *Barefoot in the Park* twenty years ago means very little to me right now. It meant a lot more to me that after writing twenty plays that I was, I think, still growing when I wrote *Brighton Beach Memoirs*. It's the changing and wanting to keep on going."

Years ago, Mr. Simon described himself as a two-headed monster with one head involved in life and the other head observing it. Success is a monster of another sort.

"Success is something that people both cheer for and then try to destroy because it is both something that they want to attain for themselves and then becomes a threat to them because they're not achieving," he says.

The success monster also preys on two-headed monsters. Playing the observer "becomes a little bit more difficult when you are the one who's being observed," he explains. "I go into a restaurant, I see people looking at me."

That's definitely one of the drawbacks of having two heads. Mr. Simon doesn't let either head get too big, though. "It's not that bad," he adds. "I'm not Robert Redford."

One reason people may begrudge Mr. Simon his success is that comedy gets no respect. The funny business may be a money business but it's hardly ever confused with high art.

Mr. Simon has a couple of theories for humor's bad rep. "The reason comedy is sometimes written off is because we see so much bad comedy," he says, making it clear that he is referring specifically to television, which happens to be where he got his start, writing for Phil Silvers and Jackie Gleason and Sid Caesar, three of the hit wits of early TV.

Comedy is what got Neil Simon into the playwriting business in the first place. There were two specific moments in his childhood that made him realize he wanted to make his living by making people laugh. The first was an outdoor showing of a Charlie Chaplin short. "I was maybe eight years old and sitting in this chair and laughed so hard I went right over in the chair, hit my head, and I was unconscious and they took me to the hospital," he recalls with a grin.

"And the next time I went to a movie theater and saw *Modern Times*, I guess it was, and laughed so hard, and I said, 'God, it would be wonderful to be able to do that to an audience.'"

However, not everyone thinks this is so wonderful. Wiping that boyish grin off his face, Mr. Simon says, "There are an enormous amount of people who have absolutely no sense of humor at all, and many of them pride themselves on it. They would say, 'I don't laugh. Nobody can make me laugh.' They think that's a sign of strength, like, 'Nobody can make me cry.'"

Okay, humorless saps, don't take this as a sign that Neil Simon has given in to your sour expectations. *But*, the fact is that the man who has caused more than a few audience members to fall out of their chairs writhing with laughter (some, undoubtedly, against their will), now says, "I don't really consider . . . that I am in certain areas writing comedy anymore."

There can be no mistaking his tone of voice. This is not a joke. This is serious—Neil Simon could be turning serious.

Just what is it that he's serious about?

"I'm certainly not into politics because you can't write a play fast enough to keep up with what politics are about," he begins. "I'm not really into major social issues because I think they change as well, and then, at least for me, you have to take a stand, a point of view, and I don't like to do that," he continues.

"The thing I write about more than anything else," he says finally, "is behavior." Behavior, of course, in a world he finds "slightly absurd."

He's not as interested in analyzing his own behavior as that of his characters. But, he does identify a highly personal strain running through his work, running, in fact, at a steady enough pace to call it a theme. It's the "shattered dreams" theme, specifically, the shattered dreams of Eugene M. Jerome, child hero of the autobiographical *Brighton Beach Memoirs*. The playwright describes it as "a certain disappointment that life didn't turn out to be what I thought it was as a child, which was a very purist attitude—that life is fair, that, as all mothers are going to tell you, everything works out for the best. I mean that is one of the all-time dumb expressions I've ever heard."

Brighton Beach Memoirs may have more laughs than some of his purest comedies. It's just that in this case he did not set out to make people laugh.

"I wanted them to remember and to be touched, or to wish for a time like that to be in our lives again, that closeness of a family, where we all can lean on each other and help each other," he says.

It so happens, however, that the time Mr. Simon is remembering in *Brighton Beach Memoirs* is not exactly the way things were. His real father worked in the garment district, like the character in the play, but unlike that character, his real father wasn't around a good deal of the time. When he was, there was often fighting. In the play, Eugene Jerome's aunt and two cousins are boarders in his house. In real life, Mr. Simon and his mother were the boarders, moving in with relatives when his father left for good.

"The relationship between my father and my mother was quite different than it is in the play," he admits, "but my relationship with him perhaps was not that different because I love my father. I was always very upset and angry and disappointed when he left home, but when he would come back, I loved being with him. I mean, he would take me to a hockey game or a baseball game—it was the greatest thrill in life."

The picture he paints of his father in *Brighton Beach* may be impressionism, but the picture of his older brother Danny is realism. As his alter ego Eugene says in the play. "I always had this two-way thing about my brother. Either I worshiped the ground he walked on or I hated him so much I wanted to kill him."

For ten years, Danny and Neil Simon were a comedy-writing team. He credits Danny as the biggest influence encouraging him to write. "He used to say, 'You're going to be one of the best writers in America,' when I was fourteen, fifteen years old," recalls Simon the younger.

Danny, who is now primarily a director and teacher, has also shown up in more than a few of his brother's plays, most notably in the guise of fastidious Felix Ungar in *The Odd Couple*. He'll be directing that play when it passes through the Mechanic on its way to Broadway this fall, only Felix will be called Florence and will be played by Sally Struthers to Rita Moreno's Olive.

Neil Simon may not go in for social issues, but he does keep up with the times. "I know for a fact that if the change in women's role in society didn't come about, there'd be no point in doing this," he says of the distaff rewrite of what has become his classic comedy of incompatibility.

You might think the key to the more serious Simon style lies in the increasingly autobiographical nature of his plays. After all, off the stage, the subject of this autobiographical drama does seem to take himself pretty seriously.

And the further adventures of Eugene Jerome are on the way. *Biloxi Blues*, which will open on Broadway in the spring, picks up Eugene's memoirs six years later, during World War II. Originally, Mr. Simon says, he intended to make Eugene's story a trilogy, although he admits, "There's not a necessity to write a trilogy. One could write a quintet, if they want."

However, the playwright insists autobiographical plays are nothing new for him. It's just that until recently they were autobiographical comedies. They started with his first play, *Come Blow Your Horn*, about two bachelor brothers. Then there was *Barefoot in the Park*, which harked back to his days as a newlywed, and later on, *Chapter Two*, based on his marriage to actress Marsha Mason, only a few months after the death of his first wife. (That marriage recently ended in divorce.) He even lumps *Last of the Red Hot Lovers* into this category, claiming that while it's not strictly autobiographical, he did share the main character's feelings "at a point when the country was going through a sexual revolution."

"When I say 'autobiographical,'" he explains, "people assume right away that everything in it was true. It isn't. You just use it as a stepping stone to a play that you want to write."

All right, if the autobiographical angle can't explain this departure from pure comedy, maybe the comedies themselves can. The funny bone may have some backbone after all.

Let's take another look at what Neil Simon has to say about comedy. For comedy to work, he points out, it's got to be dead serious to the people on stage.

"Mike Nichols used to say that to the cast," he explains. "For example, I remember the first day of *Barefoot in the Park*, when we sat around and read the play. After that first reading he said, 'I want you to forget that this is a comedy. From now on we're doing *King Lear*, and you've got to believe in it and that it's a matter of life and death.' And when I write, I always think of it that way."

As Mr. Simon would be the first to point out, there's been a serious side to his comedies all along. The difference between the new Neil and the old Neil turns out to be a matter of emphasis.

Take a look, for example, at what he has described as one of the sources of his comedy—anger. What gets him angry is pretty serious. It's not the little things in life, the things that made one of his characters feel like a *Prisoner of Second Avenue*, the things that made *The Out-of-Towners* want to go home. What gets to Mr. Simon is, among other things, stupidity.

"I wrote a whole play about stupidity, *Fools*, but not in anger," he says.

Then he's on a roll: "I get angry at people who impose on me or impose on anybody; people with a lack of sensitivity. I mean, there are obviously huge issues to be angry about—man's inhumanity to man, but we're not going to deal with that. The list gets too big. I get angry at myself a lot. I get angry at people who don't try to do their best. I get angry at people who think things are coming to them. I don't think anything is coming to anyone. I don't know where I got such a strong work ethic from, I don't think necessarily from my parents. I'm a strong believer in nature and I see that nature has certain rules that have to be obeyed. I think man is always looking for ways to break the rules so he doesn't have to work so hard. The ultimate dream for man is to work less so that he can come home to watch others work more."

Neil Simon's dream is to work forever.

He says a lot of people ask him why he keeps on writing since he's already made so much money. If it were just a matter of making money, he explains, "what would I do with money? Sit on the beach some place? You would go crazy. I mean, you would drown yourself on the third day.

"The idea is to really try to just keep on doing the work because you not only love the work, you just couldn't do without it."

Neil Simon: In Conversation with Terrence McNally

Terrence McNally / 1985

From *Broadway Song & Story: Playwrights/Lyricists/Composers Discuss Their Hits,* edited by Otis L. Guernsey Jr. (New York: Dodd, Mead, 1985), 172–83. Originally published in *Dramatists Guild Quarterly* 21 (Winter 1985): 10, 16–32. © 1985 The Dramatists Guild of America, Inc. Reprinted with permission from The Dramatists Guild of America, Inc., www.dramatists guild.com. Terrence McNally received Best Play Tony Awards for *Love! Valour! Compassion!* (1994) and *Master Class* (1995) and Best Book of a Musical Tony Awards for *Kiss of the Spider Woman* (1992) and *Ragtime* (1996).

Terrence McNally: You were born on the Fourth of July, which is very fitting for America's most popular playwright.
Neil Simon: Did you know that George M. Cohan was not born on July Fourth? He was born on the fifth, and he changed it to be the Yankee Doodle Dandy.

McNally: There are two volumes of your plays, and in one of them you talk about the writer as a split personality: as a monster that goes around observing people and writing about them, skewering their faults, *and* as a human being whom the monster observes and skewers. Today I want to talk to the human being about what the monster has wrought. For example, when you were growing up in New York City, did you go to the theater a lot? Who were your influences?
Simon: The theater did not become a part of my life until I was fifteen or sixteen years old. My family was not very much interested in the theater, so I was a movie buff. Also quite an avid reader. I never really thought much about becoming a playwright. It was much too lofty an aspiration for me, to write something that had all those plot twists and developments. It was far beyond what I imagined I could do. I would settle just for writing jokes for Earl Wilson's column. Gradually, my brother Danny and I started to work

writing sketches—monologues, at first—for the comics who at that time were playing Broadway, which was filled with the theaters like the Strand, the Roxy, the Capitol, Loew's State, Paramount. They all had the big bands, like Glenn Miller's, and the singers, like Frank Sinatra, and the comics, who always needed new material. And my brother and I, for many years when I was a teenager, wrote material for these comics. I remember the night of my high school prom, we went to a night club where the comic was performing material that I wrote—and none of the kids at my table would believe me. When I tried to get backstage later, and they didn't let me, they still wouldn't believe me.

Then Danny and I started writing sketches. I think the first job we may have gotten was for the original show in the Johnny Carson time slot, which was *Broadway Open House*, with Jerry Lester. My brother and I wrote for two nights a week, and another writer wrote the other nights.

McNally: When you were that young boy going to the movies, when did it occur to you that someone was writing the funny lines, situations, and characters? Was there a moment you realized the power of writing it?
Simon: The inspiration came from the books I read. My heroes then were Robert Benchley, Stephen Leacock, and Mark Twain. When I would do any writing, it was to emulate them. So before I began writing with my brother, I would do comic, Robert Benchley–type essays. I didn't think at that time about movies being *written*. Nobody knew screenwriters—they still don't know screenwriters.

McNally: When you started writing jokes for the comics, how did you get a joke to these people? You were very young.
Simon: Fortunately, my brother was eight years older, and he did that. I couldn't; I was scared stiff. The first radio show that we ever worked on, I would sit next to him and whisper things. The head writer, Goodman Ace, was an awesome character; I would whisper, "What if the fellow said such-and-such?" and he would say, "*What?*" and I would say, "Nothing." I did that for weeks, and finally he said, "Why do we need this kid here? He's not contributing anything." I was doing that as late as 1954. I was in my twenties, and I was whispering to Carl Reiner, working on *Your Show of Shows*. It's kind of rough sitting in a room with Mel Brooks and Larry Gelbart and Sid Caesar, and being shy. But I'm still shy.

They were such a boisterous group, extroverts all of them; it was like a cocktail party where you had to scream your line out. I was so happy when my career turned and I became a playwright. I could sit alone in a room and work without the shouting. But I type lightly.

McNally: As an adolescent, were you a funny person?

Simon: It's hard to think I was funny at that time, but I guess so. My brother was encouraging me when I was fourteen and fifteen years old. He would say, "God, that's funny," he would laugh, and he would say, "I'm telling you, someday you're going to be a top comedy writer." I never dreamed that would be possible. I can't remember a single thing that I said that was funny—or that I wrote. I remember showing him certain pieces that he liked. And I was always able to do that.

McNally: There must have been a period when you made a real decision to write for the theater.

Simon: I think it started germinating in my mind in the late 1950s. I had been writing for television and making a very good living, but I saw no future to it. I was still waiting for calls from agents saying, "Do you want to work on such-and-such a show next year?" Or I was calling them and saying, "Can you get me a movie?" and they were saying, "No, can't get you a movie until you've written a movie," you know, catch-22. So the only way was to write a play. I thought I would do it as an experiment, to see if I could put together 120 pages that made sense. And that I started around 1958.

McNally: This is *Come Blow Your Horn*?

Simon: Yes. And the 120 pages came, without exaggeration, to about twelve hundred pages. I don't mean one version of it. I wrote it ten times, maybe twenty times, from beginning to end. It had five different titles. I took it to maybe fifteen of the top Broadway producers of the day—Joshua Logan, George Abbott, David Merrick. They all liked it; all told me to fix this scene, fix that scene. The three years I spent were equivalent to a first-rate college course in playwriting, which I got from all of them. But there were then all these plays that had to be assembled into one.

   I did what was sort of suicidal in those days, doing the play in summer stock. Most plays that originated in summer stock ended in summer stock. Regional theater had not yet surfaced. But I couldn't get the play on. So I had an agent—it was the last time I had an agent, in 1961—and we tried the play at the Bucks County Playhouse in New Hope, Pennsylvania. I think, in a sense, it saved my career. If we had gone to Philadelphia with it, it would have died, and I would have been decimated and had to make a living writing *My Three Sons* for the next ten years. But the play had enough promise for me to work on rewriting it. And by the time we did the pre-Broadway production in Philadelphia, it was a much better play. I look back on it as pretty primitive now, but it was entertaining, it had a good story, good characters, and it was, in a farcical sense, very truthful. It was about my family, about myself and my brother.

McNally: You said television seemed to have no future. Did you feel that the quality of television was so low that no one could change it?
Simon: It wasn't that television wasn't good enough. At that time, which is called "The Golden Age of Television," when *Sergeant Bilko* and *Your Show of Shows* were on, there were a lot of good shows. I'm talking specifically about the light comedy shows. But that was also when Paddy Chayefsky, Tad Mosel, Horton Foote, Robert Alan Arthur—all those terrific writers—were writing wonderful plays.

But television meant doing the same thing for the rest of my life, writing what other people wanted me to write. And I had a lot of things that I wanted to say for myself, about myself. I wanted freedom of expression, and you're never going to get it in television. I had to deal not only with the comedian I was working for, but the sponsor; and the sponsor had to deal with the network. We all had someone to answer to. Writing for the theater you have no one but the public and the critics to answer to.

McNally: Did you find all the years of writing sketches and half-hour shows for television a good training for the theater?
Simon: It was great, because it taught us to work under pressure. When I worked on the Bilko show, we did thirty-nine shows a season—now it's twenty-six—and it was like writing a half-hour movie every single week. The pressure was enormous, so that later on when I got out of town to work on a play, and the first act wasn't working, I didn't panic; it was thirty or forty pages, and I felt in four weeks I could certainly do the work. Had I not had the experience turning out material week after week, it would have frightened me.

The other advantage it had was that, in those days, the quality of the material was far superior to today's shows. Today's shows, are, I think, sub-normal, most of them—the situation comedy shows. There are exceptions, of course, but not an awful lot of them. The experience you'd get now would not be first-rate. Sid Caesar, who I thought was a genius, and the writers I mentioned—and Woody Allen came on eventually—all were tops in their field. And all went on to do terrific things. I don't think situation comedy writing today is going to prepare you for a life in the theater.

In a way, I suffered the first years in the theater. I had to shake that training for getting jokes into the material instead of character. When you write a twenty-six-minute show, in which they want a lot of laughs, it's hard to create character. The Bilko show was character comedy, and situation, but it's hard to find that today.

McNally: It's interesting, what you got out of it, because so many playwrights today think that writing for television is the absolute worst thing for anyone who aspires to the theater—it teaches you a million bad habits.
Simon: I think it applies to actors and directors as well. I've seen some first-rate actors lose their abilities by working in television for so many years. They start shouting everything, they start becoming one-dimensional. And when they go back to the theater, it's tough for them to make the jump.

McNally: I worked on thirteen episodes of a show, and they say to you, "We want a joke by every third line." The laughs are nice to get, so I know how it could happen.
Simon: It's not only that so much; when you write for television, and you sit down at the typewriter and try to imagine the quintessential audience that you will be writing for on any given night, there's a possibility that it'll be forty million people. Well, it's impossible to write for forty million people— to try to reach that audience—because they have too many demands and come from too many different strata of life. Whereas, in my mind, I pick out those nine hundred or a thousand people coming to the theater, spending a fair amount of money, who want the best kind of entertainment. I find them the toughest, most critical, and also the most open audience. But you can't give them *Hee-Haw*.

McNally: The director I worked with in television was Paul Bogart, and he said, "Just remember, it's an actor's medium." That made me feel better. "They remember Lucille Ball, not who wrote or directed her shows," he said. When you got to your first play at Bucks County, you had cast approval, no words could be changed—or maybe the producers *did* tell you to change this, change that—
Simon: The theater owners, everybody. Michael Ellis and William Hammerstein produced it.

McNally: And what wasn't working about it?
Simon: Oh, tons.

McNally: And you knew it—you didn't want to blame the director, the audience, or the cast.
Simon: I had people coming up to me: "It was a bad night, it was hot in the theater," and I knew the difference—the play wasn't working. I had a man on the telephone for twenty minutes at the beginning explaining what was going on. I learned, okay, that is not the way to do the exposition. You've got to dramatize it. And I had some opportunity to fix it a little during that run, but it was in the six months afterwards, mostly, that I started to dramatize it.

McNally: This was work you did with the director?
Simon: No, I did it on my own. And we opened the revised play in Philadelphia at the Walnut. On the opening night in the middle of the first act, a man died in the balcony. I heard a woman scream, "Oh, my God, Harry!" and I said, "Oh, my God, my career." It stopped everything cold that night. But the play became a big hit in Philadelphia; we sold out for the three weeks. And we came to New York. I assumed that all New York was waiting at Grand Central Station for me. I found out that we had $175 in advance sales.

We opened, and this is how your fate can change because of the whim or ingenuity of one person. There were seven daily newspapers in 1961, and very little television coverage. There was word-of-mouth, eventually, but you lived or died by those critics. We got mixed reviews, some were good, some not good. I went down to the box office the next day—there was one woman there buying a ticket, and she found out it was the wrong play. So we didn't sell anything, and Mike Ellis and Bill Hammerstein posted the closing notice. I was heartbroken. The general manager, Wally Fried, said, "You can't close this play! The audiences love it!" He said, "Go out on the corners and give the tickets away—anybody who walks by. Get them into the theater!" And for the first week, that's what we did. We had a quarter of the house all sitting there for free—and enjoying it. They started to tell people about it, and gradually people started to buy tickets. Then we started giving out tickets to half the house. Irving Lazar, the agent, came and laughed his head off and told Groucho Marx. Groucho saw it, came backstage—I had my picture taken with him—and said: "It's one of the funniest plays I've ever seen," and the play caught on. It ran two years. Had Wally Fried not told them he believed in this play, it would have been over, and I'd be back on *My Three Sons*.

McNally: Do you wonder if you would have written another play if it had closed that first week?

Simon: Yes, because I was working in television during this, and to write I had to find weekends, nights; I had a wife and a baby to support. If those three years had gone down the drain, it would have kept me, possibly, from doing the second play. What *Come Blow Your Horn* did was subsidize my next play. When Paramount offered me the chance to do the screenplay for something like $75,000, more money than I'd ever dreamed of, I turned it down. I said, "No, I know what happens. If I go out there and write the screenplay, and it works, they'll offer me another one, and I'll end up in Hollywood." Which is not what I wanted to do. I wanted to be a playwright. So I started to work on *Barefoot in the Park*. And digressed to *Little Me*.

McNally: Was there any tone in the reviews of *Come Blow Your Horn* that this was a comedy by a television writer and therefore not a *real* playwright?

Simon: Not much. A lot of my friends in television would be quoted in the reviews as saying this was a television comedy, written by a television writer. I don't remember that as being in the reviews as a penalty to pay.

McNally: *Little Me* brought you back with Sid Caesar?

Simon: Yes, I wrote it for Sid Caesar. It was a part that required the portrayal of seven different roles, and I didn't know anyone as good as Sid. After *Your Show of Shows* went off the air, I'd stayed with Max Liebman, the producer, who was doing a series of specials—two a month. The first would be a revue, with people like Maurice Chevalier and Marcel Marceau, international stars. The other part of the month we would adapt a Broadway book show: *Best Foot Forward*, *A Connecticut Yankee*, *Dearest Enemy*—all Rodgers and Hart shows. Some Gershwin shows. The books were dated, so we got permission from the estates of these properties to update them. It was another learning experience for the theater: I learned to write books for musicals.

McNally: You interrupted *Barefoot in the Park* to write *Little Me*?

Simon: Yes, and then went back to *Barefoot*. I was lucky to have *Come Blow Your Horn* as the first show, because it was not such an awesome hit that you say, "God, what do I do now?" *Barefoot* was a huge hit; it ran four years. I had never read reviews like that. "Funniest play I've ever seen; funniest play in the last fifty years." I would sure hate that to be my first play; there's no way that you could live up to that. It would have scared the life out of me.

But having done two shows before, *Barefoot* just became my third show. It was kind of scary, but I was lucky, because I had a good idea for the next show while that was happening, which was *The Odd Couple*. So, I didn't let that success intimidate me.

McNally: With *Barefoot*, you started working with Mike Nichols, which was one of the most successful collaborations in recent history.
Simon: Mike is the most helpful director, to a writer, that I've ever worked with. And I've worked with wonderful directors—Gene Saks, Herbert Ross, Bob Fosse. They all have their individual talents, but Mike, working with a writer, is incomparable.

McNally: In what way is he most helpful?
Simon: He just makes you think differently. The first day of *The Odd Couple* we sat around a table and read the play, the first act was terrific, and the second was even better. And the producer, Saint Subber, went home; he said, "You don't need me here. I'm going out to sell theater parties, because this play is a smash." Saint didn't hear the third act, and it was a bomb. And I really panicked about that, because it had taken me three or four months to write the third act. Mike said, "I'll rehearse the first and second acts, and you go home and write a new third act." So in about four days I wrote a new third act that I told myself was brilliant. And I brought it in and Mike read it, hysterically laughing; and we sat down and read it, and it was worse than the first third act.

So for the second time I had to go back, and I didn't feel so brilliant anymore. I was getting real scared then. I came in with another version a week later, after missing the rehearsals and the rewrites needed for the first and second acts. Mike said, "No, it's not so good, but we'll have to open in Wilmington with this third act. But we'll talk on the train." Which we did. And as the train pulled in, we had pretty much evolved what the third act should be about. So I went to my hotel and spent a day and a night writing this new third act. Mike and I had breakfast, and he sat and read it—he has this wonderful giggle that makes you feel wonderful—and he said, "This is not it in its entirety, but you're on the right track. I think in here eventually will be the third act that we want."

We still had three days before we opened in Wilmington. I kept working on it. And what I had was infinitely better than what we were rehearsing, so Mike called the cast together and he said, "There is no point in performing a third act we will never perform after leaving this theater. We have a third act which is not right yet, but it will eventually be the final third act. So I want you to learn it for opening night." Some of the actors thought he was crazy; they said, "Go out there with something we learned in three days? We still don't even know the first two acts." Mike said, "You'll just have to do it." So we did it.

The first two acts went great, and the third act—we just threw it at them—survived. And I kept improving it as we went; fortunately, we had six weeks on the road with the play.

McNally: Out of town, have you ever felt panic?

Simon: Oh, yeah, I go crazy. It's happened to me on many, many shows. When you know a show is really working, when you get out of town, you prune it, you edit, you do some work. But the ones that don't seem to be working at all, you say, "What do I do? Should I just leave it?" What I do is hit rock bottom emotionally. I say, "This is a disaster, my career is over, I'll never write again, I never *want* to write again." And having hit rock bottom, there's no further place to go except to start up again. And then I get charged, I get angry that I goofed up. I say, "Maybe I can save it, maybe I can do something with it."

That's what happened with *The Gingerbread Lady* out of town. That play was a departure for me. Although *Plaza Suite* had been leaning towards a departure, *The Gingerbread Lady* really was; it was about an alcoholic trying to get herself on her feet again. So when we opened in New Haven, the audience didn't quite know how to accept the play; they were thrown by it. They were receptive, but this was not going to be a smash. When we went to Boston, it was much scarier. They were expecting another kind of play, and the reviews were not good at all. And Saint Subber called me at the restaurant where we were on opening night and said, "I think we ought to close the play." And I said, "Are the reviews so bad that we can't save it?" And he said, "Well, I think so." And when I told the cast, Maureen Stapleton was furious with me; she said, "If you close this play, I'll never speak to you again. It is a good play. It needs some work, but we'll do it. We'll learn whatever pages you give us."

But I was down at rock bottom. It was going to be my first flop, and I was devastated by it. We decided to post the closing notice, and I went to the airport to fly back to New York. But I picked up the *Christian Science Monitor*, just to see if another review had come in. And there I found an out-and-out rave for the play. It said that the author does need to make some changes, to orient audiences towards accepting the play, but it said,

"Don't close this play!" I felt spurred on by this review. I decided to take the train back to New York because the ride would take four hours; I could start working and then be able to start typing something when I arrived. And typing something meant that I was in it, in the flow.

I worked on the play, and then we came to New York with it. We weren't a hit, but we got respectful notices, and Maureen won the Tony. We had a season's run out of it. And the play has survived over the years. I made it into a film, *Only When I Laugh*, that I like. So a lot of things happened from reading that one review and being spurred on by it.

McNally: I think I read that it is one of the film adaptations of yours that you think is superior to the play.

Simon: Yes. There are two. I think *The Sunshine Boys*, which I really like as a play, is even better as a film. I had the opportunity to open up the story in a couple of key scenes: specifically, when Richard Benjamin goes to New Jersey to visit George Burns; and when they are doing the show, when we see them in the dressing room and see Walter Matthau having a heart attack and falling down the stairs. All those were visual ways of showing what was happening and worked better on the screen than they did on the stage. And I think *Only When I Laugh* was a big improvement on *The Gingerbread Lady*. Many of the other films were not nearly as good as the plays. They were written as plays and just didn't open up as films; the action was contained in an apartment or whatever.

McNally: You said with *The Gingerbread Lady* the audience's expectations made them unprepared. Have you made a conscious effort since then to solve that? I think now audiences come to your work prepared for a depth that they didn't expect in the earlier plays.

Simon: Yes. Well, in *Gingerbread Lady*, wherever there was a chance to get humor into the play, I put it there. And I don't think that was invalid, because the character was based on women I'd met, in theater and films, who had drinking problems and who were also enormously witty people. They were funnier than most of the dialogue I could write.

I remember Lillian Hellman saying, "Never try to mix comedy with drama. The critics will never buy it." And for the most part, it's true, and it really bothers me; it's been a great gripe of mine for years. Since life is neither all comedy nor all tragedy, why can't it be that way in plays? But audiences do get thrown if you start off very funny. If the play suddenly switches to something else, they say, "I'm not comfortable with this. I don't want to see this drama; get back to where it's funny."

In all our lives, we're feeling our very best, life is wonderful, and we suddenly get a phone call that's filled with tragedy. Life shifts. And I've wanted to do that on the stage: to *feel* that shift from the audience, to pull them into another area. You hear them gasp—when you do it right. When it seems organic, when it's the right thing to happen at the moment, they believe it.

McNally: Do you think you're taken less seriously as a writer because of your reputation for humor?

Simon: I'm taken less seriously by the so-called serious critics. They would, ironically, rather have me write funny. I remember when Robert Brustein saw *Plaza Suite*. The first play is a fairly serious play about a couple breaking up. The play he liked best of the three was the out-and-out farce, in which the bride is locked in the bathroom. It doesn't *really* bother me, though, because I'm going to keep doing what I'm doing as long as I can do it. And I'll let *them* deal with it.

McNally: Well, certainly your work has gotten deeper, richer, over the past few years.

Simon: There was sort of a breakthrough for me in *Brighton Beach Memoirs*. I had never tried to write a tapestry play before. Most of my plays were a confrontation between two people, and the other people around them were peripheral. I never went into much depth about the other characters. In doing *Brighton Beach Memoirs*, despite my telling it through the eyes of Eugene Jerome, the fifteen-year-old boy, I said, "This play is about every character, and I will tell each of their stories." And it's what I tried to do in the sequel, *Biloxi Blues*. I tried to treat each character as a three-dimensional character that one could possibly write a full play about.

McNally: I first felt I was seeing a new side of Neil Simon when I saw the character Linda Lavin played in *Last of the Red Hot Lovers*.

Simon: I was changing. The times were changing, society was changing, I was getting older, and I had different viewpoints. It was the middle of the sexual revolution, and people in their early forties then were saying, "I missed it! It went right by me!" So I wrote about a man who had missed it. And that play is tragicomic to me.

McNally: Did you write it with James Coco in mind?

Simon: I don't remember, really. I know I did that with Walter Matthau. I was writing *The Odd Couple* when I met Walter, and I said, "Please don't accept a job for the next year." I think I may have done the same with Jimmy Coco. Some of the producers who read the play thought it was an offbeat way of casting it, but they all missed the idea of the play. I thought Jimmy was the quintessential guy who missed the sexual revolution.

McNally: *The Good Doctor*—I felt you were present in it, as the writer speaks to the audience. That was an unusual play for you, too.

Simon: You never know where a play will come from, and that's why I do not like it when critics talk about a "typical Neil Simon play." I really don't know what it is. I think they look at your biggest hits and say they're typical. But *The Good Doctor* came out of my reading short stories by Chekhov. I read *Death of a Civil Servant*, and I had never known Chekhov was that funny. So I did some research into Chekhov and found out that when he was a young man he did comic articles every day for the newspapers.

My first idea was to find as many funny Russian short stories as I could and make an evening of them. I couldn't find enough of them, so I stuck with Chekhov's funny ones—and some other ones—till I had about fifteen pieces that I liked. We went into rehearsal, and four of them didn't work. And we were about to go to New Haven, so I had to write my own Chekhov short stories. One of them was a monologue for Marsha Mason, in which she auditions for Chekhov; one was when Chekhov takes his young son to a brothel for the first time; another was about an elderly couple, which I wrote as a lyric called "Too Late for Happiness"; and my favorite one in the play, based on a terrific piece by Chekhov, was *How to Seduce Another Man's Wife*. I had a real good time doing that, and I think I did good work with it.

McNally: The speeches of the writer to the audience are nowhere in Chekhov? That's all yours?

Simon: Bits and pieces are from Chekhov. There are lines from Trigorin, in *The Seagull*, where he says that he cannot stop writing. I identified so strongly with him, saying that when he sees a cloud and thinks it looks like a piano, it starts to turn into an idea for a story.

McNally: Do you start first with a theme, a character, a situation? All three?

Simon: All three. The theme less so. The character and the story—what it's about—come first, and I sort of discover the theme. Sometimes I discover it when I read the reviews and they tell me what it is.

Doing *Brighton Beach Memoirs*, I hadn't the slightest idea where I was going. I wanted to write about that period, write about those people, but from page to page I did not know where the story was going to go. I didn't know the father was going to have a heart attack until I got to it. And then everything seemed organic. And it was not a memory play; some of those things did not happen specifically to me.

McNally: Not knowing where it was going was atypical for you, then? Do you ever work from an outline?
Simon: No, I tried that in the beginning, and found it did not work for me. It took the fun out of the writing. I prefer to take the chance of saying, "I like this character, I like the situation, I'm just going to go with it." And I discover the play the same way the audience does. It makes me laugh sometimes: I'll write a play that way and a critic says the ending was predictable, and I'd never known the ending.

McNally: When you finish the first draft, is there anyone you show it to?
Simon: Generally my family. I show it to my wife, my two daughters—I respect their opinions greatly. And generally the producer that I'm working with, Saint Subber or Emanuel Azenberg. On occasion I've shown a play to Mike Nichols for his opinion, even though he was too busy to direct it.

I learned a lesson from *The Odd Couple*, which is to have a preliminary reading. I don't want to find out on the first day of rehearsal that I'm in trouble. I liked what I heard in the *Biloxi* reading, but I saw spots that needed rewriting in the six weeks before rehearsals started.

McNally: You've made that message very clear to other writers. Every interview you ever gave, you said, "Fix it now—not in rehearsals!"
One crazy question: I've heard that you did some work on *A Chorus Line*. Would you like to lay that one to rest?
Simon: I did. Michael Bennett was a friend of mine; we had worked on *Promises, Promises*. And he asked me to come down to the Public Theater to see *A Chorus Line* there. Well, it was a knockout; you knew it was going to be a smash. And Michael said, "Come talk to me." We went out to a Chinese restaurant, and he said, "You know, it just needs some funny things here and there. Will you do it?" And I said, "Well, it's against the Dramatists Guild

rules to do that." And he said, "What if I got permission?" So I wanted to do it. I was thrilled with the show, and it would make me feel good to make a contribution to it, as long as it didn't create trouble. I wrote not an enormous number of lines, and many more lines than he actually used. But I never took credit and I never got money for it.

I read about Moss Hart, when I was growing up, going out of town to help with someone else's play. Friends would help friends. It doesn't happen very often anymore, but I would like to do it a lot if the shows are worth saving. Mike Nichols did that with me; he came to help out with *Fools*, purely out of friendship.

McNally: I want to ask you about analysis. Did it affect you as a writer?
Simon: I've been in analysis only three or four times, always during critical times in my life. I find it invaluable, not only in getting me through those tough periods: it taught me a way to think about plays. Plays are a reflection of life, and you must think of them that way. If you think of them as artificial things, then that's what they will come out to be. So the lessons that I learned in analysis—questions I learned to ask myself—I apply to my plays when I get into trouble. I ask the characters those same questions, and I find answers for them. I'm a very analytical person, and analysis, for me, is very logical (if you can get someone to explain it to you logically). And I've applied it successfully for the most part, in my life and in my work.

Q: I'm curious about what plays you may have given up on, and why.
Simon: I have about forty plays that I've given up on. The only way for me to know if I feel like writing a play is to start to write it. I do think about it—it'll be in my head for some time—but I'll get into it, and suddenly it will hit a dead end for me. Sometimes I put it aside for a long, long time and go back and see that it's really good. That happened with *The Sunshine Boys*. After I'd put it aside, I was having dinner with Mike Nichols, and he asked what I was doing. I said I was working on a play, but it didn't seem like much. I told him the story, and he said, "You're crazy. That's wonderful." So I went home and finished the play. But the others, they just sit there, and they may sit there forever. If the play is good enough, it *demands* to be written.

Q: I saw *Fools*, and I loved it. Why do you think it closed so quickly?
Simon: We never should have done *Fools* on Broadway. I never meant for it to be done on Broadway. It was a diversion, the kind of play I write when I

don't feel like writing a play that deals with my own life. I always meant it as a children's fable, and I always wanted to do it in a regional theater. It's hard for me to do plays there, because the press comes down hard on me: "Those theaters are subsidized and exist to encourage young and experimental writers, and you're an establishment writer." So I've been sort of kicked out of that field and have to stay in the commercial field. The Goodman Theater has asked me to do plays there a number of times, so I guess if I really looked . . . But I really didn't listen to my instincts with *Fools*. I should have done it off Broadway somewhere. It has been done at the Mark Taper Forum in Los Angeles.

Q: Do you have a daily discipline?
Simon: I'm very disciplined. I work five days a week, if I can. There are so many distractions. I try to keep at it all the time, and when I'm on a new play that I really like, I don't like to get off it, especially when it really captures me. Then I will sacrifice most of my personal life to complete it. With *Brighton Beach*, I was at it night and day.

Q: Have you ever thought of directing your own material, as many writers do?
Simon: No, I have no desire to do it. I'd rather have a director that I really respect putting his input into the play. Also, I have no patience for it.

I like to walk away from a play sometimes. I won't go to a rehearsal after they've reached the point where they don't need me. I have to give the actors a chance to learn, to catch up to me. And I don't want to spend that time going over it with them; it's not what I enjoy best. I really like being alone in a room, writing.

Simon Says: A Conversation with Playwright Neil Simon

David Kaufman / 1985

From Horizon 28 (June 1985): 55–60. Reprinted with the permission of David Kaufman. David Kaufman is the author of *Doris Day: The Untold Story of the Girl Next Door* (2008) and *Some Enchanted Evenings: The Glittering Life and Times of Mary Martin* (2016).

Neil Simon and Broadway—the names are practically synonymous. Simon has three shows running concurrently on the Great White Way—*Brighton Beach Memoirs, Biloxi Blues,* and the new female version of *The Odd Couple.* Such a distinction is more of an anomaly than one might imagine. But in fact, it happened twice before. In the early 1970s Simon had three shows running simultaneously on Broadway: *Plaza Suite; Promises, Promises;* and *Last of the Red Hot Lovers.* In the mid-1960s, four Simon plays ran simultaneously on Broadway: *Barefoot in the Park, The Odd Couple, Sweet Charity,* and *Star-Spangled Girl.*

In and of itself, Simon's prolificacy is not rare. What is astonishing, however, and to all evidence unique, is that the majority of his twenty-two Broadway shows have been hits, including the ten mentioned above plus *Come Blow Your Horn* (his first play, written for the stage in 1961), *The Prisoner of Second Avenue, The Sunshine Boys, Chapter Two,* and *They're Playing Our Song.* (Though not part of the official oeuvre, he was even called in at the last minute to perform as script doctor—a capacity suggested by his nickname Doc—on *A Chorus Line,* the longest-running show in Broadway history.) Such a string of hits helps explain why he is considered the single most popular and successful playwright of all time.

Despite the celebrity and unprecedented financial reward it has brought, Simon's work has been frequently lambasted and noticeably neglected by the more serious critics. Though the occasional rave greeted the occasional show and every so often reference to Chekhov or Menander made it into a notice or two (at one point, Clive Barnes claimed Neil Simon was funnier than George Bernard Shaw ever was), for the most part, the Simon hits relied on word of mouth and thrived on popular appeal. The critics treated Simon as a contemporary Salieri in the midst of numerous potential Mozarts.

For the past fifteen years or so, he has been acknowledged as a supreme craftsman and wordsmith; a comedic writer whose concerns could not transcend the laughter he so naturally obtained; that laugh-a-minute writer who lacked the poetry and higher purpose of more enduring drama. Walter Kerr was the only respected critic who championed Simon with any consistency, as when Kerr wrote more than ten years ago that Simon's "special victory is to have discovered the exact amount of God's truth a light comedy can properly contain"—and more recently, "I swear to heaven that if I hear Mr. Simon put down one more time for his facility at coining swiftly relevant retorts, I am going to fill an entire page with one-liners every reader can recite along with me. They will all be by William Shakespeare."

Finally, all of that is changing for Simon. With his invention of Eugene Morris Jerome, who first arrived two years ago in *Brighton Beach Memoirs* (recalling the playwright's upbringing in that section of Brooklyn) and who has just reappeared in *Biloxi Blues* (capturing his experiences at boot camp in Mississippi during World War II), Simon has come of critical age. In succession, each of these plays has been received almost unanimously as his best work so far. Even John Simon, a most vituperative critic who has practically built his career on being impossible to please, proved disarmed and beguiled when he opened his review: "By George, he's done it! Incredible as it may seem—to me, anyhow—in *Biloxi Blues*, Neil Simon has written a play that is not a farce, not mostly one-liners and two-dimensional characters, nor one of those maudlin stabs at high seriousness."

For Neil Simon, this recent development represents much more than most—and especially the critics—might have imagined. As he reveals in the following interview, critical acceptance has always been important to him. Now that he's received it, he feels as if he has "broken through another wall." It's not, as some are contending, that he is writing more serious plays, but rather that he's suddenly being taken seriously.

David Kaufman: It's been said that more people have seen your plays than have seen Shakespeare. How does that make you feel?

Neil Simon: Well, in the first place, I doubt that's true. His plays have been around for four hundred years, and there've been thousands and thousands of productions of his plays. I think we tend to exaggerate a lot of things when we want to amplify a story. But even to be mentioned as being close to him is something I can only relate to by going back to my youth, when I just started to write. To think that I would ever write plays that were seen as widely as mine had never occurred to me. I took my career in stages. I never looked that far ahead, because one's aspirations would be insurmountable. When I started off writing simple comedy sketches and monologues in radio and for newspaper columns, I wasn't thinking I was going to become a world-famous playwright. And then the next stage was getting to television and finally working on comedy shows like the Bilko show and Sid Caesar's, and I kept raising my aspirations, as one does. You don't want to get stuck in one place. As good as it might be, you grow out of that experience and you start to look for a larger platform. And getting me to write that first play was a major link, because it meant giving up time and income since it took me three years to do it. Then having done that play and seeing that it took me three years, I didn't think I would have a major career in the theater because it just took too much out of me. I figured *maybe* if I was lucky, in my life I would write five plays. At the rate of one every three years, that would have been a lot.

DK: You have said elsewhere that you start roughly nine plays for every one you finish. Since you reportedly write plays without knowing where you're going or where they will take you, do you have a backlog that have been abandoned and might you resurrect any of those aborted projects?

NS: I would start fifteen, maybe, for every one I finished. There's no way that I know a play is going to catch fire until I start to write it, because you get an idea in your head and you say, Well, that sounds pretty good—but you don't know if you're going to reach a dead end until you start to write it. Emanuel Azenberg, my producer, has always said that if I got to page thirty or thirty-five in a play, then he considered it a go from that point on. I've written that much and discarded the play twice, only to come back and finish them and they proved successful—*Barefoot in the Park* and *The Sunshine Boys*. But generally, I'll write ten or twelve pages and say, No, no, no—I can see that's not going anywhere. Your mind is always way ahead of what it is that you're writing, and you can foresee what it's going to be, what's going to happen with it. I don't mean in specific detail. But it works the opposite way, too. Sometimes I get an idea and it seems so rich that I know it's a matter of selection. It was that way with *Brighton Beach*—I knew that I had rich characters and a rich situation, although I didn't have the specifics. I just took it day by day. The same thing happened with *Biloxi Blues*—I knew I had to start with them going to basic training, and by the end of the play, they would have been changed enormously by the experience. What the individual details were, I didn't know, but I didn't worry about it—I knew they would come. But usually you get an idea and you can't see down the road that far.

DK: Have you deliberately set about writing more serious plays as some people are finding?

NS: In the first place, I've been writing serious plays going back to *Plaza Suite*, which is fifteen years ago. The first act is about the breakup of a marriage, which is not handled only in comedic terms. There's a great deal of humor in it, but when I was first doing it with Mike Nichols, we kept taking out the humor. So I've been doing serious plays for a long, long time. I think the subject matter of many of the plays has been quite serious, and the handling of them was not completely serious. And the problems I was having with the critics was that they don't like you to mix the two. I guess what they're really saying is they don't mind seeing it if they believe in it and they think that you are doing it well. Some critics felt that I did manage to accomplish it, others felt that it didn't work, that it was arbitrary. So you have to go by whose decisions you agree with. The *New York Times* didn't like some of the earlier plays like *Chapter Two*, which I did like. I mean, who is to say that comedy is not basically serious? There is a point usually, and hopefully to be made in something that is comedic, but when one watches it, one laughs instead of cries, and it depends on how it's done. If you look at some of Chaplin's films, they're quite serious at the bottom. It was a good way to see how unfortunate some people were, only he had the genius to make us laugh at them. So I really hate to differentiate between serious and unserious, because I never know when it's going to come up in a play. I mean, I've never found life all serious or all comic. The best times of my life have been interrupted by some tragic news, or at least some very serious news, and vice versa. I mean, one can be in the midst of a great depression and something wonderful happens to you, and I said, Why is it not right to show that on the stage as well—to be jarred out of one thing into the other? But critics like their plays a certain way. Sometimes I might agree with them—it might seem arbitrary that you put in something serious. But *Biloxi* for some reason blended the two better than any other play except maybe *Brighton Beach*; and for the first time, I think I've gotten almost unanimously all of the critics on my side, saying, This time he's done it.

DK: How do you account for the incredibly positive response to your two most recent plays?

NS: I really made a quantum leap in *Brighton Beach* as a playwright because it was the first full-bodied play I had ever written, in terms of dealing with a group of people as individuals and telling all their stories. I think my plays in the past had focused, more or less, on two main characters—that was a problem. The peripheral people in their lives were more shadowy figures. They were there to bolster the main story. In *Brighton Beach*, I broke out of that and told everyone's story. Sometimes I just touched on it, but you knew what their lives were all about, and it was not only separate from the main people—it was also integrated with the main characters in the piece. In *Biloxi Blues* it went even further because I took people who didn't even know each other, so their lives were not yet intertwined by anything except their entering the army. And what it is that I set out to do (which is to show this boy observing life rather than participating in it) I guess was very clearly accomplished, because all of the critics seemed to hit on that; they saw the growth of the writer, which is a very hard thing to do, I think—showing a rather passive person like a writer who pictures himself invisible, become very visible to the audience as they watch him in this growing process.

DK: Have you learned anything about yourself through creating the character of Eugene Morris Jerome that you had not recognized before?
NS: I knew all this before—it just took me a long time to deal with it. For example, in earlier plays I dealt with characters who were Jewish but never specifically called them Jewish—the family in *Come Blow Your Horn* or the comedians in *The Sunshine Boys*. Their religion or faith had nothing to do, as far as I was concerned, with what was going on in their lives. Once I got into *Brighton Beach*, it seemed more important to do it. First of all, I dug much more into the truth of the matter. My mother, Kate in the play, in a sense was herself a bigot, talking about the Irish across the street and looking down on them. Well, that was one of the things that I learned growing up in New York City—that each ethnic group is always looking down on the other so that they can keep their heads above the water. So now I started to deal with it specifically. When I got to *Biloxi Blues*, I really had to deal with it, because it became a subject of the play—of anti-Semitism or antihomosexuality or anti-anything. There was a war, a smaller war, going on within the circle of the men even before they went off to fight the big war. So there I had to deal with it, which forces you into digging deeper into the truth, and I think that that's what the critics recognized and what I began to recognize in myself—that if I'm going to write plays, then I've got to deal with the

characters as absolutely truthfully as I possibly can. I did it once, though, where the audience just didn't seem to like it, and it was the most truthful I ever wrote, and that was in *Chapter Two*.

DK: I had imagined that *Chapter Two* was the most autobiographical, especially because it was soon after your wife died of cancer and it focused on your meeting Marsha Mason. It was still relatively fresh and it seemed like a personally cathartic play.
NS: It was a very painful play to write. I talked about exactly how I felt having lost my wife and remarried, and how one suffers guilt that you're still alive and suddenly in love again with a lovely, wonderful girl and wondering why this is happening to you. And in order to assuage that guilt, what the man in the play does is take it out on his new wife and try not to give her the happiness so that he doesn't share in it and then he has nothing to be guilty about. I thought that was really an important point, and I was as truthful as I possibly could be. I think, by and large, the audience responded well and some of the critics as well, but the *New York Times* and certain other papers didn't. And certainly *Chapter Two* was cathartic. So were *Brighton Beach* and *Biloxi Blues*. I can't say in what specific way without going into my whole psyche to try and understand what it is that I have expelled. But I know I felt better having written them and I enjoyed the process. *Chapter Two* was the most painful to write because it was not so long after the situation itself occurred. But most of the plays that seem to deal with my beliefs and how I feel about life are cathartic.

DK: For that matter, *Come Blow Your Horn* and *Barefoot in the Park* were autobiographical as well.
NS: *Barefoot in the Park* is autobiographical in the lightest sense. I took the situation of when I was first married, and the thing that was really close to the truth was that apartment, which was really important in the play. Since we didn't really have any major problems in our life then, I took a minor problem and blew it up into a major one, which was that they suddenly felt that they were incompatible and that the marriage was over, which is what every young newlywed couple goes through. It's that period of adjustment when you're so young, you don't even realize what life is about yet. So there was no point in getting into anything major or serious. It was meant as a light entertainment, but it was also meant to show what newlyweds are all about, and I must have done it correctly because the play has great laughing power. You know, it's twenty-five years now, almost, and the play was an

enormous success then, more than most light comedies were. I think that was the beginning of the autobiographical period for me.

DK: What of your plans for a third Eugene Morris Jerome play?
NS: I still don't know if it's going to be a trilogy. I don't know if I'll get past the second play. I wrote the first and Frank Rich, who gave me sort of a mixed review of *Brighton Beach*, still was encouraging enough to say one hopes that there will be a chapter two to *Brighton Beach*. It was sort of giving me a mandate to go ahead and write a sequel to it, which one doesn't see very often on Broadway. Occasionally, yes, as O'Neill did with the Tyrone family and Lanford Wilson with the Talley family group. I just felt I had to continue with it because I love having Eugene as a voice for the thoughts that now I am able to perceive about life, and going back to the period has been very good for me. I'm not sure specifically, but I think the third one has to begin to be about the early days of his actually writing and what it meant to him. It's a very hard thing to convey to an audience—about how you write, how it's done, and what it means to you. The only way I could do it is to show myself writing with other people, which is what I did in the early days. I don't know. I mean, I'm not planning to do it for six or eight months or maybe a year, but I would think it would be placed in the late 1940s or early 1950s. Also, I've already written about his life later on in *Barefoot in the Park* and *Chapter Two*, let's say.

DK: Why have you rewritten *The Odd Couple* for a Florence and an Olive as opposed to a Felix and an Oscar?
NS: I was besieged by actresses—many of them extremely famous and talented—asking me if they could do *The Odd Couple*, and I said, "How would you do that? You can't just change the names! It won't work. What are you going to do when the two girls from upstairs, the Pigeon sisters, come down?" And it's as though, for some strange reason, they never dealt with the fact that it had to be changed. But the idea—only because of the change in society's attitude toward women and women's changing attitudes about themselves—implied these characters have changed, so maybe it's worth doing *The Odd Couple* again, because there is now an added dimension to write about. Not just the same jokes, only women doing them, since I didn't know if they would be any funnier at all. The play is so familiar to us now that that's what I worried about more than anything. Would people be able to laugh at this couple that we've been watching for the last twenty-one years? So, I had a reading (with women) and saw the possibilities then

I rewrote some of that and then had another reading. Then I rewrote the whole play as I began to see its potential, and I kept getting rid of the old play and getting more of the new attitude about it. I'm not writing this new version in the style that I am in *Biloxi* or *Brighton*—I wouldn't tackle *The Odd Couple* anymore. Probably if I dealt with marriage and the breakup of marriage, I would deal with the real complications of what happens when people get divorced today. I still wanted to keep this a comedy, and I wanted to write it in the same style in which I wrote it in 1964, even though some of the political points have to be 1985. It's just that, every once in a while, you want to try something just for the adventure of trying it. Scene by scene, it's the exact-same play—the structure hasn't changed at all.

DK: Are you partial to any particular play or plays you've written?

NS: I'm partial to certain experiences and times in my life when I was doing them that brought me the greatest joy. I mean, it was a terrific thrill to open *Come Blow Your Horn* in Philadelphia and to see my name on one of those marquee signs for the first time in my life, having reached at least the beginning of a dream that I had when I started to write plays. But after a while, they all become the same. I mean, I like some plays better than others, obviously, but before I wrote *Biloxi*, I thought *Brighton Beach* was the best play I wrote. And the opening of *Barefoot in the Park* was an enormous thrill for me because it was a major success that I had. And I said to myself, I better enjoy this, because I won't have another one like that—it's rare that people have such a big hit. And then the next play I wrote was *The Odd Couple*, so I had them back-to-back. And then when I had it with *Brighton Beach* and *Biloxi Blues*, it was almost as much of a thrill. I think one becomes . . . certainly not blasé about it, because they're all unexpected to me. But as you get older, those same kinds of thrills are not quite the same thing. You have those early ones, and each changes your entire life. You have it at the age of fifty-seven, it doesn't change your life, it changes your retrospect, but it doesn't change my future at all. I'm surely not going to be writing plays as long as I have written plays from the beginning till now.

DK: Has any response to any of your works surprised you?

NS: I don't think I've ever been surprised. The ones that they really liked, I thought they should like. The ones that they didn't like, I was not surprised at. Come to think of it, the reception to *Fools* surprised me because I thought if it had been done somewhere else—not on Broadway, but at a community theater, for example—it would have worked better. It was meant as a children's fable and never should have been up there with the high-priced Broadway shows. And it has a life and it's going on and it's playing in repertory and in regional theaters all over the world right now. It's never been an enormous success, but I've always liked it, and I couldn't understand why most of the critics came down so scathingly on it. I think that, given a lot of time, when they get tired of doing *Barefoot* and *The Odd Couple*, they'll start to do *The Good Doctor* and *Fools* more than they'll do the others.

DK: How does it feel to know that you have achieved the most successful career in the theater?

NS: I'm six feet tall, but I guess if I were six foot six and people said, How do you feel about being six foot six? I think after a while you would say, It feels like being six foot six. It's just part of your nature. You don't think of it any differently. It came along in stages. Each one was an enormous surprise to me: that *Barefoot* would be such a big hit, and *The Odd Couple*, and then *Plaza Suite*—you know, skipping over a couple of plays now and then. But then another really big hit just kept adding on and on and on to this chain of successes. I never knew where they were going. I never knew when it would end or when the bubbles would burst. I never really thought about it. I guess I just have a very optimistic point of view. I said I'll just try harder and I think maybe I can write better and better plays hopefully. I never got scared about it. Every time you sit down to write a play, if you really spend a lot of time thinking, This is going to be a huge success, or, This is going to be a huge failure, it will frighten you either way. I just say I'll write it. So the matter of how I feel about the success still hasn't reached me, what the impact of it is. I still feel the same as I did, say, fifteen years ago. I feel a little bit better and more secure, now that I've written *Brighton Beach* and *Biloxi Blues*, because I think I've broken through another wall, but there were a lot of walls to break through in the beginning.

DK: What do you mean by "better and more secure now"?

NS: In the beginning, I had a lot of critical success plus popular success. Then the critical success sort of dropped away. It was mostly popular, bolstered by enough good reviews to get the play out to the audience, and the audience then made up their own minds. But the critics started to head away from me in other directions, saying, Here comes another whizzbang comedy and we're not that interested in whizzbang comedies. I never thought that they were whizzbang comedies, and the audience didn't take them that way. And then suddenly everything reversed with *Brighton Beach*, and on top of that, *Biloxi Blues* even more so. And so, like the Gershwin song "They Can't Take That Away from Me"—I've written them now. At least I've been to that place where I wanted to get to in my search to become a better playwright, and I've achieved it in some measure. It's not that the critical reaction has changed me. It's just pointed out to me that I have broken through another barrier as a playwright. I mean, they used to write about how much money I was earning and things like that. If you already have success, they aren't very eager to give you more success.

Neil Simon

Jackson R. Bryer / 1991

From *Speaking on Stage: Interviews with Contemporary American Playwrights*, edited by
Philip C. Kolin and Colby H. Kullman (Tuscaloosa: University of Alabama Press, 1996), 58–81.
Originally appeared in *Studies in American Drama, 1945–Present* 6, no. 2 (1991): 153–76.
Reprinted by permission. Portions of the introduction to the interview containing informa-
tion about Neil Simon's life and works available elsewhere in this book have been deleted.

This interview was conducted on January 23, 1991, in Simon's suite at the
Willard Hotel in Washington, DC, while he was preparing *Lost in Yonkers*
(then playing at Washington's National Theatre) for its Broadway opening.

Jackson R. Bryer: You always say that very early on you knew you wanted
to be a playwright.
Neil Simon: I wanted to be a writer very early on. It's not quite true about
the playwriting thing. I started writing the first play when I was thirty and
got it on when I was thirty-three, so that's fairly old to be starting as a
playwright.

Bryer: Most young people want to write poetry or want to write novels.
When you knew you wanted to be a writer, was it always writing plays that
you wanted to do?
Simon: I started out with different aims and ambitions. I grew up in the
world of radio, so the first couple of jobs I had were in radio and then television. I think I was setting my sights for film. I'm not quite sure when I
decided to do plays. I know when I actually did so, which was after years of
working on *Your Show of Shows* with Sid Caesar and *The Bilko Show*, I said
I didn't want to spend the rest of my life doing this—writing for someone
else—I wanted to do my own work. So I started writing the first play, *Come
Blow Your Horn*, and it took me almost three years to do the twenty-some
complete new versions before I got it on. When I did get it on, I said, "My

God, three years!" and I was exhausted. I had only taken other little jobs just to make a living, since I had a wife and two children. But once the play hit, *Come Blow Your Horn* subsidized the next one, which was a musical, *Little Me*, and that subsidized writing *Barefoot in the Park*, and then I was making enough money so I could do this full-time.

Bryer: So in a sense your playwriting grew out of writing for TV and radio, in that writing for TV and radio was basically writing within a dramatic form? That's what really led to the playwriting.
Simon: Right. I started off just writing jokes for newspaper columns and things and then working on *Your Show of Shows* and *Bilko*. *Your Show of Shows* was writing sketches, and *Bilko* was like a half-hour movie. So I was learning the dramatic form. Then I worked for about two years with Max Liebman, who was the producer of *Your Show of Shows*, doing specials. It was a very good education for me because we were updating pretty famous musical books of the past—*Best Foot Forward* and *Knickerbocker Holiday*. We would throw the book out completely and use the score. We would sort of follow the story line but use our own dialogue. So I was able to step in the footprints of previous writers and learn about the construction from them.

Bryer: What was the purpose of those? Were they for television?
Simon: Yes. We did about twenty of them, two shows a month. One show would be a book show. A couple of them were originals. One was *The Adventures of Marco Polo*, and we used the music of Rimsky-Korsakov. So I was really learning a lot about construction. I had made a few abortive attempts to write plays during that time—one with another writer on *The Bilko Show*—and it was going nowhere. I always had my summers off because in those days we did thirty-nine shows a year on television in consecutive weeks, and you had something like thirteen weeks off in the summer, in which I would try to write plays. And I would say, "Wow, this is tough!" Finally I went to California to do a television special—for Jerry Lewis of all people. I had quit *Your Show of Shows*—it had finally gone off the air—and so I was freelancing. I went out there for six weeks. In about ten days I wrote the whole show, and I said to Jerry Lewis, "What'll I do, I've got all this time?" He said, "I've got other things to do. Just do what you want until we go into rehearsal." And I started to write *Come Blow Your Horn*, which was almost a satirical or a farcical look at my upbringing with my parents. I was on the way, but it took three years to do that, as I said.

Bryer: As a child and as a young adult, did you read plays and did you go to the theater?

Simon: I went to the theater. I read quite a good deal. I went to the library. I used to take out about three books a week, but they weren't about the theater. It wasn't until I was about fourteen or fifteen that I saw my first play, *Native Son*, the Richard Wright book and play.

Bryer: A strange thing for a fourteen- or fifteen-year-old to go see, wasn't it?

Simon: There was a local theater in upper Manhattan, in Washington Heights, where I lived. It was called the Audubon Theatre. It used to be a movie house, and then they used it for acts—sort of vaudeville acts, but I wouldn't really call it vaudeville. They started doing that all over New York at the time when the theater was truly flourishing. You not only played Broadway, you could go to Brooklyn and Manhattan and the Bronx, and there were theaters that did their versions of plays that had closed on Broadway. So I went to this local theater and saw *Native Son* and was mesmerized by what the theater could do. I had also acted in plays in public school and in junior high school, so I had a little glimpse of that. But acting is a lot different from writing. I think that slowly, as my parents started to take me to the theater more, mostly musicals (I remember seeing *Oklahoma!* It was—for its time—so innovative and so original), in the back of my mind I thought about that. But all during those years I was working with my brother, and I thought that the only way to write a play was to do it by yourself, because one needed an individual point of view. Even if we were to write about our own family background, his point of view would be completely different from mine, and so it would get diminished somehow and watered down. When I wrote *Come Blow Your Horn*, I never even told him about it. It meant that I would have to make a break with him after ten years of writing together. The break was pretty traumatic. It was worse than leaving home, because one expects that, but this was breaking up a partnership that he started because he was looking for a partner. He doesn't like to work by himself, and he always noticed and encouraged the sense of humor I had. I didn't have a sense of construction. He had that, and I was wonderful with lines and with the comedy concepts. Finally, when I did *Come Blow Your Horn*, I knew I had to step away. Partly I think it had to do with my being married. I began to feel my own oats and wanted the separation.

Bryer: Can you speak at all about playwrights that impressed you, influenced you, early or late?

Simon: Well, it was any good playwright. I didn't have favorites. In terms of comedy I guess maybe Moss Hart and George S. Kaufman. A play that neither one of them wrote, Garson Kanin's *Born Yesterday*, I thought was a wonderful comedy, and I liked *Mr. Roberts* too. But I was as intrigued by the dramas as I was by the comedies. It wasn't until sometime later that I decided what I wanted to write was drama and tell it as comedy. I was such an avid theatergoer, especially when I first married Joan. You could go to the theater then twice a week and not catch the whole season on Broadway and even Off-Broadway. *Streetcar Named Desire* probably made the greatest impression on me, that and *Death of a Salesman*. These are not comedies. Although I knew I was not up to writing a drama as yet, I thought when I wrote something it would be from a comic point of view.

Bryer: If you could have written one play that was written by somebody else, what would that play be?

Simon: That question has been asked a lot, and I generally say *A Streetcar Named Desire*. I have a certain affinity for that play—so does everyone else in America for that matter, I think. *Death of a Salesman* I thought was maybe the best American play I've ever seen—but it lacked humor. The humor that I saw in *Streetcar Named Desire* came out of a new place for humor. It came out of the character of Stanley Kowalski saying, "I have this lawyer acquaintance of mine" and talking about the Napoleonic Code. It was the way he talked that got huge laughs, and I knew that this was not comedy. It was character comedy, and that's what I aimed for later on. If I were able to write a play, an American play, I would say it would be *Streetcar*.

Bryer: The same quality is present in *The Glass Menagerie*, too. That play also has some very funny moments in it, but they grow very organically out of Amanda and out of her situation.

Simon: Yes. Even in Eugene O'Neill, who really lacks humor, I found humor in *Long Day's Journey*, in James Tyrone's meanness with money—turning out the lightbulbs all the time and being so cheap. That was a play that I said to myself when I saw it, "I could never write that, but I would love to write like that," to write my own *Long Day's Journey*. I have an oblique sense of humor. I see comedy—or humor, not comedy (there's a difference)—in almost everything that I've gone through in life, I'd say, with the exception of my wife's illness and death. Humor has become so wide open today that it's almost uncensored on television. It's all part of the game now. As I said, *Long Day's Journey* impressed me very much early on, and the writings of August Wilson impress me very much today. There's great humor in them and great sense of character and storytelling. It's almost old-fashioned playwriting, in a way. There are not many playwrights who write the way he does.

Bryer: I think some of the humor in O'Neill comes from the Irish quality in those plays, the whole Sean O'Casey tradition of Irish drama, where the humor and the seriousness are very clearly juxtaposed. And I wonder whether there isn't something similar in the Jewish idiom, with humor coming out of serious situations. Do you feel that is a factor in your own plays?

Simon: I'm sure it is, but I find it a very difficult thing to talk about because I'm unaware of anything being particularly Jewish. This present play, *Lost in Yonkers*, is about a Jewish family, but rarely is it mentioned or brought up. But the humor comes out of the Jewish culture as I know it. It's fatalistic— everything bad is going to happen. In the opening scene the father talks about his troubles with his wife dying, being at a loss about what to do with the boys and so worried about how they're going to look well and be presented well to the grandmother. It's all out of fear. There's no sense of confidence, because he knows what he's up against. The mother is, I think, more German than Jewish, because she was brought up in Germany, and her culture is German. So one doesn't ever get a picture that she was brought up in a Jewish home in which they paid attention to the services. I would doubt very much if they were Orthodox Jews. But it's there someplace, and it's so deeply embedded in me and so inherent in me that I am unaware of its quality. When I write something, I don't think, "Oh, this is Jewish." At one time I thought I did, that I needed Jewish actors, but I found that people like Jack Lemmon or George C. Scott or Maureen Stapleton were equally at home with my material and that they gave great performances. I rarely work with Jewish actors now. There are very few of them in *Lost in Yonkers*. However, in making the film of *Brighton Beach Memoirs*, when we did not get Jewish women to play the mother and the sister, it didn't sound right. Blythe Danner and Judith Ivey, as wonderful as they are, did not sound right. To the Gentile ear it may not sound wrong, but still the audiences are aware that something is not quite organic. They don't know what it is. They can't name it. The difference came when Linda Lavin played in *Broadway Bound* and was right on the button and had the sense of truth. I think it's true too with O'Neill. He doesn't have to have Irish actors, but Jewish actors playing O'Neill would have to have a very wide range to be able to do it well.

Bryer: You have always said you stopped writing for TV because you wanted control, because you wanted to be on your own, not to have network executives and ad men running your creative life. But didn't the same sort of thing start to happen after a bit when you started to write for the stage, where producers like Saint Subber wanted you to write a particular kind of play?

Simon: Saint used terms that no longer exist—they come from the turn of the century. He talked about "the carriage trade," those people, not necessarily Jewish, maybe New York society or wealthier people, whom we wanted to appeal to as well. When I wrote *Barefoot in the Park*, I think in an earlier version I made them a Jewish family without saying so. Saint said, stay away from that because we were going to miss the carriage trade, so to speak. So maybe I was aware of it. Certainly it was in *The Odd Couple*, with Oscar Madison, only because Walter Matthau played it. I was aware of that in the beginning and then gradually got away from it until I got specifically Jewish when I was writing the autobiographical plays. In *Chapter Two*, something made me lean toward an actor like Judd Hirsch, playing the leading character, George, because I knew the cadences and the attitudes came from me. So I thought that character had to be Jewish, but I didn't call him Jewish. In these plays—I'm talking about the trilogy (*Brighton Beach Memoirs*, *Biloxi Blues*, and *Broadway Bound*) and about *Lost in Yonkers*—they are Jewish families, you can't get away from it. Some plays are just not. *Barefoot in the Park* was not necessarily at all. *The Odd Couple* has proven not to be because it's the most universal play I've written. They do it in Japan as often as they do it here now. It's done all over the world constantly because it is such a universal situation. Two people living together cannot get along all the time, and it made it unique that it was two men. It seemed like such a simple idea that you thought surely someone would have written a play about it, but no one ever had up until that time. It was the idea or concept that made it so popular and then the execution.

Bryer: Which of your plays gave you the most trouble, and which was the easiest?

Simon: *"Rumors"* gave me the most trouble because of the necessities of farce. One has to get the audience to dispel their sense of truth, and they must believe in the premise even though we know it's about three feet off the ground. It has to be filled with surprises, and it has to move at a breakneck pace. People have to be in jeopardy constantly. The minute the jeopardy stops and they can sit back and relax, it's like a train that runs out of steam. And it has to be funny every minute. It was like constructing a murder mystery, an Agatha Christie mystery in which you are kept in suspense, only it had to go at a much greater pace than any of Agatha Christie's stories. I wanted to do it because I wanted to try the form. In a sense I was buoyed by watching an interview with Peter Shaffer, whom I respect enormously. I think he's a wonderful playwright. *Amadeus* is one of my favorite plays, again a play with a great concept—an original one—about professional jealousy. The interviewer said, "Why did you write *Black Comedy*?" And he said, "Well, it was a farce, and everyone wants to write one farce in his life." I had tried bits and pieces of it. The third act of *Plaza Suite*, with the father and mother trying to get the girl out of the locked bathroom, is a farce. But it only ran for thirty minutes, and it wasn't a full-blown piece, so I wanted to try that. That was the most difficult. None of them come easy.

What happened with *Brighton Beach* was interesting. I wrote thirty-five pages and stopped and put it away for nine years. And when I came back to it, somehow the play had been written in my head over those nine years without thinking of it, so I wrote it completely from beginning to end without stopping. But that's only the beginning of the process. You can never say any play is written easily, because you write it once, and then you write it again. Then you have a reading of it, and then you go into rehearsal, in which you write it ten more times. So they all present their difficulties. But I can't think of any one play where it was really easy, where I didn't have a difficult time with it.

Bryer: Have your writing methods changed over the years? You say you wrote *Come Blow Your Horn* twenty times. Is that still true, that you write a play over and over again, or do you find that you're getting better at it?
Simon: If I do write it over and over and over again, it means that the play has some serious flaw. I wrote *Jake's Women* seven times, almost from beginning to end, before I put it on the stage, so I never really corrected the serious flaw. With this play, *Lost in Yonkers*, the first version was fairly close to what we have now. I did two more versions before we went into rehearsal, but I had less trouble with the construction of the play. It just seemed to lead to the right thing. It has to do with the beginning of the play, with how each of the characters is introduced and how each of them has his own problem. Manny Azenberg, our producer, has always said that if I reach page thirty-five, it is almost always a "go" project. Sometimes I get to page twenty-five or so, and I start to look ahead and say, "What are you going to write about? What else could possibly happen?" I've come up with some

wonderful beginnings of situations and don't always know where they're going but sort of know what they're going to be.

Billy Wilder, the director, once said to me (he was talking about a film, but I think it applies to a play as well), "If you have four great scenes, you've got a hit." He says that if you don't have those great scenes, then you're not going to make it. When I wrote *The Sunshine Boys*, the whole play came to me at once in a sense. Since I fashioned it somewhat (even though I didn't know them) after the careers of Smith and Dale, and got the premise that they had not spoken to each other in eleven years and then they were being offered this job to work together and didn't want to speak to each other, I said, "Well, they've got to get together." That's the first funny interesting conflict, then the rehearsal, then the actual doing of the show on the air. I knew that they could cause great conflict and problems with each other, and then there would be the denouement of finally getting together. I said there are those four scenes. I don't think about that all the time, but that time I knew where it was going—there was a play there—so I sat down with some sense of confidence.

Others just unfold themselves. When I was writing *Lost in Yonkers*, I knew I had these four characters in my mind. I had witnessed somebody who has this dysfunction of not being able to breathe properly, and I never thought about using it. But it suddenly came to mind in this dysfunctional family, which the mother has created. When you write, you're always trying to catch up with your thoughts. They're ahead of you, like the carrot in front of the rabbit or the horse. If it's always there ahead of you, then you know that each day that you go to work you will be able to write something. It's awful when you are writing a play and you get to page forty and you come to your office in the morning and say, "Well, what do I write today? Where does it go?" I want to leave it the night before saying to myself, "I know what that next scene is tomorrow," and I look forward to the next day.

Bryer: How do you get started on a play? Do you usually start with an idea or with a character?

Simon: First it starts with a desire, to write a play, and then the next desire is what kind of play do I want to write. When I finished *Broadway Bound*, I said, "I do not want to write another play like this right now." I've done a play that in degrees develops more seriously, because I thought that *Broadway Bound* dealt more truthfully with my family and with the kind of writing I wanted to do than anything I had done in the past. I did not have an idea for the next one, and so sometimes I just play around with an idea. I said

I wanted to write a farce, and I just sat down and thought of the opening premise. It literally started with how it looked. Most farces are about wealthy people. They're not about people who are poor, because their lives are in conflict all the time. They must be satirical—you want to make jabs at them socially. These were all fairly prominent people, and I wanted them all to show up in black tie and their best gowns, because I knew, whatever it was that I was going to write, they would be a mess at the end of the evening—either emotionally or physically—with their clothes tattered and torn. I thought of it as a mystery. I had no idea where it was going. The host had attempted suicide and was not able to tell them what happened, the hostess wasn't there, and there was no food. That's all I knew. I had read (I read a great deal of biographies of writers and artists) that Georges Simenon wrote most of his murder mysteries without knowing who was going to be murdered and who the murder was. He picked a place, a set of situations, just something that intrigued him. I think almost anyone can sit down and write the first five pages of a murder mystery because you don't have to leave any clues. You just think of some wild situation that sounds interesting. It's only the really great mystery writers who know where to take it. *The Thin Man* is one of the most complicated books I've ever read. I don't think Dashiell Hammett is given enough credit. That's really literature, that book. What was your original question?

Bryer: How you got the ideas for plays.
Simon: I never really can remember the moment, maybe with a few exceptions. *The Odd Couple* came out of watching my brother and the man he was living with at that time. They had both just gotten divorced, had decided to live together to cut down expenses, and they were dating girls. I said what an incredible idea for a play. *Barefoot* came out of my own experiences with my wife. Strangely enough, *Barefoot in the Park* started in Switzerland. The first version of it—this really happened—was when my wife and I went on our honeymoon to St. Moritz, Switzerland, met an elderly couple, and decided to go hiking with them. My wife then—Joan died in '73—was a wonderful athlete, and she and the older man were practically jumping up this mountain while his wife and I staggered behind, and I was angry at Joan for being able to jump like a goat on this mountain. Then I realized that it had too exotic an atmosphere, and I wanted to locate it in a place where one could relate to it more. I thought about that tiny apartment that we actually lived in that was five flights up and had a shower and no bath. It had a hole in the skylight in which it snowed. So I

used all of those things. You don't know that when you're sitting down to write it. It's an adventure. It's really jumping into this big swimming pool and hoping there's going to be water when you hit.

Bryer: How has the experience of writing musicals and writing films been different, and do you continue to do them when you don't need to? Why have you continued to write in collaborative situations and seemingly against the whole idea of wanting to be independent?

Simon: I do it because I think I have to keep writing all the time. Each year I want to be doing something. I wouldn't know how to take a year off and do nothing. I would feel it a wasted year of my life, unless I did something else productive that I love—but I haven't found anything. I think that even at this age I'm still growing and that I want to do as much as I can before I can't do it anymore. Again, I think, what do you want to do following what you have just done? I was about to start another play that I had in mind, but I still haven't quite licked where it's going, and I'm not ready to do it. It's not that I won't have anything on next year, but I won't have anything to work on. So I'm toying with the idea of doing a musical now, which is like a breather, even though the musical is a much more collaborative and a much more debilitating effort than anything else in the theater could be. The movies have been in the past—some of them—such good experiences that I was usually eager to do one again. The movie industry has changed enormously. I did ten films with Ray Stark. Nine of them were successful and one was terrible. But for all of them Ray Stark was the producer. He always got me a good director, always got a good cast, and was really the blocking back for me, the runner, with the studio. I almost never had to deal with the studio. This last experience I had, *The Marrying Man*, was enough to make me say I never want to do a film again.

I did have good experiences doing *The Heartbreak Kid* and *The Goodbye Girl*, even *Murder by Death*. *Murder by Death* is not a great work of art, but it's great fun. In my reveries I used to wish that I had been older in the thirties and in the early forties and could write for Cary Grant and Humphrey Bogart and Jimmy Stewart. One of the great thrills I had in Hollywood was when I met some of these people, and they said, "Gee, I wish I could have done a picture with you!" When Cary Grant said that to me, I said, "Wow, what I've missed!" Those were actors who were, I think, in some ways (the best of them) superior to some of the actors we have today, carried none of the weight that the actors do today. Now even a small star, a starlet, has something to say about the picture. I will deal with the director always, with the producer seldom but sometimes, the studio hardly ever, and with an actor never. I will listen to an actor's inabilities to find what he needs to accomplish in a part and try to accommodate that, but not because he wants to be portrayed in a certain way. On the stage Manny Azenberg and I must have fired eight to ten actors over the years because we found they were not fulfilling what we wanted. An actor's training is mostly with dead playwrights, so when they do the classics they don't expect any rewrites. I want them to feel the same thing. I rewrite more than anybody I know— I just do it over and over. I'm still giving pages and new lines on *Lost in Yonkers* and will do it until we open. But they'll always come to you and say, "I'm having trouble with this line. Can you think if there's another way of me saying it that makes it more comfortable?" I'll say, "I'll rewrite it if it makes it more comfortable for the character, not for you." When they understand that then we can find a way to do it.

To give you a really good example of the difference between films and plays for me, a director of a play will come to me and say, "What do you think about this section? I'm not so sure that this is working. Do you think you could find something else?" And I'll either agree with him or disagree with him and write it or rewrite it, but he does nothing about it until I rewrite it. He'll even come to me about a sentence or a couple of words. That play is sold to the films, and he becomes the director. He shoots the film and then invites me to the first cut, and three major scenes are missing. I say, "What happened to those scenes?" He says, "They didn't work for me." It now has become his script—it's not mine anymore. And the only way to control that is to direct your own films, which I don't want to do. I'm not a director. I don't want to spend all that time. I love writing. I hate directing. I hate hanging around the rehearsals. I do it when I'm working and I need to do something, but just to stand there and watch—I don't want to do it. So I do the films, but I'm not really very happy with them. Musicals are something else, because when you work with the best people (I worked with Bob Fosse a number of times, and I thought he was really a genius. I worked with Michael Bennett a few times, even a little bit on *Chorus Line*), that's great fun. That's like being invited to the party, so you just do it.

Bryer: You talk about rewriting. When you're readying a play like *Lost in Yonkers* and you're doing the rewriting, to whom are you responding when you do the rewrites? Is it purely your own responses when you're in the theater? Or do you also respond to critics, or the director, or an actor?

Simon: All of them. Not an actor so much, a director yes, a critic some-times. If a critic says something that's valid, and especially if it's backed up by another critic who hits on the same point, I say, "I've got to address this." When you're writing it over and over again and then you're in rehearsal and you're out of town and you start to try it, you've lost all objectivity. Now you need the audience to be objective for you (and they are totally), and you listen to them. Sometimes the actor will come to me and say, "This line isn't getting a laugh." And I say, "I never intended it to." They assume that everything they should say when the situation is comic should get a laugh. I say, "No, no, no, this is character. It's pushing the story ahead." That never happens in any of the dramatic scenes in *Lost in Yonkers*. Very few of those lines were ever changed because they don't have the difficulty in expecting a reaction from the audience. I rewrite just watching what it is that I hear wrong. And sometimes I can watch a play, and after about eight or nine performances, I say, "I don't like that." There was a producer who once said to me, "Only look at the things that don't work in the play. The good things will take care of themselves, don't worry about that. Don't say, 'I know this stuff doesn't work, but look at all the good things I have." He said, "The bad things'll do you in every time." So I concentrate on the bad things. And after I get whatever I think is unworthy of the play out, then I start to hear it more objectively. I stay away for two or three performances and come back and say, "We need something much better than that." When you first see that play up on a stage for the first time in front of an audience, all you care about is that the baby is delivered and is well and has all its arms and legs and moves. They you say, "Okay, now starts its education."

Bryer: I teach a course in modern American drama, and many of the play-wrights in the course, people like John Guare and Beth Henley, are consid-ered by the "establishment" to be serious playwrights who write plays that contain comic moments. Neil Simon, on the other hand, is considered a writer of funny plays that are occasionally serious. That strikes me as unfair because, especially in the most recent of your plays, like the trilogy and now *Lost in Yonkers*, the proportion of humor to seriousness is, if anything, less comedy than in, say, *Crimes of the Heart*.
Simon: *Crimes of the Heart* is a comedy.

Bryer: Yes, but Henley is considered a serious playwright.
Simon: I don't consider it necessarily unfair. I just think it's inaccurate. Unfair means that I'm being picked on for not writing serious, which is

better than comedy, which I don't hold to be true. For the most part I think I have written, with the exception of *"Rumors"* and the musicals (starting even with *The Odd Couple*), a serious play that is told through my own comic point of view. There are no serious moments in *The Odd Couple*, but when I first sat down to write it, naïve as this may be, I thought it was sort of a black comedy, because in most comedies up to that point, there were always women in the play and a romantic relationship. Here there were none—the relationship was between these two men. *Plaza Suite*, with a husband and wife getting a divorce after twenty-three years, was basically a serious play that had comedy in it. The audience at that time was so trained to laugh at what I wrote that, in Boston, Mike Nichols and I kept taking out all the funny lines in the first act—and they found other places to laugh.

I write with a sense of irony, and even with lines that are not funny, sometimes the audience senses the irony, when they are sophisticated enough, and they see the humor. That's why I always need really good productions for the plays to work. I once met a woman who said, "You know, I've never been a fan of yours," and I said, "Oh, that's okay," and she said, "Now I'm a big fan!" and I said, "What happened?" She said, "Well, I come from"—it was either Wyoming or Montana—and she said, "I've only seen dinner theater productions of your plays, in which they would play all the plays on one superficial level. They played it all as comedy, and then I read the plays, and I said, this isn't comedy at all." I remember people walking out of *Prisoner of Second Avenue* confused, because some would say, "This wasn't funny." I didn't mean it to be funny—I thought it was a very serious subject, especially at that time. It was the beginning of people being so age-conscious, with the man of forty-eight years old losing his job and finding it very difficult to start all over again, which is true even today. That to me was a serious play that had a great deal of comedy.

I use the comedy in a way to get the audience's attention and then sort of pull the rug from underneath them. That's how I view life. Things are wonderful, things are going along just great, and then a telephone call comes and just pulls the rug from under you. Some tragic thing, some tragic event, has happened in your life, and I say if it can happen in life I want to do that in the theater. It took a long time to convince audiences and critics that one could write a play that way. I remember reading Lillian Hellman saying, "Never mix comedy and drama in the same play; the audiences won't understand it." They say to me, "What are you writing?" and I'll mention something, and they say, "Is it comedy?" I say, "No, it's a play." They say, "Is it a drama?" and I say, "It's a play. It has everything in it."

Bryer: When you look back over your career to date, how has Neil Simon changed as a playwright? In other interviews you've mentioned the idea of the tapestry play, that you're now writing about more than two people as the focus of the plays. I assume that's one way, but are there other ways that you see your plays changing?

Simon: Well, in a glacier-like way. They move slowly. I don't make sudden overnight changes. I think back to *Chapter Two*, which was the story of the guilt a man feels who has lost a spouse and who feels too guilty or is made to feel too guilty by his children or other relatives to go ahead in another relationship. There were people who spent the next fifteen or twenty years or the rest of their lives never moving on with it. In my own case I was encouraged by my daughters to move on when I met somebody else. But still you get that kick of guilt, not a high kick, a kick in the gut, of guilt much like the survivors of the Holocaust, when those who lived felt guilty all their lives. So the man in the play was not able to give himself the enjoyment and the latitude of exploring this new relationship without always pulling in the guilt of being alive and his wife being dead. Around that point it's what I started to look for in almost every play. I think if there's any change, it's that way. It's not necessary for me to be conceived of as a serious playwright, because the word is so bandied about I think that it gets misinterpreted, "serious" meaning the intention is lofty. It isn't any loftier than comedy can be, but I don't write a pure comedy anymore, with the exception of *"Rumors,"* where I intentionally did. I try to write plays about human emotions. I don't write plays about society. I find I can't. They become very current plays, and I like plays to be able to last for fifty or a hundred years or so. These are plays that contain serious subject matter. *Lost in Yonkers* is very well disguised, not that I meant it to be, but I couldn't open up the play showing the tragic side of Bella. It only came out when she was confronted with this chance to better her life and she didn't quite know how to do it and didn't get the permission of her mother, who was the one who stunted her growth in the first place. That has to be built to, and I see how the audience is taken by surprise as it goes on. If they leave after that first act, they say, "It's nice, it's funny, it's cute." And then the second act just hits them so hard. It's what you leave the theater with, not what's going on in the beginning of the play, that's important.

Bryer: Perhaps this analogy will seem far-fetched to you, but one could say that it took O'Neill almost his whole creative life to write a play like *Long Day's Journey*, where, as he said, he "faced his dead at last." He had started to do it with *Ah, Wilderness!* in a more lighthearted way. *Ah, Wilderness!* and *Long Day's Journey* are really the same play, but one is weighted toward a comedic treatment and the other toward a more tragic approach. It seems to me that you could say the same thing about *Brighton Beach Memoirs* and *Broadway Bound*. *Brighton Beach Memoirs* is your *Ah, Wilderness!*, and *Broadway Bound* is your *Long Day's Journey*. You started to confront your family directly in *Brighton Beach*, particularly through Eugene's narration in a comic way, and then in *Broadway Bound* you did so much more seriously.

Simon: There was a really valid reason for that. With *Brighton Beach* my mother was still alive, so she could come and enjoy it and *Biloxi Blues* as well. She died after that, so she never saw *Broadway Bound*. I would not have written *Broadway Bound* if my parents had been alive. I couldn't have put them up on the stage in that way. I don't think I put them in an unsympathetic light certainly, but in a truthful one in a way. I was probably harsher on my father than I was on my mother. At that time in our lives, I really think she was the one who caused the anguish in the family. But I have more of an understanding of him now, having lived through some of the same things myself.

Bryer: So you think it was basically the death of your mother that enabled you to write *Broadway Bound* when you did?

Simon: It freed me to do it. I reveal things about her, her inability to be close and emotional. I don't remember ever being hugged by my mother as far back as being a child. I always knew that she loved me, but she was unable to show emotion. I did talk about something that happened to my mother personally, that she was burned in a fire. The grandfather talks about that. I don't go into it in *Broadway Bound*, but it must have affected their marriage very much—how she was scarred. She was actually scarred on the front, not on the back, as in the play.

Bryer: And you never could have done that if she'd been alive?

Simon: No, I couldn't. When O'Neill wrote *Long Day's Journey*, he put it in a drawer and said it couldn't be done until twenty-five years after his death, which didn't happen of course. His wife had it done. I sort of felt that way. *Chapter Two* was cathartic for me. It helped me get rid of my own guilt by sharing it with the world. But *Broadway Bound* was not cathartic. It was an attempt to try to understand my family and my own origins. It's a play of forgiveness, and I didn't realize it until somebody associated with the play—the set designer or a costume designer—said after the reading, "It's a love letter to his mother." I had a very up-and-down relationship with my mother. I used to get angry at her very often, and I loved her too, but there was no way for either one of us to show it—and so there it is on the stage. I remember in real life once I gave a surprise birthday party for my mother— she really was surprised—and we brought out the cake. She couldn't smile or say, "This is wonderful." She just looked at me as she was about to cut the cake and said, "I'm still angry with you from last week when you did such and such." It was the only way she could deal with it. So when I wrote the play, what I had to do after listening to the first reading when I didn't have that scene about George Raft, I said, I've got to show the other side of my mother, show her when she was happy. I like that when, in the second act of the play, you begin to show what really is information that happened way before that, to give it late in the play.

Bryer: Do you have a favorite among your own plays? The last one you wrote?

Simon: Yes, it's generally that. It suddenly becomes the one that you're working on. But when I think of my favorite, I think about what my experience was when I wrote it and put it on. Was that a good time in my life, in my personal life and in doing the play? With some of the plays I had terrible times doing the play yet the play came out very well. Other times it was great fun doing it. I think the greatest kick I got on an opening night— when I knew I was sort of catapulted into another place in my life—was the opening night of *The Odd Couple*. It was accepted on such a high level by everyone. It was what you dream about—Moss Hart in *Act One*—the hottest ticket in town. That night was a terrific night!

Bryer: What about as a craftsman? Which of the plays are you proudest of as a piece of writing?

Simon: Structurally I like *The Sunshine Boys*, and I like this one structurally.

Bryer: *The Sunshine Boys* is my favorite Simon play so far, because of the integration of comedy and seriousness and because of the organic nature of that integration. Maybe it's an accident of the subject matter because you're dealing with comedians.

Simon: You're dealing with comedians, which gives you license for them to be funny. But the seriousness in the play was inherent too. It wasn't always written about because you knew that they were old, you knew they couldn't deal with things. One was really fighting for his way of life to continue; the other was quite satisfied to be retired and live in another way. So there was something classic about it. It just seems to hark back to another period in time. That play is done by more national theaters in Europe—in England or even Germany—because they relate to it in some part of their own culture, to the old vaudevillians and what's happened to them. They've died out. That's another play that sat in the drawer for six months after I wrote twenty-five pages of it, until I had lunch with Mike Nichols and said, "I'm kind of stuck. I have a play." I started to tell him the idea, and he said, "That sounds wonderful!" That's sometimes all I need—that's like a great review. "You really like that, Mike?" "Yes." And I went ahead and wrote the whole thing.

Bryer: Can you think of plays that exceeded your expectations and plays that you had great expectations for that never reached them once you saw them on stage?

Simon: That's an interesting question because I think I always know what the reception is going to be. I'm rarely surprised. Sometimes I write a play knowing it's not going to succeed. There's a psychological subconscious will to fail after writing four or five hits—you don't deserve that much. I pick a subject matter that is so far out—something that I would not do right now. Not one that's more dangerous and that's taking more of a chance with an audience, but one that's almost guaranteed not to be commercially successful (not that I always know when it's going to be). *The Odd Couple* and *Barefoot in the Park* fooled me because they were so early in my career. I didn't know what to expect. When they were both such big hits, I was really shocked. But a play that I knew I wanted to write for a reason other than artistic or commercial success was something like *God's Favorite*.

God's Favorite was my way of dealing with my wife's death. It was *Waiting for Godot* for me. I could not understand the absurdity of a thirty-nine-year-old, beautiful, energetic woman dying so young. It was railing at God to explain to me why He did this thing, so I used the Book of Job. One critic cried on television in his anger: "How dare you do this to the Book of Job!" Yet there were critics like Walter Kerr, a devout Catholic, who loved it, just adored it. And so I wasn't too surprised that we weren't a major success, but I learned in hindsight that it was not a Broadway play. It should have been done Off-Broadway, as *Fools* should have been. *Fools* I did in a way like "*Rumors.*" Again it was farce in a sense. I just loved the premise. It's almost Hebraic culturally, like the towns written about by Sholem Aleichem in which there were stupid people (without ever going into the reasons why), and I had a curse in my town. I thought it was good. Mike Nichols came up and did it. We had a good time. If we had done it in a small theater, it would have been fine—Playwrights Horizons or something like that—but not with the expectations of a Broadway audience, paying whatever it was at the time, expecting a certain kind of play.

I remember when we did *The Good Doctor*, which was another play written during my wife's illness, when they discovered that she would not live. I was just sitting up in the country, and I wanted to write to keep myself going, and I read a short story by Chekhov called "The Sneeze." And just to kill time I dramatized it. And I said, "Gee, this would be fun, to do all Russian writers and do comic pieces—or non-comic pieces—by them." I couldn't find any, so in order to give unity to the evening, I decided to do Chekhov, because he had written so many newspaper pieces where he got paid by the word. And I found as many of them as I could. Then when I tried them out of town, some of them didn't work. So I wrote my own Chekhov pieces, and some of the critics pointed them out and said, "This one is so Chekhovian," which wasn't his at all! I don't mean that as flattery to me but as not knowing by some of the critics. I remember a woman in New Haven coming up the aisle and she said to me, "This isn't Neil Simon." So I asked, "Do you like it, or do you not like it?" She said, "I don't know. It's just not Neil Simon." I have to overcome their expectations of me so that they don't get to see what they want to see. It's like going to see Babe Ruth at a baseball game. If he hits two singles and drives in the winning run, it's not a Babe Ruth game.

Bryer: How do you feel about the current relationship between the theater and film and TV? It's a cliché that television is ruining the theater, that we are a culture of filmgoers and not theatergoers. Do you feel those are valid kinds of observations? You once said you thought the biggest obstacle to theater was the price of theater tickets. Do you think it's really that?

Simon: That's one of them. It's only one of them. No, there's enough money around, I think, for people to go to Broadway theater. I think we've lost the writers more than anything. David Richards of the *New York Times* recently said to me, "Do you realize you may be the only one left around who repeatedly works for the Broadway theater?" And I said, "Well, they're all gone." Edward Albee hardly writes at all. Arthur Miller has grown older and writes occasionally for the theater but rarely for Broadway—it's usually for Lincoln Center or someplace else. David Mamet now would rather direct and write his own films. Sam Shepard was never a Broadway writer. There are no repeat writers—the Tennessee Williamses, the George S. Kaufmans, or even Jean Kerr in terms of comedy. You talk to anybody today, especially in California, and they will use writing as a stepping stone to becoming a director. They want to be directors. It has to be about control. Even a promising young writer like John Patrick Shanley has a big success with *Moonstruck* after he had small success in the theater. We had said this is an interesting playwright. He does *Moonstruck* and then he wants to direct— so he does *Joe Versus the Volcano*, and I'm sure he just wants to keep on directing. Nora Ephron writes a couple of movies that are nice, and now she wants to direct. I have no desire to direct at all. I see the soundness of it, in terms of movies. As I said before, I have no control over what goes on up on the screen or what's cut later. Between the director and the actors you lose all of that.

It's almost a mystery as to what's happened in the theater. I think it's just changing. It's becoming regional theater, and the plays are in a sense getting smaller, not necessarily in their scope. *Six Degrees of Separation* is a wonderful play. I really like that play. I'm not so sure, if it had opened on Broadway at the Plymouth Theatre, that it would have gotten the kind of attention, the demands for seats. It's viewed from a different perspective when it's presented in an Off-Broadway atmosphere. You see what happens when they transfer plays. One of the few that transferred fairly well was *The Heidi Chronicles*, but even when you're watching *The Heidi Chronicles*, you say this isn't really a Broadway play. That could be a misnomer too, because it makes it sound crass and commercial, but *Amadeus* is a Broadway play, and I think it's a great play. I think most of Peter Shaffer's plays are wonderful plays: *Five Finger Exercise* and the one about the Incas, *The Royal Hunt of the Sun*. Tennessee Williams didn't write Off-Broadway plays except at the end of his career when the plays got smaller in their scope. *Cat on a Hot Tin Roof* is a beautiful play, but it's got size to it, and there is no one around who does that anymore. It's changed, I guess maybe the way painting has changed. I don't know who the great portrait painters are anymore, if they exist at all. I think it's economics that changes it. In the theater now they are catering to an international audience. Who comes to America now but the people who have money—the Japanese or the Germans? They don't all understand English, but if they go see a musical like *Cats* they don't have to. Even *Phantom of the Opera*—if you don't understand it you can still enjoy it. If a play runs two years, it is amazing. Most musical hits will run ten years now. You can't get *Cats* out of that theater. *Phantom* will be there forever. It will be interesting to see what happens with *Miss Saigon*, because it has this amazing anti-American number. When I saw it in London, you could almost cheer it, but if, when it opens in March, this war [the Gulf War] is still going on, there may be some repercussions.

Bryer: One of the things that occurred to me when I was watching *Lost in Yonkers* the other night is that you're one of the cleanest playwrights I know, even though you write about very intimate things.

Simon: You write to what fits the play. There are all sorts of four-letter words in *"Rumors"* because these are very contemporary people. In *Lost in Yonkers* you're dealing with the 1940s, and you're not only trying to emulate a play that might have existed in that time, but certainly what life was like at that time. And that kind of language, street language, I at least didn't hear that much. I never heard it at home, except maybe in a violent argument between my mother and father. It's interesting to watch playwrights like Tennessee Williams and Arthur Miller who never resorted to that language but found another language that was more potent. In doing *The Marrying Man* with Kim Basinger and Alec Baldwin, which was just an awful experience, she did this scene in which she was sitting in a box at the opera in Boston. She used to be Bugsy Siegal's girlfriend but is found by this guy who's a multimillionaire, and they got married—they're forced to get married through no intention of their own. Later on they fall in love and get remarried. She's sitting in Boston, and a man in the box is annoying her as she's sort of kissing the ear of Alec Baldwin. He keeps shushing her, and she says, "Oh, come on, this opera isn't even in English, you can't understand it." And he goes on, and finally she ad-libs, "Oh, go fuck yourself." And I said, "Wait, you can't say that." It had nothing to do with my thinking that the language is offensive, but it's so wrong for the character and for the tone of the movie. It's a movie that takes place in 1948. It's okay when the Alec Baldwin character and his four cronies are in the car. They use all sorts of language, but for her to use it in that place seemed so wrong for me. So it wasn't being prudish about anything. You've just got to use it where it's got some weight. Sometimes I would use "fuck you" or whatever it is once in a play, and it has much more impact that just using it all the way through. I like it when David Mamet does it sometimes, as in *American Buffalo*. It is said so often that it is no longer offensive. It bothers some people I know—they don't want to hear it. But it never bothers me. I think he writes in such wonderful rhythms and cadences that the language is so important, so precise.

Bryer: Linda Lavin once said apropos of *Last of the Red Hot Lovers*, in which she was then appearing: "People come to the theater to see their lives

verified. They haven't been offended. The life they lead hasn't been challenged, it's been reaffirmed." And I think you once said, "recognition" is what you'd like to see your plays be all about. Let me be a devil's advocate and say that one should come out of the theater upset, as Edward Albee insists. I don't mean necessarily emotionally upset, but something should have changed. You shouldn't have been patted on the head, you should have been disturbed. *Lost in Yonkers* can be a very disturbing play in that way.
Simon: Oh, absolutely.

Bryer: Do you think you've changed in that respect?
Simon: Yes. I remember that when I did *Plaza Suite* and I wrote the first act about the husband who's having the affair with the secretary, the general manager for the play read it and said, "You can't do this play." I said, "Why not?" He said, "Do you know how many men come from out of town and meet their secretary or somebody and come to this play. They'll be so embarrassed." I said, "Good, that's what I want to do. I want to shake people up." So I don't think I was trying to reaffirm middle-class values. In *Last of the Red Hot Lovers* the man was trying to have an affair. I found him sort of a pitiful character, not even being able to break through that. I saw him in a way as an Everyman who finally had the courage to try to break out but didn't know how to do it. Sometimes those labels stick with you. But as I said, it's a glacier. It moves along and it changes and it pulls along the debris with it. I don't think I write that way. I think why I get bandied about a lot by critics is because of the success ratio. There must be something wrong when it appeals to so many people around the world. They hate it that I've become a wealthy person from the plays.

Bryer: You can't be any good if you're wealthy!
Simon: Yes. I remember at the time reading about Tennessee Williams's wealth, which was relative compared to today's market, but he was a fairly wealthy man because he was so successful. But he also took such chances with plays like *Camino Real*. He was a poet, and he made his reputation on plays like *The Glass Menagerie* and *Streetcar Named Desire*. It's because I do write plays that for the most part are so popular. I never mind a bad review from a good critic who has liked some of the work in the past and then says, "No, you didn't do it this time." I say that's valid, and I can accept it. I don't expect a rave from Frank Rich. Frank Rich always will find fault. He's tough to figure out, because he'll write a very middling review of *Brighton Beach* and talk about its faults and at the end of it say, "One hopes there will be a

chapter two to *Brighton Beach*." He finds fault with the play, yet he wants to see a sequel to it! I had no intention of writing a trilogy, I just wrote *Brighton Beach*. When I read his notice, I said, "Well, I'll do another play." You still don't think about a trilogy, because if the second play fails, who wants to see the sequel to a failure? So I wrote *Biloxi Blues*, which he loved. It won the Tony Award, and so I did the third one, which he again then finds fault with by saying, "I missed it being a great play." He gives it a negative sounding review by saying it almost reaches great heights but doesn't.

You have to steel yourself. You become very thick-skinned after a while, because you're out there naked and they are writing about you personally. They don't write about your work as much as who you are in the reviews. In a way I think the theater has been changed a lot by critics who are now looking to make names for themselves. It bothers me that critics are hailed as personalities. Siskel and Ebert, good critics or bad critics, it makes no difference to me, I hate that they are celebrities and have such power. Fortunately there are so many people who write reviews for films, and people generally make up their minds to go see a film before they go read the reviews. Not so with the theater. The reviews mean everything. If you get a bad review in the *New York Times*, you can still exist, but you've got to overcome it.

Bryer: No, that's not exactly true. *You* can still exist. Neil Simon can still exist. A lot of other people can't with a bad review in the *Times*.
Simon: Well, it depends on the play. There have been a few that have existed without it, but it's very hard. Rich loved *Biloxi Blues*, and the first day after *Biloxi Blues* opened, we did an enormous amount of business, twice what we did on *Brighton Beach Memoirs*. But *Brighton Beach Memoirs* ran twice as long as *Biloxi Blues*. The audience seeks out what they want, and *Brighton Beach*, next to *The Odd Couple*, is played more than any play I've ever done. There is something about the idealization of the family in that play that we all dream about. They know it's an idealization. It's like looking back on your family album and seeing it better than it was.

Bryer: But it's not *Ah, Wilderness!* It's not that sappy.
Simon: Well, those were sappier days.

Bryer: There's a lot of what happens in *Broadway Bound* underneath the surface of *Brighton Beach*.
Simon: Oh, yes—the mother's hurt when she finds out that the father has had this heart attack and that the boy has lost all the money.

Bryer: What do you think you've done differently in *Lost in Yonkers*? What would you say has inched the glacier forward with this play?

Simon: I've written about much darker people than I ever have before. I've written about normal people in dark situations before—the death of spouses, the break-up of marriages (tragedies in proportion to their own lives at that time, as in *Brighton Beach*), anti-Semitism and antihomosexuality in *Biloxi*. But in this play I really wrote about dysfunctional people and the results of a woman who was beaten in Germany and who, in order to teach her children to survive, teaches them only to survive and nothing else. That's much further than I've gone in any other play, so it's deeper. It's why I want to do a musical next year, because I need really sure footing to go on to the next place. That doesn't mean I need to write about people even more dysfunctional, but as a matter of fact the play that I've been working on and haven't been able to lick quite yet is about two people in a sanitarium who have had breakdowns and find solace in each other almost more than in the doctor. I've written about thirty pages of it, and I've had it there for two years, and I'm anxious to write it. But each play comes when its time is ripe. Who knows? If at some point I lose faith in the musical I'm working on, I'll probably go back and start to write that play. Right now all I want to do is get out of Washington, go home, rest, come back, do the stuff in New York. Then I'll forget all about *Lost in Yonkers*. They all become a piece of the past for me. I've learned from them, and then they only come up in interviews like this, when you talk about them. I don't think of the plays. I don't try to remember or go back or ever read them and see what I've done to see how I could do that again. I want to go to some other place. I'm just hoping that there'll even be theater enough around for people to want to go see these plays.

The Art of Theater X: Neil Simon

James Lipton / 1992

From *Paris Review*, no. 125 (Winter 1992): 167–213. © 1992 by The Paris Review, used by permission of The Wylie Agency LLC. James Lipton is the dean emeritus of the Actors Studio Drama School at Pace University, and from 1994 to 2018 was the host, executive producer, and writer of the Bravo TV series *Inside the Actors Studio*.

Legend has it that on his deathbed the actor Edmund Gwenn answered director John Ford's "What is dying like?" with a reflective, "Dying is easy. Comedy is hard."

By any measure—quantity, quality, popular success, renown—Neil Simon is the preeminent purveyor of comedy in the last half of the twentieth century. Like the work of most writers of comedy, from Aristophanes to Woody Allen, Simon's humor is written to be spoken. And heard. For Simon the art of humor is both communal (each member of the audience in league with all the other members of the audience) and collegial (playwright and performers in league with the audience—a relationship Simon will describe as a "shared secret"). Fielding, Twain, and Thurber can be savored in one's lap, but verbal, visual humor, like misery, loves company. Simon is not only skillful at his craft but prolific as well. He is the author of more than twenty plays, including *Come Blow Your Horn*, *Barefoot in the Park*, *The Odd Couple*, the Brighton Beach trilogy, *Prisoner of Second Avenue*, *Plaza Suite*, and *Lost in Yonkers*.

These pages are the winnowing of sixteen hours of taped conversation in Simon's office on the second floor of a Spanish colonial apartment building in the Beverly Hills flats—several miles, a thousand vertical feet, and a dozen social strata below the Bel Air hilltop home Simon shares with his wife Diane and their daughter Bryn.

The writer's no-nonsense work space, impersonal in its laidback Southern California setting, is conspicuously empty (no secretary, no phone calls, no distractions) but intensely personal in the memorabilia that have, as Simon explains, "sort of gravitated" there over the years.

Halfway through the tour of the apartment Simon stopped abruptly and remarked, in apparent surprise, on how many of the room's furnishings date from the house on Manhattan's East Sixty-Second Street where he lived with his first wife, Joan: chairs, tables, photographs, paintings—some painted by Joan, a framed letter from her, written in cryptic, Joycean prose and signed, "Klarn." The baseball paraphernalia on display reflects another side of Simon's life. His substantial collection of antique caps and autographed balls, with a recent emphasis on Bobby Bonilla, would knock the knee-socks off the playwright's baseball-mad alter ego, Eugene Jerome.

There are the usual theatrical souvenirs and a few unusual ones: a telegram from the president of Columbia University informing Simon of his Pulitzer Prize for *Lost in Yonkers*, a Neil Simon *Time* magazine cover, a poster from the Moscow production of *Biloxi Blues*, signed by the cast, "Dear Neil Simon, We love you and your plays. We had worked on this performance with enjoy."

"Doc" Simon, so called from his childhood habit of mimicking the family doctor, is tall and fit, despite the chronic back problems that have curtailed his tennis playing in recent years. We sat at a massive, polished tree-stump coffee table covered with the tools of his trade: pens neatly stacked (by the cleaning woman, he hastened to stay), scripts, finished and unfinished, books, and the long pads on which he writes. We laughed frequently as we discussed his plays, opinions, and past. Even when the talk turned as serious as some of his recent scripts, the face that peered over the tree stump like a Bronx leprechaun bore two indelible Simon trademarks: the eyes of an insatiably curious and slightly guarded child, shielded by horn-rimmed glasses, and a faint, constant, enigmatic smile. What is this man smiling at? Perhaps the shared secret.

Interviewer: Lillian Hellman once said she always began work on a play with something very small—a scene, or even two vague lines of dialogue whose meaning was utterly unknown to her. What starts *you*, what makes you think there's a play there?

Neil Simon: As many plays as I've written—twenty-seven, twenty-eight—I can't recollect a moment when I've said "This would make a good play." I never sit down and write bits and pieces of dialogue. What I might do is make a few notes on who's in the play, the characters I want, where it takes place and the general idea of it. I don't make any outlines at all. I just like to plunge in. I'll start right from page one because I want to hear how the people speak. Are they interesting enough for me? Have I captured them? It goes piece by piece, brick by brick. I don't know that I have a play until I've reached thirty, thirty-five pages.

Interviewer: Have you ever started thematically?

Simon: I *think* about thematic plays, but I don't believe I write them. Nothing really takes shape until I become specific about the character and the dilemma he's in. *Dilemma* is the key word. It is always a dilemma, not a situation. To tell the truth, I really don't know what the theme of the play is until I've written it and the critics tell me.

Interviewer: Every playwright, every director, every actor, speaks about conflict. We're all supposed to be in the conflict business. When you speak of dilemma, are you talking about conflict?

Simon: Yes. In *Broadway Bound* I wanted to show the anatomy of writing comedy—with the older brother teaching Eugene, which was the case with my brother Danny and me. Stan keeps asking Eugene for the essential ingredient in comedy, and when Eugene can't answer, Stan says, "Conflict!" When he asks for the *other* key ingredient, and Eugene can only come up with, "*More* conflict?" Stan says, "The key word is *wants*. In every comedy, even drama, somebody has to want something and want it bad. When somebody tries to stop him—that's conflict." By the time you know the conflicts, the play is already written in your mind. All you have to do is put the words down. You don't have to outline the play, it outlines itself. You go by sequential activity. One thing follows the other. But it all starts with that first seed, conflict. As Stan says, it's got to be a very, very strong conflict, not one that allows the characters to say, "Forget about this! I'm walking out." They've got to stay there and fight it out to the end.

Interviewer: You said that it isn't until you get to page thirty-five that you know whether or not you've got a play. Are there times when you get to page thirty-five and decide the conflict isn't strong enough, and the play disappears to languish forever in a drawer?

Simon: I've got infinitely more plays in the drawer than have seen the lights of the stage. Most of them never come out of the drawer, but occasionally one will, and it amazes me how long it has taken to germinate and blossom. The best example would be *Brighton Beach Memoirs*. I wrote the first thirty-five pages of the play and gave it to my children, Nancy and Ellen, and Marsha, my wife at the time. They read it and said, "This is incredible. You've got to go on with it." I showed it to my producer, Manny Azenberg, and to Gordon Davidson, and they said, "This is going to be a great play." I knew the play was a turn in style for me, probing more deeply into myself, but maybe the pressure of the words "great play" scared me, so I put it away. Periodically, I would take it out and read it, and I wouldn't know how to do it. After nine years I took it out one day, read the thirty-five pages, picked up my pen and the pad I write on, and finished the play in six weeks. I have the feeling that in the back of your mind there's a little writer who writes while you're doing other things, because I had no trouble at that point. Obviously, what had happened in the ensuing years in my life made clear to me what it should be about. Somewhere in the back of my head I grew up, I matured. I was ready to write that play. Sometimes it *helps* to have some encouragement. Once I was having dinner with Mike Nichols, and he asked, "What are you doing?" I said, "I'm working on a play about two ex-vaudevillians who haven't worked together or seen each other in eleven years, and they get together to do an Ed Sullivan Show." He said, "That sounds wonderful. Go back and finish it." So I did. It was as though a critic had already seen the play and said, "I love it." But there are many, many plays that get to a certain point and no further. For years I've been trying to write the play of what happened to me and the seven writers who wrote Sid Caesar's *Your Show of Shows*. But I've never got past page twenty-two because there are seven conflicts rather than one main conflict. I've been writing more subtext and more subplot lately—but in this situation *everybody* was funny. I didn't have somebody to be serious, to anchor it. I always have to find the anchor. I have to find the Greek chorus in the play, the character who either literally talks to the audience or talks to the audience in a sense. For example, Oscar in *The Odd Couple* is the Greek chorus. He watches, he perceives how Oscar behaves, and he comments on it. Felix then comments back on what Oscar is, but Oscar is the one who is telling us what the play is about. More recently, in the Brighton Beach trilogy, I've been *literally* talking to the audience, through the character of Eugene, because it is the only way I can express the writer's viewpoint. The writer has inner thoughts, and they are not always articulated on the stage—and I want the audience to be able to get inside his head. It's what I did in *Jake's Women*. In the first try out in San Diego the audience didn't know enough about Jake because all he did was react to the women in his life, who were badgering him, trying to get him to open up. We didn't know who Jake was. So I introduced the device of him talking to the audience. Then he became the fullest, richest character in the play, because the audience knew things I never thought I would reveal about Jake—and possibly about myself.

Interviewer: Will you return to the *Show of Shows* play?
Simon: I do very often think about doing it. What was unique about that experience was that almost every one of the writers has gone on to do really major things: Mel Brooks's whole career . . . Larry Gelbart . . . Woody Allen . . . Joe Stein who wrote *Fiddler on the Roof* . . . Michael Stewart who wrote *Hello, Dolly!* . . . it was a group of people only Sid Caesar knew how to put together. Maybe it was trial and error because the ones who didn't work fell out, but once we worked together it was the most excruciatingly hilarious time in my life. It was also one of the most painful because you were fighting for recognition, and there was no recognition. It was very difficult for me because I was quiet and shy, so I sat next to Carl Reiner and whispered my jokes to him. He was my spokesman, he'd jump up and say, "He's got it! He's got it!" Then Carl would say the line, and I would hear it, and I'd laugh because I thought it was funny. But when I watched the show on a Saturday night with my wife, Joan, she'd say, "That was your line, wasn't it?" and I'd say, "I don't remember." What I *do* remember is the screaming and fighting—a cocktail party without the cocktails, everyone yelling lines in and out, people getting very angry at others who were slacking off. Mel Brooks was the main culprit. We all came in to work at ten o'clock in the morning, but he showed up at one o'clock. We'd say, "That's it. We're sick and tired of this. Either Mel comes in at ten o'clock or we go to Sid and do something about it." At about ten to one, Mel would come in with a straw hat, fling it across the room and say "Lindy made it!" and everyone would fall down hysterical. He didn't need the eight hours we put in. He needed four hours. He is, maybe, the most uniquely funny man I've ever met. That inspired me. I wanted to be around those people. I've fooled around with this idea for a play. I even found a title for it, *Laughter on the 23rd Floor*, because I think the office was on the twenty-third floor. From that building we looked down on Bendel's and Bergdorf Goodman and Fifth Avenue, watching all the pretty girls go by through binoculars. Sometimes we'd set fire to the desk with lighter fluid. We should have been arrested, all of us.

Interviewer: If you ever get past page twenty-two, how would you deal with Mel and Woody and the others? Would they appear as themselves?
Simon: No, no, no! They'd all be fictitious. It would be like the Brighton Beach trilogy, which is semi-autobiographical.

Interviewer: It feels totally autobiographical. I assumed it was.

Simon: Everyone does. But I've told interviewers that if I meant it to be autobiographical I would have called the character Neil Simon. He's not Neil. He's Eugene Jerome. That gives you greater latitude for fiction. It's like doing abstract painting. You see your own truth in it, but the abstraction is the art.

Interviewer: When did you realize there was a sequel to *Brighton Beach Memoirs*?

Simon: It got a middling review from Frank Rich of the *New York Times*, but he said at the end of it, "One hopes that there is a chapter two to *Brighton Beach*." I thought, he's asking for a sequel to a play that he doesn't seem to like!

Interviewer: Are you saying Frank Rich persuaded you to write *Biloxi Blues*?

Simon: No, but I listened to him saying, "I'm interested enough to want to know more about this family." Then, Steven Spielberg, who had gone to see *Brighton Beach*, got word to me, suggesting the next play should be about my days in the army. I was already thinking about that, and I started to write *Biloxi Blues*, which became a play about Eugene's rites of passage. I discovered something very important in the writing of *Biloxi Blues*. Eugene, who keeps a diary, writes in it his belief that Epstein is homosexual. When the other boys in the barracks read the diary and assume it's true, Eugene feels terrible guilt. He's realized the responsibility of putting something down on paper, because people tend to believe everything they read.

Interviewer: *The Counterfeiters* ends with the diary André Gide kept while he was writing the book, and in it he says he knows he's writing well when the dialectic of the scene takes over, and the characters seize the scene from him, and he's become not a writer but a *reader.* Do you sometimes find that your characters have taken the play away from you and are off in their own direction?

Simon: I've *always* felt like a middleman, like the typist. Somebody somewhere else is saying, "This is what they say now. This is what they say next." Very often it is the characters themselves, once they become clearly defined. When I was working on my first play, *Come Blow Your Horn*, I was told by fellow writers that you must outline your play, you must know where you're going. I wrote a complete, detailed outline from page one to the end of the play. In the writing of the play, I didn't get past page fifteen when the characters started to move away from the outline. I tried to pull them back

in, saying, "Get back in there. This is where you belong. I've already dia-
grammed your life." They said, "No, no, no. This is where I want to go." So, I
started following them. In the second play, *Barefoot in the Park*, I outlined
the first two acts. I said, "I'll leave the third act a free-for-all, so I can go
where I want." I never got through that outline either. In *The Odd Couple*,
I outlined the first act. After a while I got tired of doing even that. I said, "I
want to be as surprised as anyone else." I had also read a book on playwriting by John van Druten, in which he said, "Don't outline your play, because
then the rest of it will just be work. It should be joy. You should be discovering things the way the audience discovers them." So, I stopped doing it.

Interviewer: Gide writes about being surprised by the material coming up on
the typewriter. He finds himself laughing, shocked, sometimes dismayed . . .
Simon: Sometimes I start laughing—and I've had moments in this office
when I've burst into tears. Not that I thought the audience might do that.
The moment had triggered a memory or a feeling that was deeply hidden.
That's catharsis. It's one of the main reasons I write the plays. It's like analysis without going to the analyst. The play becomes your analysis. The writing of the play is the most enjoyable part of it. It's also the most frightening
part because you walk into a forest without a knife, without a compass. But
if your instincts are good, if you have a sense of geography, you find that
you're clearing a path and getting to the right place. If the miracle happens,
you come out at the very place you *wanted* to. But very often you have to go
back to the beginning of the forest and start walking through it again, saying, "I went that way. It was a dead end." You cross out, cross over. You meet
new friends along the way, people you never thought you'd meet. It takes
you into a world you hadn't planned on going to when you started the play.
The play may have started out to be a comedy, and suddenly you get into
a place of such depth that it surprises you. As one critic aptly said, I wrote
Brighton Beach Memoirs about the family I *wished* I'd had instead of the
family I *did* have. It's closer to *Ah, Wilderness!* than my reality.

Interviewer: When did you realize that *Brighton Beach Memoirs* and *Biloxi
Blues* were part of a trilogy?
Simon: I thought it seemed odd to leave the Eugene saga finished after
two plays. Three is a trilogy—I don't even know what two plays are called.
So, I decided to write the third one, and the idea came immediately. It was
back to the war theme again, only these were domestic wars. The boys
were having guilts and doubts about leaving home for a career writing

comedy. Against this played the war between the parents. I also brought in the character of the socialist grandfather who was constantly telling the boys, "You can't just write jokes and make people laugh." Against this came Blanche from the first play, *Brighton Beach*, trying to get the grandfather to move to Florida to take care of his aging, ill wife. To me, setting people in conflict with each other is like what those Chinese jugglers do, spinning one plate, then another, then another. I wanted to keep as many plates spinning as I could.

Interviewer: What exactly do you mean when you call the Brighton Beach trilogy semi-autobiographical?

Simon: It means the play may be based on incidents that happened in my life—but they're not written the way they happened. *Broadway Bound* comes closest to being really autobiographical. I didn't pull any punches with that one. My mother and father were gone when I wrote it, so I did tell about the fights, and what it was like for me as a kid hearing them. I didn't realize until someone said after the first reading that the play was really a love letter to my mother! She suffered the most in all of it. She was the one that was left alone. Her waxing that table didn't exist in life, but it exists symbolically for *me*. It's the abstraction I was talking about.

Interviewer: Speaking of abstraction, there's something mystifying to audiences—and other writers—about what the great comedy writers do. From outside, it seems to be as different from what most writers are able to do as baseball is from ballet. I'm not going to ask anything quite as fatuous as "What is humor?" but I *am* asking—is it genetic, is it a mind-set, a quirk? And, most important, can it be learned—or, for that matter, taught?

Simon: The answer is complex. First of all, there are various styles and attitudes towards comedy. When I worked on *Your Show of Shows*, Larry Gelbart was the wittiest, cleverest man I'd ever met, Mel Brooks the most outrageous. I never knew what I was. I *still* don't know. Maybe I had the best sense of construction of the group. I only know some aspects of my humor, one of which involves being completely literal. To give you an example, in *Lost in Yonkers*, Uncle Louie is trying to explain the heartless grandmother to Arty. "When she was twelve years old, her old man takes her to a political rally in Berlin. A horse goes down and crushes Ma's foot. Nobody ever fixed it. It hurts every day of her life, but I never once seen her take even an aspirin." Later, Arty says to his older brother, "I'm afraid of her, Jay. A horse fell on her when she was a kid, and she hasn't taken an aspirin yet." It's an almost exact repetition of what Louie told him and this time it gets a huge laugh. That mystifies me. In *Prisoner of Second Avenue*, you knew there were terrible things tormenting Peter Falk. He sat down on a sofa that had stacks of pillows, like every sofa in the world, and he took one pillow after the other and started throwing them angrily saying, "You pay eight hundred dollars for a sofa, and you can't sit on it because you got ugly little pillows shoved up your back!" There is no joke there. Yet, it was an enormous laugh—because the audience identified. That, more or less, is what is funny to me: saying something that's instantly identifiable to everybody. People come up to you after the show and say, "I've always thought that, but I never knew anyone *else* thought it." It's a shared secret between you and the audience.

Interviewer: You've often said that you've never consciously written a joke in one of your plays.
Simon: I try never to think of jokes as jokes. I confess that in the early days, when I came from television, plays like *Come Blow Your Horn* would have lines you could lift out that would be funny in themselves. That to me would be a "joke," which I would try to remove. In *The Odd Couple* Oscar had a line about Felix, "He's so panicky he wears his seatbelt at a drive-in movie." That could be a Bob Hope joke. I left it in because I couldn't find anything to replace it.

Interviewer: Have you ever found that a producer, director, or actor objected to losing a huge laugh that you were determined to cut from the play?
Simon: An actor, perhaps, yes. They'll say, "But that's my big laugh." I say, "But it hurts the scene." It's very hard to convince them. Walter Matthau was after me constantly on *The Odd Couple*, complaining not about one of his lines, but one of Art Carney's. He'd say, "It's not a good line." A few days later, I received a letter from a doctor in Wilmington. It said, "Dear Mr. Simon, I loved your play, but I find one line really objectionable. I wish you would take it out." So, I took the line out and said, "Walter, I've complied with your wishes. I got a letter from a prominent doctor in Wilmington who didn't like the line . . ." He started to laugh, and then I realized, "You son of a bitch, *you're* the doctor!" And he was. Those quick lines, the one-liners attributed to me for so many years—*I* think they come purely out of character, rather than out of a joke. Walter Kerr once came to my aid by saying "to be or not to be" is a one-liner. If it's a dramatic moment no one calls it a one-liner. If it's gets a laugh, suddenly it's a one-liner. I think one of the complaints of critics is that the people in my plays are funnier than

they would be in life, but have you ever seen *Medea*? The characters are a lot more dramatic in that than they are in life.

Interviewer: You've also said that when you began writing for the theater you decided to try to write comedy the way dramatists write plays—writing from the characters out, internally, psychologically . . .

Simon: Yes. What I try to do is make dialogue come purely out of character, so that one character could never say the lines that belong to another character. If it's funny, it's because I'm telling a story about characters in whom I may find a rich vein of humor. When I started writing plays I was warned by people like Lillian Hellman, "You do not mix comedy with drama." But my theory was, if it's mixed in life, why can't you do it in a play? The very first person I showed *Come Blow Your Horn* to was Herman Shumlin, the director of Hellman's *The Little Foxes*. He said, "I like the play, I like the people, but I don't like the older brother." I said, "What's wrong with him?" He said, "Well, it's a comedy. We have to like everybody." I said, "In *life* do we have to like everybody?" In the most painful scene in *Lost in Yonkers*, Bella, who is semi-retarded, is trying to tell the family that the boy she wants to marry is also retarded. It's a poignant situation, and yet the information that slowly comes out—and the way the family is third-degreeing her—becomes hilarious, because it's mixed with someone else's pain. I find that what is most poignant is often most funny.

Interviewer: In the roll-call scene in *Biloxi Blues* you riff for several pages on one word, one *syllable*: "Ho." It builds and builds in what I've heard you call a "run."

Simon: I learned from watching Chaplin films that what's most funny isn't a single moment of laughter but the moments that come on top of it, and on top of *those*. I learned it from the Laurel and Hardy films too. One of the funniest things I ever saw Laurel and Hardy do was try to undress in the upper berth of a train—together. It took ten minutes, getting the arms in the wrong sleeves and their feet caught in the net, one terrible moment leading to another. I thought, there could be no greater satisfaction for me than to do that to an audience. Maybe "Ho" also came from sitting in the dark as a kid, listening to Jack Benny's running gags on the radio. In *Barefoot in the Park*, when the telephone man comes up five or six flights of stairs, he arrives completely out of breath. When Paul makes *his* entrance, *he's* completely out of breath. When the mother makes her entrance, *she's* completely out of breath. Some critics have written, "You milk that out-of-breath joke too much." My answer is, "You mean because it's happened three times, when they come up the fourth time they shouldn't be out of breath anymore?" It's *not* a joke, it's the natural thing. Like "Ho." Those boys are petrified on their first day in the army, confronted by this maniac sergeant.

Interviewer: Do you pace the lines so the laughs don't cover the dialogue or is that the director's job? Do you try to set up a rhythm in the writing that will allow for the audience's response?

Simon: You don't know where the laughs are until you get in front of an audience. Most of the biggest laughs I've ever had I never knew were big laughs. Mike Nichols used to say to me, "Take out all the little laughs because they hurt the big ones." Sometimes the little laughs aren't even *meant* to be laughs. I mean them to further the play, the plot, the character, the story. They're written unwittingly . . . strange word to pick. I cut them, and the laugh pops up somewhere else.

Interviewer: When did you first realize you were funny?

Simon: It started very early in my life—eight, nine, ten years old—being funny around the other kids. You single out one kid on your block or in the school who understands what you're saying. He's the only one who laughs. The other kids only laugh when someone tells them a joke: "Two guys got on a truck . . ." I've never done that in my life. I don't like telling jokes. I don't like to hear someone say to me, "Tell him that funny thing you said the other day." It's repeating it. I have no more joy in it. Once it's said, for me it's over. The same is true once it's written—I have no more interest in it. I've expelled whatever it is I needed to exorcise, whether it's humorous or painful. Generally, painful. Maybe the humor is to cover the pain up, or maybe it's a way to share the experience with someone.

Interviewer: Has psychoanalysis influenced your work?

Simon: Yes. Generally I've gone into analysis when my life was in turmoil. But I found after a while I was going when it *wasn't* in turmoil. I was going to get a college education in human behavior. I was talking not only about myself; I was trying to understand my wife, my brother, my children, my family, anybody—including the analyst. I can't put everything in the plays down to pure chance. I want them to reveal what makes people tick. I tend to analyze almost everything. I don't think it started because I went through analysis. I'm just naturally that curious. The good mechanic knows how to take a car apart; I love to take the human mind apart and see how it works.

Behavior is absolutely the most interesting thing I can write about. You put that behavior in conflict, and you're in business.

Interviewer: Would you describe your writing process? Since you don't use an outline, do you ever know how a play will end?

Simon: Sometimes I think I do—but it doesn't mean that's how the play *will* end. Very often you find that you've written past the end, and you say, "Wait a minute, it ended *here*." When I started to write *Plaza Suite* it was going to be a full three-act play. The first act was about a wife who rents the same suite she and her husband honeymooned in at the Plaza Hotel twenty-three years ago. In the course of the act the wife finds out that the husband is having an affair with his secretary, and at the end of the act the husband walks out the door as champagne and hors d'oeuvres arrive. The waiter asks, "Is he coming back?" and the wife says, "Funny you should ask that." I wrote that and said to myself, "That's the end of the play, I don't want to *know* if he's coming back." That's what made me write three one-act plays for *Plaza Suite*. I don't *like* to know where the play is going to end. I purposely won't think of the ending because I'm afraid, if I know, even subliminally, it'll sneak into the script, and the audience will know where the play is going. As a matter of fact, I never know where the play is going in the *second act*. When *Broadway Bound* was completed, I listened to the first reading and thought, there's not a moment in this entire play where I see the mother happy. She's a miserable woman. I want to know *why* she's miserable. The answer was planted in the beginning of the play: the mother kept talking about how no one believed she once danced with George Raft. I thought, the boy should ask her to talk about George Raft, and as she does, she'll reveal everything in her past.

Interviewer: The scene ends with the now-famous moment of the boy dancing with the mother the way Raft did—*if* he did.

Simon: Yes. People have said, "It's so organic, you had to have known you were writing to that all the time." But I *didn't* know it when I sat down to write the play. I had an interesting problem when I was writing *"Rumors."* I started off with just a basic premise: I wanted to do an elegant farce. I wrote it right up to the last two pages of the play, the denouement in which everything has to be explained—and I didn't know what it was! I said to myself, "Today's the day I have to write the explanation. All right, just think it out." I *couldn't* think it out. So I said, "Well then, go sentence by sentence." I couldn't write it sentence by sentence. I said, "Go word by word. The man sits down and tells the police the story. He starts off with, 'It was six o'clock.'" That much I could write. I kept going until everything made sense. That method takes either insanity or egocentricity—or a great deal of confidence. It's like building a bridge over water without knowing if there's land on the other side. But I do have confidence that when I get to the end of the play, I will have gotten so deeply into the characters and the situation I'll find the resolution.

Interviewer: So you never write backwards from a climactic event to the incidents and scenes at the beginning of the play that will take you to it?

Simon: Never. The linkages are done by instinct. Sometimes I'll write something and say, "Right now this doesn't mean very much, but I have a hunch that later on in the play it will mean something." The thing I always do is play back on things I set up without any intention in the beginning. The foundation of the play is set in those first fifteen or twenty minutes. Whenever I get in trouble in the second act, I go back to the first act. The answers always lie there. One of the lines people have most often accused me of working backwards from is Felix Ungar's note to Oscar in *The Odd Couple*. In the second act, Oscar has reeled off the laundry list of complaints he has about Felix, including "the little letters you leave me." Now, when Felix is leaving one of those notes, telling Oscar they're all out of cornflakes, I said to myself, "How would he sign it? I know he'd do something that would annoy Oscar." So I signed it "Mr. Ungar." Then I tried "Felix Ungar." Then I tried "F.U." and it was as if a bomb had exploded in the room. When Oscar says, "It took me three hours to figure out that F.U. was Felix Ungar," it always gets this huge laugh.

Interviewer: Felix Ungar also appears in *Come Blow Your Horn*. I wanted to ask why you used the name twice.

Simon: This will give you an indication of how little I thought my career would amount to. I thought *The Odd Couple* would probably be the end of my career, so it wouldn't make any difference that I had used Felix Ungar in *Come Blow Your Horn*. It was a name that seemed to denote the prissiness of Felix, the perfect contrast to the name of Oscar. Oscar may not sound like a strong name, but it did to me—maybe because of the *K* sound in it.

Interviewer: So you subscribe to the *K*-theory expressed by the comedians in *The Sunshine Boys*—*K* is funny.

Simon: Oh, I do. Not only that, *K* cuts through the theater. You say a *K*-word, and they can hear it.

Interviewer: Let's talk about the mechanics of writing, starting with where you write.

Simon: I have this office. There are four or five rooms in it, and no one is here but me. No secretary, no one, and I've never once in the many years that I've come here ever felt lonely, or even alone. I come in and the room is filled with—as corny as it might sound—these characters I'm writing, who are waiting each day for me to arrive and give them life. I've also written on airplanes, in dentist's offices, on subways. I think it's true for many writers. You blank out whatever is in front of your eyes. That's why you see writers staring off into space. They're not looking at "nothing," they're visualizing what they're thinking. I never visualize what a play will look like on stage, I visualize what it looks like in *life*. I visualize being in that room where the mother is confronting the father.

Interviewer: What tools do you use? Do you use a 1928 Underwood the way real writers are supposed to? Or a computer? You mentioned using a pad and pencil . . .

Simon: I wrote my early plays at the typewriter because it was what writers looked like in *His Girl Friday.*

Interviewer: Lots of crumpled pages being flung across the room?

Simon: Yes. But my back started to get so bad from bending over a typewriter eight hours a day, five or six days a week that I couldn't do it anymore, so I started to write in pads. Then a curious thing happened. I was in England and found that they have pads over there with longer pages and thinner spaces between the lines. I liked that because I could get much more on a single page. At a single glance I could see the rhythm of the speeches. If they're on a smaller page with wide spaces you don't get a sense of the rhythm. You have to keep turning. So, I write in these pads. Sometimes I write on both sides of the page, but I always leave myself lots of room to make notes and cross things out. I'll write about three pages, then go to the typewriter and type that out. Then the next day I'll read those three pages again and maybe not like them, and go back to the notebook—write it out, make changes, and then retype it. The typing is boring for me, but I can't use a word processor. It feels inhuman. It seems to me that every script comes out of a computer looking like it was written by the same person. My typewriter has its own characteristics, its own little foibles. Even there, I black out parts and write marginal notes. I'd like it to be neat, but I don't like to send it to a professional typist because they invariably correct my purposely made grammatical errors. I try to write the way people speak, not the way people *should* speak.

Interviewer: When you're writing dialogue, do you write it silently or speak it aloud?
Simon: I never *thought* I spoke the lines until my family told me I did. They said they could walk by and tell if it was going well or not by the rhythm of it. I guess I want to see if I'm repeating words, and, because I write primarily for the stage, I want to make sure the words won't be tripping badly over some tongues.

Interviewer: Do you play the parts, I mean, *really* play them and get into them?
Simon: Yes. When I wrote the Sergeant Bilko show my father asked me naively, "Do you just write Sergeant Bilko's lines or do you write the other lines too?" When you write a play, maybe even a novel, you become *everybody*. It may seem like I only write the lines spoken by the character who is like Neil Simon, but, in *Lost in Yonkers*, I'm also the grandmother—and Bella. And to do that you have to *become* that person. That's the adventure, the joy, the release that allows you to escape from your own boundaries. To be Grandma every other line for a couple of pages takes you into another being. It's interesting how many people ask, "Was this your grandmother?" I say, "No, I didn't have a grandmother like that," and they say, "Then how do you know her?" I know what she *sounds* like. I know what she *feels* like. The boys describe it when they say, "When you kiss her it's like kissing a cold prune." I describe her in a stage direction as being a very tall, buxom woman. But she doesn't necessarily have to be tall and buxom. She just has to appear that way to the boys. You can't really use that as physical description, but it will convey something to the actress.

Interviewer: And to the actors playing the two boys.
Simon: Yes. Those directions are very important.

Interviewer: Family seems to be more than a predilection or interest, it is a near obsession with you. Even if you're writing about a couple, in comes an extended family of friends or the blood-related aunts, uncles, cousins, fathers, and mothers with which your plays abound. Is that because family has played such an important role, for good and ill, in your life?
Simon: Well, for one thing, it's a universal subject. For example, when *Come Blow Your Horn* was playing, the theater doorman, a black man in his sixties,

was standing in the back of the theater, laughing his head off. I went over to him after the play and asked, "Why were you laughing so much?" He said, "That's my family up there." I don't write social and political plays, because I've always thought the family was the microcosm of what goes on in the world. I write about the small wars that eventually become the big wars. It's also what I'm most comfortable with. I am a middle-class person, I grew up in a middle-class neighborhood. I try now and then to get away from the family play, but it amazes me that I've spent the last thirty-one years writing plays primarily about either my family or families very close to it. Maybe the answer is that at some point along the way you discover what it is you do best, and writing about the family unit and its extensions is what I do best.

Interviewer: Your introduction to the first published collection of your work is called "The Writer as Schizophrenic." The word *observer* comes up repeatedly in your conversation, your interviews, and, especially, in your plays. Have you always seen yourself as an outsider, an observer?
Simon: Yes, that started very early, when my parents would take me to visit family. They'd offer me a cookie or a piece of fruit, but no one *spoke* to me, because they knew I had nothing to contribute. I wasn't offended. I just thought it was the accepted norm. And that led me to believe that I was somehow invisible. On radio shows like *The Shadow*, there *were* invisible people. And movies were coming out—*The Invisible Man*, with Claude Rains. To me, invisible seemed the greatest thing you could be! If I could have one wish, it was to be invisible. First of all, you could go to any baseball game you wanted to. Free. You could go into any girl's house and watch her get undressed! But it works another way too. It means there's no responsibility. You don't have to integrate, to contribute. This becomes a part of your personality.

Interviewer: Does that detachment apply to your personal relationships as pervasively as to your work?
Simon: I'm not quite sure who I am besides the writer. The writer is expressive, the other person can sit in a room and listen and not say anything. It's very hard for me to get those two people together. In the middle of a conversation or a confrontation, I can suddenly step outside it. It's like Jekyll turning into Mr. Hyde without the necessity of taking the potion. It's why the Eugene character speaks to the audience in the trilogy: because, in a sense, he is invisible. The other characters in the play don't see him talking to the audience. They go right about their business. As I wrote it, I thought: I'm now living my perfect dream—to be invisible.

Interviewer: In *Barefoot in the Park,* Corie says, "Do you know what you are? You're a watcher. There are watchers in the world, and there are doers, and the watchers sit around watching the doers do."

Simon: In all three of my marriages I've been accused of this separation. "You're not listening to me. You're not looking at me." When you asked about where I write, I said anywhere. I just stare into space. That's happened when I was talking to my wife. I could be looking at her and not thinking about what she's saying. It's rude. It's selfish, I guess. But it's what happens; some other thought has taken its place. One of the worst and most frightening examples of that was the first time I was ever on television. I went on the Johnny Carson show. I was standing behind that curtain, hearing them give my credits. Then they said, "And here he is, the prolific playwright, Neil Simon." I walked out and froze. I thought, my God, I'm out here, I've got to deliver something, I've got to be humorous, that's what they expect of me. I sat down opposite Johnny Carson, and he asked his first question, which was fairly lengthy. After the first two words I heard *nothing.* I only saw his lips moving. I said to myself, "I've got all this time not to do anything. In other words, while his lips are moving, I'm all right." So, my mind just wandered. I was looking around, saying, "Well, forty million people are watching me, I wonder if my brother's going to watch this, what's he going to think of it?" When Johnny's lips stopped, I was on. But I had no answer because I'd never heard the question. So, I said something like, "That reminds me of something Johnny," and went into something completely irrelevant that fortunately was funny, and we just seemed to move on with the conversation. It happens while I'm speaking to students at a college or university. I'll be talking. I'll look over the room and see one face not interested, and I'm gone, I'm lost. I wish I were out there, sitting among the invisible, but I'm up there having to deliver. The demands of coming up with something every minute are difficult. In a sense, being in this office, I am invisible because I can stop. When I'm writing, there's no pressure to come up with the next line. I always need that escape hatch, that place to go that's within myself. I've tried coming to terms with it. I feel, as long as it doesn't bother someone else, I'm happy with it. When it *does* bother someone else, then I'm in trouble.

Interviewer: And your characters share this watcher/doer problem?

Simon: Felix in *The Odd Couple* isn't a watcher—or a doer. He's stuck. He's reached a certain point in his life and developed no further. *Most* of my characters are people who are stuck and can't move. The grandmother in

Lost in Yonkers has been stuck for the last seventy years. The mother in *Broadway Bound*—she's *really* stuck.

Interviewer: I remember George in *Chapter Two* saying, "I'm stuck, Jennie . . . I'm just stuck some place in my mind, and it's driving me crazy." Going back to *Barefoot in the Park*, Corie's pretty hard on your surrogate Neil when she tells him he's not a doer. But, come to think of it, what could be more venturesome and brave—or foolhardy—than the real Neil opening a play on Broadway and exposing it to the critics and the audience?
Simon: It *is* the most frightening thing in the world—and it was almost a matter of life and death for Joan and me with *Come Blow Your Horn*. If it had failed I would have been forced to move to California and become a comedy writer in television. But I don't worry about it anymore, and I think not being fearful of what's going to happen has allowed me to write so much. If I *do* worry, I say I won't do the play, because that means I don't think it's that good.

Interviewer: Is the opposite true? Can you anticipate a hit?
Simon: I never think of the plays as being hits when I write them. Well, I thought *"Rumors,"* of all plays, would be a really good commercial comedy if I wrote it well. I thought *The Odd Couple* was a black comedy. I never thought it was going to be popular, ever.

Interviewer: It's your most popular play, isn't it? All over the world.
Simon: Yes. And I thought it was a grim, dark play about two lonely men. I thought *The Sunshine Boys* wouldn't be a popular play, but it was very well received. *Chapter Two* was another one I doubted, because when you touch on a character's guilt, you touch on the *audience's* guilt, and that makes them uncomfortable. Yet the play turned out to be very successful because it was a universal theme. *Lost in Yonkers* is an enormous success, but I thought I was writing the bleakest of plays. What I liked about it was that I thought it was Dickensian: two young boys left in the hands of dreadful people. What I was afraid of was that I would hear words like *melodrama*.

Interviewer: You heard "Pulitzer Prize." There are several plays that don't seem to fit in your canon. In plays like *The Good Doctor*, *"Rumors,"* *Fools*, and *God's Favorite* you seem to have a different agenda, there's a different relationship between you and the play than the one you've described. Could that explain their lack of critical and popular success?

Simon: I wrote *The Good Doctor* soon after I learned my wife had a year and a half to live. She didn't know that. On the advice of the doctors, I'd elected not to tell her, and I wanted to keep on working, so it would seem to her that everything was normal. I was reading Chekhov's short stories and decided, just for practice, to translate one of them into my own language, my own humor. I knew it was a diversion. After a performance, a woman grabbed me in the foyer and said, "This is not Neil Simon!" *Fools* was an experiment that didn't work. *God's Favorite* is an absurdist black comedy about Job that was written as on outcry of anger against Joan's death. My belief in God had vanished when this beautiful young girl was dying. I wasn't Archibald MacLeish. I thought it would be pretentious for me to try to write something like a dramatic *J.B.* So, I wrote it as a black comedy, and it did help me get through that period. Sometimes you write a play just for the sake of working at it. It's my craft. I'm allowed to go in any direction I want. I hate being pushed into certain places. Walter Kerr once wrote that he thought I was successful because I didn't listen to what was in fashion in the theater and went my own way at my peril, and that sometimes I suffered for it, and at other times I broke through. With *Lost in Yonkers* I suddenly heard from critics who said, "This is a new voice for Neil Simon. We want you to go deeper and deeper into this area." At the same time other critics complained, "I don't like this as much. It's not as funny as the old plays." They wanted *Barefoot in the Park* and *The Odd Couple.* I could have spent my whole life writing the *Barefoot in the Parks* and *Odd Couples*, which I certainly don't denigrate, because I love them—but, where would I have gone with my life? I would have been standing still, grinding out the same story time after time after time. What I've done, I think, is take the best of me and the best of my observations and try to deepen them to reform them and reflesh them. At some point along the way you discover what it is you do best. Recently I've been reading Samuel Beckett's biography. When he was about forty-four years old, he said he wanted to write monologue. It was his way of expressing himself to the world. *He* was shy, too. In a sense, I think many of my plays are dramatized monologues. It's like sitting around the fire and telling you the story of my life and my father and my mother and my cousins and my aunts. In *Lost in Yonkers* I know I'm *one* of those two boys, probably the younger one. Who that grandmother is, who Aunt Bella is, with her adolescent mind, I don't know.

Interviewer: You seem to be saying that *Lost in Yonkers* is even less autobiographical than the Brighton Beach trilogy.

Simon: I'd say *Lost in Yonkers* isn't autobiographical at all. You asked me earlier whether I write thematic plays. I don't, but I have a feeling that in *Lost in Yonkers* there was a theme within me that was crying to get out, a common denominator that got to everybody. In the last fifteen, twenty years, a phrase has come into prominence that didn't exist in my childhood: dysfunctional family. My mother's and father's constant breakups seemed to show little concern for my brother and me. It was like coming from *five* broken families. That pain lingers. Writing plays is a way of working out your life. That's why I can never conceive of stopping, because I would stop the investigation of who I am and what I am.

Interviewer: You have the reputation of being a tireless, even an eager, rewriter. How much of the rewriting is done during the first drafts of the play, and how much do you rewrite after the play has gone into rehearsal?

Simon: I would say that I do no fewer than three to four major rewrites on a play before we go into rehearsal. I write the play, put it aside, take it out six months later, read it. By then I've forgotten everything about the play. It's as though someone had sent it to me in the mail and I'm reading it for the first time. I can tell right away what I don't and do like. That becomes a very easy rewrite: you just get rid of the stuff you don't like. Then we start auditions for actors, so I keep hearing the words every day. After a while I can't stand some of them, and I start to rewrite, so, in later auditions, the actors get a better script to read. I finally say it's the last draft before we go into rehearsal, and we have a reading of the play in a room with just the producer, director, and a few of the other people who will work on the play, one month before rehearsal. At that reading we have the entire cast, so now I know what it's going to sound like. Based on that reading, I'll do another major rewrite. It's rare that I would ever do what they do in musicals: "Why don't we switch scene four and scene two?" I write in a linear way, so that everything falls apart if you take anything out. Sometimes, if even a few sentences come out of the play, something suffers for it later on. Once the play opens out of town, the most important rewriting begins, based on not only the audience's and the out-of-town critics' reactions, but the reactions of ourselves, the actors, and some people we've invited to see the play and comment. I also listen—if I can, to the audience's comments on the way out of the theater. That becomes harder now that I've lost my invisibility.

Interviewer: How do you remain objective with all those voices in your ear?

Simon: Mostly it's my own intuition. I bring in rewrites no one has asked for. I'll suddenly come in with five pages, and the director and the actors will say, "You didn't like the other stuff?" I'll say, "I think this is better." If you bring in seven pages, maybe three will work. That's a big percentage. You're way ahead of the game. An analogy for it would be if you were in college and took a test, and your grade came back. You got a 63 on the test, and they say, "Come back tomorrow. You'll be given the exact same test. There'll be no new questions." Well, you're going to get an 84 on the second test. You'll have had chances to fix it. That's what happens to a play. Day by day, it gets better and better. In the case of *Jake's Women*, in the first production a couple of years ago, there were a lot of things wrong. It was miscast, I had a director I was unfamiliar with who didn't really understand my process. We opened with a play that was about a 62 on a possible grade of 100. I brought the play up to about a 78. As we got toward the end of the run, just prior to going to New York, I thought, you can't get by in New York with a 78. You need at least a 96 or 97. So, I said to everyone, let's just pull it. And we did. I thought it was dead forever, because I'd put so much into it and wasn't able to save it. Two years later I took another crack at it and did a major rewrite in which, as I've told you, I had Jake speak to the audience. The play took a whole new turn. I thought it was finally up in the 90-percent bracket.

Interviewer: If a play is truly flawed, how much can you do to improve it?

Simon: Well, in the case of something like *The Gingerbread Lady*, which *was* a flawed play, the producer was going to put up a closing notice in Boston. Maureen Stapleton, who was starring in the play, came to me and said, "If you close this play I'll never speak to you again." She said, "This is a potentially wonderful play. It needs work but don't walk away from it!" I thought, what a reasonable thing to say, because all it amounted to was more of my time. The producer said he wanted to close, to save me "from the slings and arrows of the critics in New York." I said, "I can take the slings and arrows. I've had enough success up to now. I'll *learn* from this one." What finally made up my mind, after reading three terrible reviews in Boston, was, while waiting at the airport for my plane, I picked up the *Christian Science Monitor*, and the review was a letter addressed to me. It said, "Dear Neil Simon, I know you're probably going to want to close this play, but I beg of you, don't do it. This is potentially the best play you have written. You're going into a whole new genre, a whole new mode of writing. Don't abandon it." So, I called the producer and said, "Please don't close the play. Let's run in Boston and see what happens." Then, I didn't want to get on a plane and arrive in New York an hour later; I wanted a four-hour trip on a train, so I could start the rewrite.

By the time I got to New York I had rewritten fifteen pages of the play. I stayed in New York for a week and came back with about thirty-five new pages. And we went to work. The play was never a major success, but we did have a year's run, and sold it to the movies. Maureen Stapleton won the Tony Award, and Marsha Mason, who played the lead in the film version, got an Oscar nomination. So, something good came out of persevering.

Interviewer: Your plays have become darker in the last several years. Is this a sign of maturity or a wish to be taken seriously, since comedy generally isn't as highly regarded as so-called "serious plays?"

Simon: Maybe the plays matured because *I* matured. I *do* want to be taken more seriously, yet I want to hear the laughter in the theater. The laughs are very often the same gratification to the audience as letting themselves cry. They're interchangeable emotions.

Interviewer: Most of the darker plays take place in your childhood. Does that mean that your childhood was dark, or that your view of your childhood and perhaps of the world has darkened as you've matured?

Simon: My view of my childhood was always dark, but my view of the world has darkened considerably. The darkness in my plays reflects the way the world is *now*. The darkness in the plays, strangely enough, seems more beautiful to me. I think anything that is truthful has beauty in it. Life without the dark times is unrealistic. I don't want to write unrealistically anymore.

Interviewer: What do you consider your strongest suit as a writer? And what in your view is your weakest suit?

Simon: I think my blue suit is my weakest.

Interviewer: I knew it would come to this.

Simon: I think my greatest weakness is that I can't write outside of my own experience. I'm not like Paddy Chayefsky who could go off and do six months of research and then write something extremely believable. I'd *like* to write about Michelangelo, but I don't *know* Michelangelo. I don't know what his life was like. I wish I could extend myself, but I don't think that's going to happen. I might play around with it from time to time. Those are the ones that wind up in the drawer.

Interviewer: If you ever have a fire sale of the contents of that drawer, call me. What would you say is your particular strength?

Simon: I think it's construction. Maybe what I write is outmoded today, the "well-made play"—a play that tells you what the problem is, then shows you how it affects everybody, then resolves it. Resolution doesn't mean a happy ending—what I've been accused of. I don't think I write happy endings. Sometimes I have *hopeful* endings, sometimes optimistic ones. I try never to end the play with two people in each other's arms—unless it's a musical. When I was writing three-act plays, a producer told me the curtain should always come down on the beginning of the fourth act. A play should never really come to an end. The audience should leave saying, "What's going to happen to them now?" As the plays progressed, some people wanted darker endings. Some critics even said the ending of *Lost in Yonkers* wasn't dark enough. But I can't write a play as dark and bleak and wonderful as *A Streetcar Named Desire.* I fall in some gray area. There is so much comedy within the dramas or so much drama within the comedies.

Interviewer: In her interview for the *Paris Review*, Dorothy Parker said she got her character names from the telephone book and obituary columns. Do you have a system for naming *your* characters?
Simon: There was a time I used to take baseball players' names. The famous ones were too obvious, so you had to take names like Crespi. There was a guy named Creepy Crespi who played for the St. Louis Cardinals. Crespi would be a good name, although I've never used it.

Interviewer: It's got a nice *K* sound in it.
Simon: Yes. I try to name the character the way the character looks to me. I spend more time on the titles of plays than on the names of the charac-ters. What I've tried to do over the years is take an expression from life that has a double entendre in it, for example, the musical *Promises, Promises*, so that every time people speak the words it sounds like they're talking about your play. Or *The Odd Couple*—sometimes people say, "They're sort of an odd couple." If you mention an odd couple now, you think of the play. I've seen the words maybe a thousand times in newspapers since, and it seems as if I originated the term, which, of course, I didn't. *Come Blow Your Horn* comes from the nursery rhyme. *Barefoot in the Park* came from what the play was about. There's a line in the play that comes from my life, when Joan used to say to me, "Stop being a fuddy-duddy. Let's go to Washington Square Park and walk barefoot in the grass." *Chapter Two* was, literally, the second chapter of my life, after my wife Joan died, and I married Marsha. *Prisoner of Second Avenue* was a good title for a play about a man who loses

his job and is left to live in that little apartment on Second Avenue while his wife goes to work. He has nothing to do but walk around the room 'til he knows exactly how many feet each side is—so he's literally a prisoner. *The Gingerbread Lady* is a bad title. I liked the title and then had to make up a phrase about the gingerbread lady to make it fit. The film title was better: *Only When I Laugh. The Star-Spangled Girl* was a better title than a play. I liked *Last of the Red Hot Lovers*. It seemed familiar. It comes from Sophie Tucker's slogan, "Last of the Red Hot Mamas." *Lost in Yonkers*—I love the word Yonkers, and I wanted to put the play in a specific place. I said to myself, "*What* in Yonkers?" These boys are lost, Bella is lost, this family is *all* lost . . . in Yonkers. *Jake's Women* is literally about a man named Jake and three women. Again, there's the *K* sound in Jake.

Interviewer: Let's talk about stage directors. How much can a director help a play? Or, conversely, hurt it?

Simon: Well, in the early days, I worked principally with Mike Nichols. He was after me day and night. "This scene isn't good enough. Work on this. Fix this." He'd call me at two or three in the morning, to the point where I'd say, "Mike, give me a chance, leave me alone. You're on my back all the time." But, I always knew he was right. I wasn't that experienced a playwright. The way I work now—with Gene Saks—the conversion is generally short. He might say to me, "There's something wrong with this scene." I'll say, "I know what you mean. Let me go home and work on it." I'm much less influenced by the director now than I was before. I depend on the director in terms of *interpretation* of the play. With the Brighton Beach trilogy and *Lost in Yonkers*, I watched with clenched fist and teeth as Gene was directing, thinking, that's wrong, it's all wrong what he's doing. Then, suddenly, I *saw* what he was doing, and said, "Oh God! He has to go step by step to get to this place, trying all his things, the way *I* would try them at the writer's table."

Interviewer: How much do actors influence you? Is it ever the case that the personality of an actor influences you to remold the character to the actor, playing into what you now perceive to be the actor's strength?

Simon: I might do that. But what I try to do in terms of rewriting is always to benefit the *character*, not the actor. There's something an actor sometimes says that drives me crazy: "I would never do that." I say you're *not* doing this, the *character* is. The one thing I always look for is the best actor, not the funniest actor. I rarely, rarely cast a comedian in a play. The best comedian I ever had in a play was George C. Scott. He was funnier than anybody in the third act of *Plaza Suite* because he was playing King Lear. He knew the essence of comedy is not to play "funny." I remember, at the first reading of *Barefoot in the Park*, the whole cast was laughing at every line in the play. When we finished the reading, Mike Nichols said, "Now forget it's a comedy. From here on we're playing *Hamlet*."

Interviewer: I notice in the printed plays that you use ellipses, italics, and all-caps. I assume the ellipses are meant to tell the actors when you want them to pause, the italics are meant to give emphasis, and that all-caps for added emphasis, even volume.

Simon: Yes. They are a first indication to the actor and the director. Some of those emphases change enormously in the rehearsal period, but I also have to worry about what's going to be done in stock and amateur and European productions, so I hope it's a guide to what I meant. *The Prisoner of Second Avenue* opens in the dark. All we see is a cigarette, as Mel Edison comes in. The part was played by Peter Falk. He sat down on the sofa, took a puff of the cigarette, and in the dark we heard, "Aaaahhhhhhh." I don't know how you're going to be able to spell that, but it's got a lot of *h*'s in it—a *lot* of them. It got a huge laugh because the audience heard two thousand years of suffering in that "Aaaahhhhhhh." When Peter left and other actors played the part, they would go, "Ahh." There weren't enough *h*'s, and the line wasn't funny. People tell me that when they study my work in acting class, the teachers have to give them the sounds, the nuances, the way the lines are said. I guess Shakespeare can be said a thousand different ways, but in certain kinds of lines—for example, that run on "Ho" in *Biloxi Blues*—everything depends on the timing of it. I've always considered all of this a form of music. I wish I could write tempo directions, like *allegro* and *adagio*. That's why I put dots between words or underline certain words, to try to convey the sense of music, dynamics, and rhythm.

Interviewer: Do the critics ever help you, shedding light on your work, regardless of whether they're praising or damning it?

Simon: Walter Kerr gave me one of the best pieces of criticism I've ever had. In the first line of his review of *The Star-Spangled Girl*, he said, "Neil Simon didn't have an idea for a play this year, but he wrote it anyway." That was exactly what had happened. Elliot Norton was very helpful to me in Boston with *The Odd Couple*. His title of the opening night review was, "Oh, for a Third Act." He wasn't going to waste his time telling everyone how good the first two acts were. His job, he felt, was to make me make the third act better. And his suggestion to me was to bring back the Pigeon sisters. I said, "Good idea," brought back the Pigeon sisters, and the play worked. More important than the reviews, it's the audience that tells you whether or not you've succeeded. A week prior to the opening of the play you know if it's going to work or not. If 90 percent of the critics say it doesn't work, well, you already knew that without having to read the reviews. On the other hand, the opening night of *Little Me*, Bob Fosse and I were standing in the back of the theater. The producers had allowed a black-tie audience to come from a dinner to the theater. They'd eaten, they'd had drinks, they all knew each other—that's the worst audience you can get. About three-quarters of the way through the first act, a man got up, so drunk he could hardly walk, and staggered up the aisle looking for the men's room. As he passed Bob and me, he said, "This is the worst piece of crap I've seen since *My Fair Lady*!" Go figure out what *that* means.

Interviewer: Maybe the reason comedies like *Barefoot in the Park*, *The Odd Couple*, and *The Sunshine Boys* are sometimes underrated is quite simply that the audience is laughing at them—rather than worrying, weeping, learning—or doing any of the other virtuous things an audience is reputed to be doing at a drama. However, I think most writers would agree that it is relatively easy to make people cry and very, very hard to make them laugh.

Simon: Billy Wilder, whom I respect enormously, once confided in me, "Drama's a lot easier than comedy." He found some of the brilliant dramas he wrote, like *Sunset Boulevard*, much easier to write than the comedies. Comedies are relentless, especially a farce like *Some Like It Hot*. "*Rumors*" was the most difficult play I ever wrote because not only did every moment of that play have to further the story, complicate it, and keep the characters in motion—*literal* motion, swinging in and out of doors—but the audience had to laugh at every *attempt* at humor. You don't have five minutes where two people can sit on a sofa and say, "What am I doing with my life, Jack? Am I crazy? Why don't I get out of this?" You can do that in a drama. You can't do it in a farce.

Interviewer: Do you make it a point to see the plays of other playwrights?
Simon: When I was in my late teens and early twenties, I went to the theater a lot. There was always a Tennessee Williams play to see or a great English play. It was such an education. I learned more from bad plays than from good ones. Good plays are a mystery. You don't know what it is that the

playwright did right. More often than not you see where a work fails. One of the things I found interesting was that a lot of comedy came from drunks on the stage. If a character was drunk he was funny. I thought, wouldn't it be great to write characters who are as funny as drunks, but are not drunk. In other words, bring out the *outrageousness* of them, and the only way you can do that is to put them in such a tight corner that they have to say what's really on their minds. That's where the humor comes from.

Interviewer: Are you a good audience for other people's work? Do you laugh in the theater? I know some writers who are just not good audiences. Would you call yourself a good audience?

Simon: I'd call myself a *great* audience. I'm appreciative of good work, no matter what its form—comedy, drama, musical. I saw *Amadeus* four times. *A Streetcar Named Desire* I could see over and over. When I'm in England I go to some of the most esoteric English plays, plays that never even come over here, and I'm just amazed at them. I've recently caught up with the works of Joe Orton. I love Tom Stoppard's plays *Jumpers* and *Travesties*, and I admire the work of Peter Shaffer. If it's good theater, yes, I'm the best audience. I'm out there screaming.

Interviewer: Comedy has changed in a very noticeable way in the last thirty years. Subjects and language that were taboo are now almost obligatory. Do you think that indicates progress?

Simon: I like the fact that one can touch on subjects one wouldn't have dealt with in years gone by. The things that Lenny Bruce got arrested for you can find on any cable station today. Television situation comedy doesn't seem as funny to me as what Chaplin and Buster Keaton did without words. There are a few good comedians, but by and large I don't think comedy is a lot better today.

Interviewer: You seem to exercise a certain constraint over the language of your plays. Even *Biloxi Blues* doesn't use the kind of profanity and obscenity I remember from my days at that same airfield.

Simon: I think to say *fuck* once in an entire play in much more shocking than to say it sixty times. Four of the last five plays I've written took place in the thirties and forties, when profanity wasn't used on stage—or in the home. The fifth play, *"Rumors,"* is contemporary, and it's *filled* with profanity. But I don't need profanity. I love language, and I'd rather find more interesting ways to use it than take the easy way out.

Interviewer: Every playwright has fingerprints. You've mentioned thinking of your plays in musical terms, and one fingerprint of yours seems to be the "aria." At a certain point in almost every one of your plays a character *in extremis* launches into an extended list of all the catastrophes that are happening to him. In *Come Blow Your Horn*, Alan says, "You're using my barber, my restaurants, my ticket broker, my apartment, and my socks. How's it going, kid? Am I having fun?" In *Plaza Suite* the father explodes, "You can take all the Eislers, all the hors d'oeuvres and go to Central Park and have an eight-thousand-dollar picnic! I'm going down to the Oak Room with my broken arm, with my drenched, rented, ripped suit and I'm going to get blind!" Are you aware of doing that?

Simon: Yes, it's a fingerprint. You'll notice that those arias always come near the end of the play. The character has reached the point where he can't contain himself anymore, and everything comes spurting out, like a waterfall, a cascade of irritations. Just mentioning one of them wouldn't be funny, but to mention *all* the irritations wraps up a man's life in one paragraph.

Interviewer: The words you use to describe your comedy are words that are generally associated not with comedy at all, but with tragedy. You've talked about catharsis and your characters exploding when they can't bear the pain anymore.

Simon: Yes. That's why I don't find television comedy very funny—because it's hardly ever about anything important. I think the weightier comedy is, the funnier it is. To me, Chaplin's films are masterpieces. Remember him running after a truck with the red warning flag that has fallen off it?

Interviewer: And he doesn't see hundreds of rioting radicals falling enthusiastically in behind him . . .

Simon: So he gets busted and goes to jail as their leader.

Interviewer: Maybe when the record is written a hundred years from now it will turn out that all our comedy writers, from Chaplin to Keaton to you and Woody Allen, were writing tragedies. What's the cliché? Comedy is tragedy plus time. How fine is the line between tragedy and comedy?

Simon: It's almost invisible. I think Mel Brooks is one of the funniest people in the world, but when he makes a picture like *Spaceballs*, he's telling us, "This is foolishness. No one is in danger," so the audience knows it's too inconsequential to laugh at. But when he does a picture like *High Anxiety* or

Young Frankenstein there's something at stake. He's taken a frightening idea and twisted it, so we're able to laugh at it.

Interviewer: Here comes a difficult question . . .
Simon: As long as it doesn't have to do with math.

Interviewer: I don't know a writer who wouldn't say that—or a musician who isn't *good* at math. Because music is mathematical, I guess.
Simon: But so are plays. As surely as two plus two is four, the things you write in the play must add up to some kind of logical figure. In *Broadway Bound*, when Stan is teaching Eugene the craft of comedy, Eugene says, "It's just a comedy sketch. Does it have to be so logical? We're not drawing the plans for the Suez Canal," and Stan says, "Yes we are. It's not funny if it's not believable."

Interviewer: Well, now that we've covered math and logic, here's the difficult question. You write repeatedly about an uptight man and a liberating woman: is that because it's a reflection of your relationship with the women in your life—or because you feel it's a common and important theme?
Simon: The answer is quite simple. It's because I'm an uptight man who's been married to three liberated women. Joan was the first liberated woman I ever met and the most unconventional. She introduced me to more ways of looking at life than I'd ever dreamed of. She was more adventuresome than I'd ever been. She would jump from a plane in a parachute, and I'm the uptight man who would say, "You're crazy." Marsha was the same way. She was a feminist and had me marching in parades with a flag, yelling for women's rights. It's not that I didn't believe in women's rights, but I'm not an activist. Diane is an environmentalist, an ecologist, and also a fighter for the rights of women. Go over all the plays. With the exception of *The Odd Couple* and *The Sunshine Boys*, you'll find that the women are not only stronger but more interesting characters than the men. Again, the men are usually the Greek chorus. That's me sitting there, little Neil, born Marvin, observing the world—verbally, from a very safe place, which is what the man does in *Barefoot in the Park*, which is what he does in *Chapter Two*, in almost every play.

Interviewer: In the theater, in films, rugged men usually liberate unfulfilled women. From what you say, your plays reverse that convention.

Simon: Yes. I never feel threatened by women. I have enormous respect for them. I would also usually rather be with them than with men. I'm not much of a male bonder. I have male friends, obviously. I belong to tennis clubs. But in a social situation, I'd generally rather talk to a woman because it's like a play: you're getting the opposite point of view. You talk to a man, you're getting your own point of view. It becomes redundant. But when you're with a woman, that's when the sparks fly, that's when it's most interesting.

Interviewer: Plays these days are usually in two acts rather than three, and you are using more and shorter scenes. Is that the result of changes in stage technology? Are you being influenced by film?

Simon: I think I've been influenced by films, which have been influenced by television and commercials. Today you can see a one-minute commercial with about forty setups in it. There's a need to pace things differently because the audience's attention span has grown shorter. *Biloxi Blues* was the first major example of that because I had fourteen set changes. What also helped speed things along was that I started writing plays with larger casts, so there were many more entrances and exits. Also, having a narrator makes big time-leaps possible. I *am* influenced by new technologies and techniques, but that doesn't mean I'm following the fashions. It just means that I'm moving to another phase in my career—I'm becoming less literal and more abstract.

Interviewer: You've mentioned finding your characters waiting for you every time you walk into your office. Dickens complained that he hated to end his books because he didn't want to say good-bye to the characters he'd been living with.

Simon: That's why I don't go back to see my plays again, because they belong to someone else—to the actors and the audience. That process happens in a series of events. First, you finish writing the play, and everyone reads it. Then you go into rehearsal. Day by day, it slowly becomes the director's and the actors'. They're still asking me questions. I'm still participating. I'm still the father of these children. They get onstage, and soon the play is finished. They no longer need me! I feel locked out, I'm not part of them. After the play opens, I'm almost embarrassed to go backstage, because it's the place that belongs to the director and the actors. I'm just the man who introduced the characters to them. It's a very, very sad feeling for me. What happens eventually—it may sound cold—is that I disown them. I have no interest in seeing the plays again. In fact, it's painful, especially, when a play has run for a long time and new actors have come in to replace the original cast. When I walk into that theater, it's as if I were picking up my family album, and turning the pages to see my mother and father and aunt and cousins—and I say, "This isn't my family!" So, you give it up and go on to the next play.

Interviewer: And the next. And the next.
Simon: Every time I write a play it's the beginning of a new life for me. Today as I listen to you read excerpts from these plays and talk about them, it makes me feel nostalgic about how wonderful those days were—but I'm enjoying *these* days of writing, even though I see that the sun is setting.

A Life in the Theater

Peter Marks / 1992

From *Newsday*, March 22, 1992, *FanFare Magazine*, pp. 6–7, 41. Reprinted with permission, Newsday LLC. Peter Marks is the theater critic of the *Washington Post* and has been a theater critic for the *New York Times*.

Near the end of *Jake's Women*, there is a scene so heartbreaking you wonder how Neil Simon found the composure to write it.

The scene is enacted in the mind of the show's protagonist, Jake, a writer played by Alan Alda, who longs for a connection that no longer exists and imagines a meeting that can never be.

On the sofa in his apartment, Jake conjures a reunion of his dead wife and the daughter she never got to see grow up. The two women emerge from the shadows of the stage and meet in the middle, the imagined daughter melting in tears at the sight of the imagined mother. In a play filled with the usual supply of trademark Simon laugh lines, the moment stands out as a wise, tender lesson in the art of wishful thinking.

And never fails to move the playwright.

"It gets to me every time I see it," Simon says of his own handiwork. "They suddenly meet and look at each other and they say: 'Ahhhhh.' It touches me. Because you have created something that we wish we could create for ourselves. I mean the wonderful thing about the imagination is that you can do the impossible."

Sitting in his gracious, sun-dappled apartment above Park Avenue, his feet propped up on a small, blue ottoman, Simon talks wistfully about the pivotal scene in *Jake's Women*, his latest play, the twenty-sixth he has brought to Broadway and the first since his biggest critical triumph, *Lost in Yonkers*, which won both a Pulitzer and Tony last year. He speaks animatedly about the intricate mechanics of the scene and the play, a departure for the author in that it takes place almost entirely in the mind of its title character, a book writer in his fifties whose first wife died young and who is now experiencing the breakup of his second marriage.

What he does not talk about without a lot of prodding is the scene's emotional underpinnings, which—not surprisingly for Simon—mirror those of his own life. His first wife, Joan, died of cancer nearly twenty years ago, when their daughters were ten and fifteen. He has since remarried three times—twice to the same woman—but his friends have said through the years that Simon has never really recovered from Joan's death at the age of thirty-eight.

It does not seem much of a leap to suggest it is Simon himself who is experiencing this wrenching reunion with his wife through his play. But Simon resists the attempt to pin him down.

"Maybe," he says a bit remotely, after a long silence. "Maybe that's a thing in it. My wife is gone, and my daughter is around. Well, I have two daughters; I mean, if I made it two daughters, the play certainly would be autobiographical, and I don't think it is. I don't think a person's thoughts are autobiographical."

Can Simon really believe anyone with even a cursory knowledge of his life won't immediately identify with him as Jake? While the playwright says he's baffled by the world's obsession with verisimilitude, personal history is a hallmark of his work and the basis for some of his most acclaimed. He portrayed his first marriage in *Barefoot in the Park*, his military service in *Biloxi Blues*, his second marriage in *Chapter Two*, his growth as a comedy writer and the relationship to his parents in *Broadway Bound*.

Despite Simon's protestations, journalists, friends, and relatives alike are forever doing reality checks, ceaselessly trying to chart his characters and plot lines on the map of his life—and he wishes they would stop.

"You know that when my brother first saw *Broadway Bound*, he said, 'Is that how you see me, short and fat?' I said, 'No, Danny, Jason Alexander just happened to be a good actor. If we had found a tall guy, who was six-feet-one, I would have hired him, too.' Even my brother, who's that close to me, he assumes—everybody assumes—that what's up onstage is exactly what you wanted."

Don't get him started. "I'll tell you the worst one of all. I have a cousin, they're retired in Florida. Sees all the plays when they come there. *Broadway Bound* came, I was sure she was going to love it. She said, 'Well, I had trouble with it.' I said, 'Really, why?' She says, 'That's not the way your father would have dressed. He would never have worn a brown suit like that. He always wore dark gray suits.' I said, 'That's why you didn't like the play?'" Simon laughs and shakes his head at the memory.

It's not difficult to see his point, that people mistake his plays for his life, but it's also not hard to see why people are intrigued by the connection. After all, his current wife, Diane Lander, did get him to sign a prenuptial agreement promising he wouldn't use their life together in his plays. They live principally in Los Angeles with Lander's young daughter, while Simon comes to New York half a dozen times a year.

"She explained that very well," Simon says. "She said, 'I didn't want our marriage to be the subject of a play, I want our marriage to be a marriage.'" Clearly, the issue is evolving. Two weeks ago, Simon, profiled on CBS's *60 Minutes*, said he did not think the agreement would hold up, because he had already used the manner in which they talk to each other in his writing. A week later, he backed off his statement, saying he would honor his wife's wishes. Sort of. "She says, 'If I'm going to be put up there as subject matter, I think it's going to interfere with the marriage,' and I agree with her, and I doubt very much if I would write about that marriage," he says.

Still, the playwright seems to waste very little material. In a December 1986 cover story about Simon in *Time* magazine, his younger daughter, Nancy, said she and her sister had warmed immediately to actress Marsha Mason—whom Simon married shortly after his first wife's death—partly because "We needed to become a family again." In *Jake's Women*, Jake's daughter, Molly, confronted with his second wife-to-be, utters the very same words.

His new play comes to Broadway at a time when Simon, who was born sixty-four years ago on the Fourth of July, is at the top of his game. With *Yonkers* and the Brighton Beach trilogy, he has added to his canon a series of richly textured plays that not only have contributed to the commercial success that has made him one of the world's richest playwrights but also have yielded a level of acceptance by critics that eluded him earlier in his prolific career. He was pigeonholed for so long as a comedy writer that he had felt slighted by those whom he believed wrongly consigned his work to some lesser category of art. "Well, I don't try to write comedies anymore. I write plays," he says.

He recalls the time he bumped into movie critic Pauline Kael while waiting for a cab on a New York street. She had never been kind to his movies, and so the moment was a tad awkward.

"She said, 'I've given you a lot of bad reviews' . . . and I said, 'Yes, you have,'" he recounted. "She says, 'Well, you come to bat so often.'"

Simon still bats more often than anyone else in contemporary American drama, keeping three or four projects in the bullpen in various stages of development. In the works now are a musical based on his 1977 movie, *The Goodbye Girl*, with music by Marvin Hamlisch, a movie version of *Yonkers*, with Mercedes Ruehl and Richard Dreyfuss, and a new play "about eight young men in their twenties who work together," which he says he is not ready to discuss. And tomorrow night, the TV-movie version of *Broadway Bound* will be broadcast at 9:00 on ABC. Although the first two plays of the trilogy were made into feature films, Simon says *Broadway Bound* was too expensive for the big screen, because it required extensive outdoor period sets of New York City.

His newest Broadway play opens Tuesday at, appropriately enough, the Neil Simon Theater on West 52nd Street, the only Broadway theater named for a living playwright. In essence, *Jake's Women* is the story of the troubled marriage of Jake and his second wife, Maggie. As Jake tries to sort out his feelings about her, he mentally summons other women in his life—his psychiatrist, his daughter, his sister, his girlfriend, and, most importantly, his first wife, Julie—who in the course of the play help him let go of the past and find his way. The cast of the Broadway production includes Helen Shaver as Maggie, Tracy Polan as twenty-one-year-old daughter Molly and Kate Burton as Julie. Burton, oddly enough, knew Simon's first wife when she was a child in England, where the Simons had lived for a time.

"The whole play," Simon says, "is about Jake regaining some sort of health, being in a healthy mental environment." It is also, as its title suggests, about a man who has more complex relationships with women than with men. "I was surrounded in my life by women," he says. "Obviously, there was my father, and I had a brother, but as I grew older and married Joan, Joan's father died, and my father died. When we got together, it would be me and Joan, her mother and my mother, and our two daughters. And I was the only man there. And it was that way for years."

For a time it looked as if *Jake's Women* would be the first Broadway-bound Simon play to die on the road. Two years ago the play had what Simon says was a "pre-Broadway tryout" at the Old Globe Theater in San Diego, a run that was cut short after near-unanimous pans and what the playwright himself thought was a misguided production that starred Peter Coyote as Jake and Stockard Channing as Maggie. The *Los Angeles Times* called the show "as flat as the Mojave Desert."

While Simon loved Channing, he believed Coyote was miscast. "A number of people in the cast were wrong, the director was wrong, the set was certainly wrong. So I pulled it off." At the time, Emanuel Azenberg, the show's producer, was quoted as saying the play had lost $550,000, and about 70 percent of that was Simon's own money. The production left such a bad taste in the author's mouth that he doubts he would attempt another play there.

The experience may have left him down on San Diego, but not on his play. He put the script away and went to work on *Lost in Yonkers*, which was not unusual behavior for Simon, who wrote the first thirty-five pages of *Brighton Beach Memoirs* and then shoved the script in a drawer for nine years "because I didn't know how to write it."

But *Jake's Women* refused to stay in the drawer. Simon says he was haunted by the play, and what tormented him most of all was the reunion scene between mother and daughter, not only because of its emotional power, but because he knew he'd written a terrific scene.

"The play was in my mind, but I didn't know it," says the playwright, who is affable but serious in person. "It's like that line in my play, 'My mind has a mind of its own.' I really believe that's true."

Simon returned to the material more than a year ago and rewrote from scratch, retaining only the basic outline of the play. He had taken consolation in a review by a critic from a small alternative weekly in California, "who gave us our only really promising review, who sort of told me what he thought the play should be." The reviewer, he says, recommended the set be more stylized, so that the women who pop into Jake's mind could have their say and leave the stage artfully.

In an era when it is fashionable for creative people in theater and movies to announce they don't read reviews, it is surprising to hear Simon declare he not only reads his critics, but he takes some of their advice. "This critic was being very supportive, saying I think what you have to do is this, and this is the way I would do it, and it made great sense to me."

As far as Simon is concerned, the breakthrough in whipping the play into shape came when he decided to have Jake speak directly to the audience, a conventional theatrical device he used to great effect for his wise-cracking hero, Eugene Jerome in *Brighton Beach Memoirs* and *Biloxi Blues*. But while Eugene's remarks were comments on the action around him, Jake uses the stage as a confessional. "In the original play, Jake didn't talk to the audience at all," he says, "so we didn't know enough about him. It was the only way I could get inside of Jake's brain so the audience would understand him."

And of course, he lingered over the delicate meeting of the dead mother and her daughter. He loved the notion of an imagined reunion that could be, for an audience, emotionally real: "The intimacies that [Julie and Molly] have are so wonderful that I am positive the audience sits and watches and think it's really happening."

After Alda did a reading of the play and agreed to take the part of Jake, Simon and Azenberg, eschewing the West Coast, where Simon had unveiled most of his recent work, took the play to the North Carolina School of the Arts in Winston-Salem last month. Audiences during the sold-out run were enthusiastic, the playwright says. The early critical reaction, however, has been mixed. *Variety*, in its review of the North Carolina production, said the play "lacked the substance" of the playwright's other recent works but nonetheless predicted it had "the requisite star power and audience appeal to become a success."

Waiting for the opening and the Broadway critics, Simon says he feels the usual trepidation, but nowhere near the pressure he once felt. Sure, the financial stakes are a lot higher than when he opened his first Broadway play. *Come Blow Your Horn*. In 1961, that show cost about $75,000; in 1992 *Jake's Women* has come in at $1.1 million.

"There was so much riding on my life," he says. "I mean, *Come Blow Your Horn*: I stood in the back of the Brooks Atkinson Theater in 1961 and said, 'My life is riding on this play.'"

Now, he says, he thinks about writing a book about his life. There is so much more about him, he says, that he has not gotten into his plays. But the man who has put so much of his life onstage worries he doesn't have the skills for book-length self-revelation. "I read Arthur Miller's autobiography. It said, 'On June 27 my father was having a chocolate ice cream soda, and he said, 'What are you doing with that hat?'" he says facetiously. "Now how does he remember that?"

Neil Simon shifts in his chair, thinking better of it. "It would take me well over a year to write, and I would have to not write a play or a movie," he says, shaking his head. "I'm not in such a rush to do an autobiography."

Neil Simon

Jackson R. Bryer / 1992

From *The Playwright's Art: Conversation with Contemporary American Dramatists*, edited by Jackson R. Bryer (New Brunswick, NJ: Rutgers University Press, 1994), 221–40. Reprinted with permission. Portions of the introduction to the interview containing information about Neil Simon's life and works available elsewhere in this book have been deleted.

This interview took place on May 29, 1992, in Neil Simon's office in Beverly Hills, California.

Interviewer: What about playwriting, either when you started or now, appeals to you particularly?
Simon: That's a good question. I've never thought about it. From the first day I saw a play or a musical, the theater was the way I wanted to express myself. When I started writing for myself as a young boy of thirteen, fourteen, or fifteen, I was writing dialogue, I wasn't writing prose. I think that maybe what attracted me to it was the immediate response that you get from an audience. They tell you right away whether they like it or are moved or appreciate the humor in it. I like the idea of it being live as opposed to it being filmed. The idea of being a screenwriter didn't appeal to me from the beginning as it does to most people who are growing up today and who have aspirations to be in the arts.

Interviewer: Since you've been writing plays, have you ever been tempted to do anything else—write a novel or write poetry?
Simon: Certainly not poetry. I couldn't see where I would get more satisfaction than from doing a play, its being so malleable that I could play around with it all the time during rehearsals or readings or whatever. With a novel, it seemed like such a lonely life; there's no one. It's between you and the person that buys the book. They're sitting someplace in Poughkeepsie reading this and you don't know what they think about it unless you get a letter. It's

not that I need the approval. I just want to have that byplay between the two of us, that we are communicating in one way or another.

Interviewer: What about the collaborative aspects of theater? Do you get a lot of satisfaction out of that, or is it a frustration? When the play begins to go into rehearsal and you're working with other people, is that part of the attraction of being a playwright?

Simon: Well, it works both ways. It is attractive when you have a really good director and you have a first-rate cast. Then you say, "I've got the best of everything." But there are days when you're sitting there and you say to yourself, "No, that's not what I meant at all," and you're frustrated. You don't want to say anything yet because you want to give them the time and the space. Sometimes I can jump in and say to the director, "No, that's not really what I wanted," and he will say, "Well, what do you want?" or "Let me try it this way and see." I keep forgetting that they have an overview more than I have because I've been on that play for a year and they may bring something new to it that I hadn't imagined, which is why I don't want to direct my own plays. Then I'm very grateful, but I would say, generally speaking, that when a play opens, 95 percent of what's up there is what I have approved of. With a film, I'm at the mercy of the director, and what comes out on the screen is about 10 percent of what I approved of.

Interviewer: With a play, what's the other 5 percent? Is the other 5 percent stuff you wished weren't there?

Simon: There's only 95 percent in anything in life.

Interviewer: Do you regard the rehearsal period as extremely significant to you as a playwright?

Simon: Yes, but with me it starts even before then. After everybody reads it—the director, the producer, the people that I'm concerned with for their opinion on it—we have a reading either a month or two months prior to rehearsals. So I have heard the play for the first time rather than waiting for that first day to find out that the second act doesn't work at all. If I'm going to find that out, which I have found out many times, I really have a good amount of time to sit down and correct it. With *Brighton Beach*, on the first day of reading, which was six weeks before rehearsal, I cut out a main character and put in another scene between the boy and the mother. That turned out to be the most important scene in the play, but I had the time to think about it and do it. Then, once I go into rehearsal, I have those four weeks. I don't have every minute of those four weeks; I figure I have the first two weeks to keep changing and improving, and then you've got to let the actors' and director's work start to give it life. Then I go away for a few days and come back, and I'm looking at it much more objectively.

When you get out of town and you start to put it on the stage, the first couple of dress rehearsals look like garbage, and you don't want the curtain ever to go up. Then it goes up and, like the doctor coming out of the lab and giving you the results of your test, you find out all night long what's positive and what's negative. You get to fix that, but you have to be patient there, too, because maybe you got an audience one night that responded a certain way, as opposed to waiting for two, three, or four performances and seeing what regularly grabs the audience or when the coughing starts and they are not really with the play. You can even disregard what they're saying and pay attention to what you feel inside and say, "I don't like that." I'm very open to any changes as long as they make sense, not just to me. You hear it and you say, "Of course, that's a good idea," as opposed to just listening to anybody because you're so anxious to have it turn out to be a good result.

Interviewer: Do you think it's more a question of response because it's comedy?
Simon: Well, it's the easiest response. They laugh or they don't laugh, but sometimes it's the wrong kind of laugh. In *Plaza Suite*, when I did it first with Mike Nichols, they were laughing too much, and Mike and I kept cutting out laughs; but when we cut them out we got laughs in other places where we didn't mean to get them. They wanted to laugh because I had presented a very identifiable situation to them and it made them uncomfortable; sometimes when an audience is uncomfortable, they laugh. They laugh with it, they laugh from their own perspective. They're sitting next to their wife that they've had the same kind of argument with, and they're embarrassed by it, and rather than turn away they'll laugh at it as though it didn't mean them. It means other couples.

Interviewer: Do you sometimes get surprised by where you get laughs?
Simon: Many times I've sat in the back of the theater with a director, and we'll hear this huge laugh, and we'll turn to each other and shrug out shoulders. There are laughs that I've had in plays that have run two or three years and I still don't know what they're laughing at. That doesn't happen a lot, but there are one or two lines where I say, "I don't get it." At first, I didn't get it in *Biloxi Blues* when the character Wykowski, one of the fellow soldiers who

is not Jewish, was having some problems with Eugene and with the other boy, Epstein, and he said in a derogatory way, "It's always the Jews who wind up with the money." It got a big laugh from the audience, and I said, "Why are they laughing at that?" I meant that to be a real swipe, but the character who was saying it was such an obvious bigot you couldn't take him seriously. As he explained it, we're all kikes, wops, japs, niggers; he grew up on the streets, so none of those things were offensive to him and he could just easily say it. When the audience laughed at it, I said, "Are they laughing because they agree all Jews have the money or because of how obvious a bigot he was?" I still don't get it. Why are they laughing?

Interviewer: What about the opposite? Are there scenes where you wanted them to laugh but they didn't laugh?

Simon: Well, I have to examine that too because they may be very touched at that moment. You have to take into consideration what has preceded it; if they are in a frame of mind where they are very moved at what's happened, you could have the funniest line in the world and they're saying, "I don't want to laugh at that." It's as if someone just said to you, "I have terrible news. My mother just died," and I say, "Oh God, I'm so sorry," and you say something funny. They won't hear what's funny. Why you would want to be funny I don't know. It's possible that you might say something funny; but in terms of an audience hearing that, they don't want to have anything to do with it.

Interviewer: So you can be surprised by that in rehearsal or in the reading of a play, where you realize it wasn't the right time for that to happen?

Simon: One of the most tricky things that I ever wrote that came out really right was in *Lost in Yonkers*. The character named Bella, the sort of emotionally arrested girl, is trying to tell her mother and family that she wants to marry this young man who is obviously retarded and she wants to borrow five thousand dollars to open a restaurant. He is obviously illiterate, so it is sad, but there is a certain comical notion about it, and the rest of the family are being so difficult with her; they are standing instead of sitting. The audience is laughing and laughing until Bella says this one thing that just stops it. When her brother Louie asks, "What is this guy after? What more could he want?" she says, "He wants *me*! He wants to marry me." The audience stops laughing because they know that's when to stop. They know what she is going to say is going to be so powerful and poignant that you wouldn't dare laugh at it.

Interviewer: That brings up something else I was going to ask you. What does using comedy enable you to do as a playwright? Herb Gardner has said it gets the audience's attention so he can get the serious stuff across. That scene which you just describe is an example of that, isn't it? We're paying attention to Bella at that moment, so that when she does say something serious, it gets our attention.

Simon: Yes, I would say that would be an answer for me, too, except it sort of denigrates comedy. It's like saying it's just a setup to get to the more important things, and I don't think that's necessarily true. I think that comedy can be just as important as the drama in the play, because when you start puncturing those balloons of pomposity and the audiences laugh at it, you're also making some important points.

Interviewer: You've talked in other interviews about the irony in the humor you use. Would you say that that's the way you look at life and that that's the way the comedy comes through in the plays?

Simon: I think so. I think there is nothing as absurd in the world as life. The most incongruous things happen. I mean, you just watch where this country is going right now and you say, "Well, we're just heading for a crash. Why don't we turn right?" But we're not turning right. Or "Turn left" or whatever; but you see, we're going right into the sea. I'm putting that on a grand scale, but behavior interests me more than anything. I think in any play that I've ever written the people all have options to behave in another way; they don't, and that's what makes it so funny and so poignant. It's people who generally get themselves in all of the problems. There are the few who are going to get hit by the plane that falls out of the sky; some can say that they take that fatalistic approach by saying, "Well, they should have known better than to have been in that spot where the plane was going" or "It was destiny that you were going to get hit." I don't believe in that, but I do believe that 95 percent of the trouble that we do get into is caused by ourselves.

Interviewer: What gets you started on a play? Has that changed over the years? Do you hear something? Do you read something?

Simon: A seed is planted, and when the seed starts to flower a little bit, then you start to see what it's like. You can't start writing based on the seed; you say, "Oh, there's something in there." *Lost in Yonkers* was quite a different play when I first thought of the idea. I wrote twenty pages of it and I said, "It's not going anyplace," and I put it aside and went on to other things. It was starting to germinate and grow, so that the next time when I went back

I realized what was wrong. In the first version, the girl was not retarded and the young boy who came to live there was alone, and I said, "Wait a minute. I need him to talk to somebody, so it might as well be two brothers who are in this predicament." Bella was just a spinster. When I made her the emotionally arrested person that she was, it was not for convenience, but it was because the grandmother has done this to them. So you started out thinking what nature had done to these people—or their environment or their background.

Interviewer: What was the germ of the idea that got you started on the play?
Simon: It takes a chain of events to happen. I thought about an uncle that I had never met who apparently was a bookkeeper in a garment business that was owned by some Mafia people. One day he disappeared because he obviously knew too much. The character fascinated me; he was obviously not a gangster himself. He was just a bookkeeper, but he disappeared and the family never heard from him again. So I started to write about that; the play I was going to write was called "Louie the Gangster." Louie the Gangster now turned into that uncle who was really a gangster, and I said, "What if a kid was left by his father because the mother died, and he was being brought up in the house where the gangster lived who was corrupting the kid's morals, and the kid finally fought against it? Okay," I said, "there's something in there." But eventually that became only a very small part of the play; he didn't really corrupt the kids, but the brother was really needed there to show again what the grandmother had done to that family. He was the one who pushed and instigated Bella's ability to speak up against the family.

Interviewer: Is that typical of how the plays have started?
Simon: Yes.

Interviewer: Was *The Sunshine Boys* simply suggested by the career of Smith and Dale?
Simon: For years before I wrote *The Sunshine Boys*, I had wanted to write a play about two partners in business. I started three or four different plays about partners in business. They owned something in the garment center, they were in the furniture business; it was a really good idea. They were two partners who were both making equal amounts of money but one was living like a king. He had a great house on the beach, he had a great car; and the other guy had nothing. So after about twenty years he said, "I think this guy is stealing from me." I thought it was a great idea, but it evolved into these

two vaudevillians who had nothing to do with money or one being richer than the other. Generally in a lot of my plays, two people are in major confrontation with each other, like in *The Odd Couple* or *Barefoot in the Park* or *The Sunshine Boys*. That's how the play evolved, but you never sit down and think of an idea and start writing it. At least I don't.

Interviewer: And it never ends up where it starts? Has there ever been a play where from start to finish of the writing process it stayed pretty much the same? *The Odd Couple*, for example, was essentially the same play from when it started to where it ended, wasn't it? It was the idea of writing about your brother, who had recently separated from his wife and was sharing an apartment with another man.
Simon: Yes, but I had the wives in it in the first draft. You go through all of these drafts and you don't go all the way through the play. You get to a certain point and you say, "Uh-oh, it just stopped; the light went out. It's going in the wrong way." And I kind of like that. The most dangerous play that I ever wrote was *"Rumors,"* because all I had in mind was that I wanted to write a farce, and I knew that farces had to be about wealthy people because they're never about poor people in trouble. There are some, of course, but the classic ones, the Molière farces, are primarily about the upper classes. So I pictured ten people or eight people dressed in black ties or gowns, because I knew that by the end of the evening they would be torn to shreds emotionally and physically. I went page by page setting up a situation not knowing where it was going until I got to the last scene. The interesting thing is, you do know where it's going, but it's something in the back of your mind that says, "I don't know what I'm not going to tell you yet, but just keep going and you'll get it."

Interviewer: Do the characters take over the play at certain times?
Simon: Yes, because if you're going to be truthful you can't start putting words in their mouth that you know they wouldn't say just because it's convenient for the plot. The minute something sounds wrong you know you're making it up (even though you know you're making it all up anyway). When that character is so well delineated and drawn so well, they can only say certain things; their minds will only take them to a certain level.

Interviewer: *The Sunshine Boys* is my favorite Simon play. That's why I keep talking about it.
Simon: I loved writing *The Sunshine Boys*. It was a play that allowed me to be outrageously funny but also dramatic at the same time, because these

two old codgers were very poignant to me. They were tragic figures in a way, but they were so funny also. They really didn't know after a while whether what they were saying was funny or was from the act, because they talked in life in the same rhythms that they did in the act for forty-five or fifty years.

Interviewer: Wouldn't you say that's the kind of situation that you are always looking for, the kind of situation where you can be both poignant and comic? Isn't that the reason there are so many family plays, because families are by definition almost always both poignant and amusing?

Simon: I suppose so. I'm always looking for a comic idea that has a dramatic subtext to it. If it's just funny, I'm not really interested. I'm starting now to work on a play about when I worked on *Your Show of Shows* with Sid Caesar. There are seven or eight people in the play. They are all writers, and they are all funny in their own way, so I have a license to kill in a way. Eight really funny people could be too much, but underneath it there is some pain there about what's going on in their own lives, in what's going on in the life of the star, and also what's going on in the world. It was during the McCarthy era. One of them is Russian-born and makes jokes about it, but they are scary jokes. As long as I know I have that good solid foundation underneath it, then the humor is the gravy and you're still telling a story.

Interviewer: That's the irony, of course, isn't it—that at the same time it's funny there is something serious going on, and you can never forget either?

Simon: I know. People have told me that they've seen plays of mine in, let's say, dinner theaters and never gotten the subtext because the actors and the directors aren't good enough. As Mike Nichols or Gene Saks would say to the actors, "Okay, we've heard all the jokes on opening day; now we start playing this as a drama." At a dinner theater they would play it as comedy; that subtext would be gone because they're just looking to get the laughs from the audience. A play can be destroyed, and that's why I would never go to see a play in a dinner theater.

Interviewer: You never go see your plays in nonprofessional situations, do you?

Simon: No, I don't. I rarely go back to see my own play in the second year of the play when the third cast is playing. It's not fair to them; you may get somebody who's wonderful in it, but I don't have any more interest in the play. It's gone; it's like an ex-lover. She's gone and out of your life and you move on to something else. I don't want to see it again. I don't want to watch my movies, even the good ones. Once in a while I can watch a certain one. I like watching *The Goodbye Girl* a lot; it seems to hold up for me. But I don't even read my plays anymore.

Interviewer: Could you talk a little about the difference between being a playwright when you started and now? It's been thirty years and, obviously, getting the play on is more difficult now.

Simon: It was sheer terror in the beginning, especially with the first play. It was life or death: if the play failed, my career as a playwright was over because I had no money. I had quit television, which was subsidizing me and my family; and if *Come Blow Your Horn* had failed, I would have had to move to California (because all of television was moving to California), work in situation comedies, I guess, and maybe try to get into movies. But it paid enough for me to start to write the next one, which was *Barefoot in the Park*. *Barefoot* was a huge hit, but still I didn't feel comfortable. I lost all of the rights to *Barefoot* because I had a lawyer who advised me to sell the rights to Paramount Pictures, including the film rights to the next play I wrote, which was *The Odd Couple*, for some capital gains money because they said, "Look, you'll never write another play after this anyway; and, if you did, what chance would there be that it would be a hit? Who's going to write three hits in their life?" So I took the money and I don't own *Barefoot in the Park* anymore, and I never received a single cent from all of *The Odd Couple* on television for five years! I never saw any of the millions of dollars that went with it; but *The Odd Couple* was even a bigger hit than *Barefoot*, so I said, "Okay, I'm going to stay in this business." But you still don't know when you're going to be secure and be able to make a living. Robert Anderson, who wrote *Tea and Sympathy*, said, "You can make a killing in the theater, but you can't make a living in it." I was determined to stay in the theater, and I went out and did some films, but I always came back to the theater, and I didn't have any flops for a long time. Even *The Star-Spangled Girl*, which was not a well-received play, got its money back. *Gingerbread Lady* finally got its money back; so I was making a living, and then eventually making a killing. Then, when I suddenly felt, "Okay, I'm secure now. I can do this," then comes the new feeling: "Well, maybe it's going to start to go away now; you're not going to be able to do it anymore."

Interviewer: Is that terrifying?

Simon: No, that's not terrifying anymore; there's anger that I still have to face the *New York Times*, which never gives me a good review. I sort of count on them; they're very dependable in that way. I don't think I'd put on something that I thought didn't have some chance or didn't have some major redeeming qualities; there's no point in doing it.

Interviewer: One thing that differentiates you from most playwrights is that they depend on the regional theaters to get their plays started, and many of them depend on the regional theater even after their plays start— to revive them and keep them in front of the public. Your plays are pretty much Broadway plays. You try them out on the road, but once they go to Broadway, that's it. Of course, they're done subsequently. That puts you in a very different position from, say, a Wendy Wasserstein or a Herb Gardner who need Seattle Rep working on their plays. How do you feel about the repertory theater system, even though you are really not part of it?

Simon: I'm not part of it, but I think it's a great system. I love the repertory theater. *Jake's Women* would have been gone had I not done it in a repertory theater in San Diego—the Old Globe. I saw the faults and the virtues in the play, and even though I lost money on it (because it was on the way to Broadway, so the contracts were pre-Broadway contracts), I believed in the play, and so we just did it again. The play was saved by those enormous rewrites and by the recasting we did. One of the reasons I don't go through the repertory route is because I subsidize at least half of my own plays. I found out early on that people were making a ton of money on plays like *The Odd Couple*. I was making my royalty, which was good, but the backers were making more money than I was. I'm not a good businessman, but I thought the only good investment is one which I could control, so the plays I felt pretty good about I would put a certain amount of money into, and the plays I felt really good about I'd put even more money in. It was not only for me, it was for my family; I really put my family's money in there, too, but there aren't many playwrights who can afford to do that. I think Shakespeare did it.

Interviewer: But on a smaller scale.

Simon: Well, the shilling wasn't worth as much then.

Interviewer: There is another question we have asked other playwrights, and, again, in your case it doesn't really apply: Is Broadway still your goal? A number of them said no. They didn't care anymore if their play was done on Broadway, if it got good productions at four or five major repertory theaters. Obviously, your aim with all of your plays still is to take it to New York and have it be a big success. Is there a reason for that?

Simon: Well, no. Sometimes I intended not to go that way, but I was sort of pushed. I never wanted *The Good Doctor* to go to Broadway; I thought it was an Off-Broadway play. It was an adaptation of Chekhov's short stories, and I knew it was not going to be a big hit. I couldn't see lines around the block waiting to get in to see my adaptation of Chekhov's short stories, although I thought we did a good job with it. It does well in repertory theaters and with amateur companies now. Another play was *God's Favorite*, which was a play that I didn't think would be successful at all but was a play I wanted to write. It was sort of a dark version of the Book of Job and I wrote it shortly after my first wife, Joan, had died. It was a way for me to deal with the absurdity of a beautiful thirty-nine-year-old woman dying; it was a clash between me and God. Again I said, "I don't see the audiences lining up to see this dark comedy," but the producer and other people said, "They're going to like this. It should go on Broadway; you can't do this Off-Broadway." I don't know how the critics would have treated me if I'd gone Off-Broadway. They might have said, "Oh, he doesn't like this one well enough to do it on Broadway, so we assume it's not good enough," and I didn't want that obstacle, so we did it on Broadway. I don't regret it now, but I think the play might have fared better had we not.

The standards for Off-Broadway are different, not less; the quality has to be there, but sometimes you see an Off-Broadway play and you say, "This is wonderful but it wouldn't make it on Broadway." *Driving Miss Daisy* is a perfect example, because it was all illusion; they just used chairs and made believe they were driving. On Broadway, they would have said, "Why don't they have the car?" They're spending more money, and they want to see the money spent on the sets. I don't know what that criterion is, but it's worse now than it's ever been. When I first started writing plays, there were many more avant-garde plays that today you would see Off-Broadway that you would see on Broadway then because you didn't have to gross a lot to keep it running. You could run for a whole season doing half-a-house, but today it's hit or miss, and if you don't have a blockbuster hit you fail. Many of my earlier plays, with the exception of the really big hits, would not have lasted in today's world. *The Gingerbread Lady*, which was doing half-a-house all the time, ran a full season and won a Tony Award for Maureen Stapleton. It's a different business now; it's like the movies. When I first went to the movies as a kid you went to the movies and that was it; you didn't care about how well the movie was doing. Now you open up the *New York Times*, and *Basic Instinct* did $100 million. Who cares? Does the public really care what that picture did? I don't understand it. It's all hype. It's because we have shows like *Entertainment Tonight* and people are just so needy to get show business news, I guess. It's all Cinderella stories: "Oh look, Sylvester Stallone is going to make $12 million!" They resent him for making it, but they think that it's possible, it could happen to them, I suppose.

Interviewer: But it doesn't hurt you as a playwright that you've become a celebrity, does it? And isn't it kind of nice that a playwright can be a celebrity?
Simon: Well, there are very few playwrights that are celebrities, that are well known. Arthur Miller is well known; but unless you are on television a lot you don't become a celebrity—and the only way you become a celebrity in a sense is doing those talk shows.

Interviewer: Doesn't your celebrity status come from your work? It would seem that if playwrights can be celebrities, then somebody values what they do.
Simon: I think there is something special and unique in my story because it is kind of a Cinderella story. There's not a lot of people who really make it big in today's theater world as a playwright. We have some wonderful playwrights, but they don't write a lot. The story is not that I've done something incredible; I just think that it's my job. I like writing the plays, but it's unusual that a playwright would become a celebrity. The celebrated writers in this country are mostly the novelists like Stephen King or the ones who write those love stories or, in other days, Ernest Hemingway or Scott Fitzgerald. Screenwriters nobody knows; they are just anonymous people.

Interviewer: Do you think, then, that the theater as an art form is in trouble with the public, or do you think it's in a bad way or a good way in terms of its competition with the other arts?
Simon: I've heard that it's been in trouble for the last twenty years, and it's probably been in trouble for the last two hundred years or two thousand. It's in trouble now because the demands of making it a hit sometimes make one diminish the play to give the audiences something they want instead of being very artful about it. I don't know if that's a conscious effort on the part of the playwright or the producer or the director: let's go for the jugular, let's really make this a hit. One can do that a little bit easier, I think, with musicals because they are purely an entertainment form. A play that will probably win the Tony Award this year, *Dancing at Lughnasa*, I thought was a wonderful play, but it didn't have a long run on Broadway; it's still running, but hardly anybody is going to see it. The Tonys will help them, but I don't

think the theater could support a lot of plays like *Dancing at Lughnasa*. People want something bigger. Numbers are the name of the game now.

Interviewer: Do you think this spring has helped—with all the serious plays that have opened—or is that just a coincidence?
Simon: What serious plays have opened this year apart from *Dancing at Lughnasa*?

Interviewer: *Death and the Maiden* is running, but that's because it has all those movie stars in it.
Simon: You couldn't get that play put on, not in America, without them. You could in England, but I don't think you could in America. That would be an Off-Broadway play in America without those stars.

Interviewer: Talk a little bit about your actual writing process. Do you write every day? Do you work on more than one thing at a time?
Simon: Sometimes I have to work on more than one thing at a time because I get to a certain point with something. Let's say it's a film I'm working on, and I don't know if we're going to be doing the film, so I get sidetracked, and I go back to something I really want to do. I've been working on this play *Laughter on the 23rd Floor*, and I was perturbed that I had to stop to go on to do something else. *Lost in Yonkers*, the film, is being made; I have to have meetings and auditions, so I stop working and I lose the run that I'm getting. Following that, we're doing *The Goodbye Girl*, the musical; I've been working on the book for that for a year with the composers. That doesn't mean you work every day for a year, but I took two months to do the first draft, and then I stopped to let them catch up and do the songs. I would go to see them in New York, and then I would get back to the play I'm writing. So I'm doing two or three things at the same time, but my mind is really only on the one thing until I really have to do *The Goodbye Girl*. Then all the attention and focus will go to that.

Interviewer: If you had your druthers, would you be working on one thing, or do you really enjoy working on lots of different things at once?
Simon: Well, if I had my druthers, I'd rather just write the play if it means forgoing doing the other things. I think I can do both, because the play doesn't have to go on next year and I could write it over a period of two or three years. *Brighton Beach* was written over a period of nine years. It didn't get put aside for other projects; I just got stuck on it, which is liable to

happen when I get to the second act of *Laughter on the 23rd Floor*. I haven't started it yet; I don't even know what's going to happen yet, so it may take me a while to get into it. Also, there's so many things that come at me now, offers to do things that are very promising, that sound like interesting projects or people. A prominent director wants to do a film of *Jake's Women*, and ordinarily I would think that would be a very difficult one to do. I'm not sure I will do it, but I'll have a meeting next week with the director. Because he's such a good director, maybe he can see a way of putting that on film; so I get sidetracked.

Interviewer: Do you consider yourself a kind of workaholic in that you really need to keep working to be happy?

Simon: Well, if you consider any man who goes to work five days a week on a job, doesn't work on the weekends, and doesn't work at nights a workaholic, then I'm a workaholic. I'm not working at night, I don't work on the weekends, I don't work on holidays, and I don't work nine to five. I work four hours a day, but I don't come into this office for any other reason but to work.

Interviewer: How have you changed your writing method over the years since you started writing plays?

Simon: When I started, I didn't know how to find my way. I didn't know how to start the play; I didn't know when I was on the wrong track. I was such a virgin at it that I always needed to go to someone and say, "Is this any good?" After ten or twelve pages, I was showing everybody! No one has seen a page of *Laughter on the 23rd Floor*, and I'm finishing the first act. No one saw a page of *Lost in Yonkers* until I finished it; I just went ahead. I'm more reticent to show things to people now anyway, because, even if they love it, they put a responsibility on you: "This is great. What happens in the second act?" "Well, I don't know." I don't want to go through that, so I just show them the whole thing. I've written twenty-seven plays in thirty-one years. When I worked in television, I would do thirty-nine shows a year. Granted that it was with other writers like *Your Show of Shows*—because it was on thirty-nine weeks a year. Those were long seasons. I did that for years; working on *The Bilko Show*, we did thirty-nine shows a year; they were half-hour shows, but they were tough. When I quit it all to write plays, I said, "A play a year? That's all I have to do? That sounds like a vacation." It was, comparatively; and even though sometimes they took me years to do and I would do them over and over again, I just kept at them. There have been playwrights that have written as many or more than I have: Tennessee Williams and maybe Sam Shepard—they've written in the twenties. Shakespeare wrote thirty-seven, I think; George Bernard Shaw wrote fifty-some plays. I don't think it's such an enormous output of work; it's just that people will say to you sometimes, "You've made enough money. Why do you keep doing it?" They miss the whole point of it. If Willie Mays could still play ball and hit .320, wouldn't he still be playing, not even for the money? If he could run back and catch the fly ball at fifty-six, he would do it, like in *Damn Yankees*.

Interviewer: Do you get unhappy if you can't work?
Simon: I admit to taking the pad with me on vacation. Lately, I've been trying to do other things when I go on vacations. I'll read more or take crossword puzzles or something to take my mind off of things, but it's hard for me not to do some work. I was going through my stuff the other day with my secretary, and I found on the stationary of Sandy Lane in the Bahamas that I wrote out the entire outline for *The Prisoner of Second Avenue*. I must have done it on the beach. My wife Joan was sitting on the beach reading a book then; and for me it was just as pleasurable to do this. I didn't feel I was working, but I was feeling young then and I had the energy to do it. The rest of the day we played tennis and went swimming.

Interviewer: Would you do that now?
Simon: Possibly, but not as much. If I were alone on the plane going to London for business, I might work; but I'm starting to do it less on airplanes. I'd rather read a book or something. I find I'd rather come back to the office. I am getting older, and I find it tiresome to be working that much. I want to be doing other things.

Interviewer: Is part of the reason for that that now you're more confident when you come in here you will have something to say? Then, if you didn't get it down while you were sitting on the beach, you might have thought that you wouldn't ever get it down. Now you know it will come eventually.
Simon: Yes, I think so. People say, "Why don't you get a word processor?" which I don't have. I have a typewriter over there. And I say, "Why?" And they say, "Well, you could work faster." The last thing that I want to do is work faster. I work fast enough as it is. I want to slow down the writing process so I can think about what I'm doing. I don't want to sit over the typewriter or any machine for hours, because it just ruins your back and your health if you don't get up and walk around. I'll walk around and sit

in a chair with a writing pad and just sort of jot down things and write it out. There's the tactile beauty, I think, of coming down here and feeling the pen on the paper.

Interviewer: It's amazing how many writers still talk about that.
Simon: Yes, it's important. I think if you took the brush away from the painter, he would be miserable—even if there were another way to paint. I'm sure there is now, like you throw it at the canvas.

Interviewer: Well, we've got to talk about critics.
Simon: Now this gets to the R-rated part of the conversation!

Interviewer: You are a playwright whose work survives despite Frank Rich. Is there anything that can be done about the critical situation in this country?
Simon: This is hard to make clear to somebody because it's about negative reviews. I accept negative reviews, which I have received, when I see what they are saying. For example, Walter Kerr wrote of *The Star-Spangled Girl*: "Neil Simon didn't have an idea for a play this year, but he wrote it anyway." That was his first sentence, and I bought it completely. He was right, because I felt the idea I had was not really good. The producer I had at that time kept saying, "It's a wonderful idea." I could always write funny dialogue, and after ten pages he said, "This is wonderful," but I knew that the typewriter felt like each of the keys were ten pounds. I knew what I wrote was not really first-rate stuff. I will take that kind of criticism as productive and say, "Don't do that, Neil. Write something better, reach a little higher." The next play I did was *Plaza Suite* and I felt, "Okay, now I'm doing something worthwhile."

But when I come up against somebody like Frank Rich, who I think is a completely biased critic—a very intelligent man and a very good writer, but biased certainly against me and against other people and very pro other people (other playwrights, other actors, other directors)—for whatever reasons (they don't make any difference), I never learn anything about my plays. He never shows me where I went wrong or what I can do better, whereas Elliot Norton in Boston, when he saw *The Odd Couple* for the first time and I was sort of stuck in the second act, wrote: "Why don't you put those Pigeon sisters in there?" Of course, he was seeing something that was still in the working process as opposed to what Frank Rich sees. I said, "But of course, bring back the Pigeon sisters." That's a light comedy, and you can deal with that differently; but Frank Rich will tear the plays apart from his point of view of life, not "Is this a good play?" Maybe a critic can't write from any other place besides his point of view, but if I have one that is so diametrically opposed to how I see life I get maybe one good review in the last nine or ten plays from him—and almost all of those plays have been successful to one degree or another. John Simon doesn't bother me as much because he works on a rather esoteric magazine. People know reading that that it's not going to send people to the theater or deter them from going; so I can sometimes learn more from John Simon, who is equally intelligent and sometimes more honest because he doesn't have to worry about the masses that Frank Rich is writing for. I'm as angry with the rave reviews that Frank Rich gives to plays that nobody seems to like—or acting performances or directors or concepts; it's the way he sees the theater. He would rather that there were no Broadway with the exception of a few musicals; *Guys and Dolls* is fine to do, but when you do theater you'd better do something really smart.

Interviewer: What makes a good critic?
Simon: A man who comes with a clean slate to the theater; his mind is not prejudiced one way or the other. One who feels, "I hope I'm going to be entertained tonight, but if I'm not, I'll say so." If I can't predict what the critic is doing to say, he's a good critic; but if I know before the show opens what his response will be, he's not a good critic. I can guarantee you, with the next three shows that I write, with the exception of one (I shouldn't say because I'll jinx it), I'll get a bad review from the *New York Times*; so I say he doesn't help me as a critic or he doesn't help me as a playwright, and I want to be helped always as a playwright. I want to say, "Ah, I see what he means. That's what I should be doing." I just have to forget about that, and I go by the ones who I think are intelligent. I'd feel the same way about somebody who was so pro-me that I learned nothing from him. I haven't found that critic yet, but if there was one who just loved everything I did, I'd say, "He doesn't really mean anything, and I can't learn from him."

Walter Kerr was always the guidepost because I guess I batted .500, which is not a bad average for him—fifty-fifty: half he liked and half he didn't like. Some of the ones he liked were some of the ones that none of the audiences liked, like *God's Favorite*. There's a man who's a devoted Catholic, a very religious man, who saw the absurdity of the Book of Job. The new kinds of critics seemingly want to make a name for themselves by being very negative to the establishment. I guess that's an ongoing thing for centuries. The minute that you become establishment you become a target. Sometimes the new gets a better shot at things than the establishment, unless the establishment gets so old and is about to die or about to quit that you have to say, "Hey, the guy's still got something in him"—like when Hemingway wrote *The Old Man and the Sea*.

Interviewer: What about other playwrights? I'm not talking about Shakespeare and Shaw and Chekhov, but I mean your contemporaries. Have you learned from other playwrights?
Simon: No, I can only learn from other plays, because I can't put any consistency on anybody's work including my own. There haven't been a lot of really good plays lately, but I like plays like *The Heidi Chronicles* and *I'm Not Rappaport*. I like August Wilson's plays a lot; probably I like him more consistently than any other contemporary playwright.

Interviewer: Why is that, do you think?
Simon: Well, because they are about a race that I'm not a member of except the human race, and that's the part I identify with. It's the fact that they're black and have a completely different cultural background from me, and it still affects me and I am pulled by it, and I see the honesty of his writing for the most part. Some things I don't always get, but the fact that he is a working playwright, that he turns them out all the time, that he set a goal for himself of writing maybe ten or twelve plays on the growth of black culture in this country, that he's at it all the time, and that the quality is always superior. He's never going to make millions of dollars from his plays because they're not lined up around the block and selling out, but they win prizes. He's won two Pulitzer Prizes, which he deserves.

Interviewer: What about the quality of them as plays appeals to you?
Simon: For one thing, they are both very dramatic and very funny. I haven't seen any of them that weren't funny, and the humor is so rich. In *Fences* I was very moved, and there's wonderful humor in *The Piano Lesson*; it's very touching and moving and terrific drama and a wonderful story. It's like sitting around a campfire and listening to a man tell the story of life.

Interviewer: You've also mentioned Peter Shaffer in earlier interviews.
Simon: I'm a major fan of Peter Shaffer's. One of the reasons I wrote *"Rumors"* is because he said on a television show, when somebody asked him why he wrote *Black Comedy*, that every playwright wants to write one farce in his lifetime. Here is the man who wrote *Royal Hunt of the Sun* and *Five Finger Exercise*; you could go down the list of them and, of course,

Amadeus. I think he's a major playwright. I liked *Lettice and Lovage*; the critics said that it wasn't big enough. I really identified with that because it's a terrific play. I wished I had written that play. It's very English, but he was writing about the decay of our society, the breaking down of, not the status quo, God knows, but of the things that are beautiful in life and fighting out against it. He loves London as I love New York. He sees London decaying, as I see New York and, God knows, Los Angeles (that I don't love that much to begin with) decaying. I think Peter Shaffer is first-rank.

Interviewer: Let me give you a sentence: "The biggest impediment to a healthy theater scene today is—"
Simon: No people.

Interviewer: No audiences coming, you mean?
Simon: I don't like questions like that, because I have to answer. It's like saying, "All right, I'll tell you what's wrong with the American theater." I don't think there is anything wrong with the American theater. You just show me the play, and I'll tell you what I think is right or wrong about that play. The American theater is made up of all these different parts—playwrights and actors and everything else.

Interviewer: Do you think if a good play is written, people come to see it?
Simon: Oh, sure. There's August Wilson's plays. They're on Broadway, and they've also had the benefit of touring around the country. He rewrites, he fixes them up, and they have long lives. They'll be playing those plays forever. As long as somebody like him can be around and profit in the American theater, there's nothing totally wrong with the American theater.

Interviewer: Do you picture an audience when you write a play, or is that kind of a destructive thing to do?
Simon: I picture an ideal audience. They don't always show up—some nights they do—but they're the ones who give you a fair shake and can tell you the truth. I don't think a play keeps running if the audience doesn't like it; there's no name big enough to keep an audience coming all the time. For example, with the slams that *Death and the Maiden* got: I know a lot of people want to see those stars, but if that play were directed and acted badly, the people wouldn't be coming. I think there's a lot of quality up on that stage. I do write for an audience. I picture in my mind very tough people sitting there. I don't think that I'm someplace in the San Fernando

Valley where they just want to see *Encino Man* or something. I'm thinking of a really sophisticated audience. I tried out my last two plays in Winston-Salem, North Carolina—both *Lost in Yonkers* and *Jake's Women*. With the new play, *Laughter on the 23rd Floor*, by the nature of the material—they are twenty-six-, twenty-seven-, twenty-eight-year-old young men sitting in a room—the language is going to be salty, to say the least. I don't think I would go down there, because the last time we went down there a woman said of Helen Shaver in *Jake's Women* that she would've liked it better if her skirt weren't so short.

Interviewer: So you basically, in a sense, visualize a New York audience, which is a tough audience, a sophisticated theater audience.

Simon: They are tough and sophisticated, but you can give them the corniest musical in the world and they probably will go to that longer than they will go to the sophisticated play.

Interviewer: But, in a way, you have two New York audiences. You have a tourist audience and you have a New York audience. There is a hard-core New York audience who have been going to the serious theater for years, and there are the tourists who are primarily going to the musicals.

Simon: They do seem to stay consistent. The ones that came twenty-five years ago to *Barefoot in the Park* and *The Odd Couple* come now to *Lost in Yonkers* and *Jake's Women*. They're the same people, only their children have grown up and their children are going to the theater now. They have the same responses. I loved the audience that came to *The Odd Couple*, but it must have been in the play. It was a very fresh play at that time, that kind of comedy; we didn't have a conventional love story in the play, which was fairly new then. That's the kind of audience I hope I can get, but you get theater parties, and you need them because you can't exist without them. Half the audience is theater parties. They come mainly because it's a social event. The men aren't interested in being there. Most of the time they don't know what play is playing or even if it's a musical; so they're not as good as the ones who line up and buy tickets. If you could just get a fresh audience every night who bought tickets because they want to see this play, that's the best audience you can get; and you can get them in New York.

Interview with Neil Simon

Mike Wood / 1997

This is an edited version of an interview conducted on January 30, 1997. It is published with the permission of Mike Wood and courtesy of Independence Community College and the William Inge Center for the Arts. Mike Wood was executive director of the Media Resources Center at Wichita State University. Between 1987 and 2014, he was writer/director of twenty Tributes to the Inge Award winners at the annual William Inge Theater Festival in Independence, Kansas; Neil Simon received the Inge Award in 1997.

We are in Neil Simon's office in Beverly Hills as he walks in. He points out a number of photographs from his life and career. They are the early comedy teams he worked with; his Drama Critics Circle Award; dancing photos; a poker club group which includes Chevy Chase, Carl Reiner, Steve Martin, and others; the dance scene from *Broadway Bound*; Simon theater posters of productions in the US and overseas including in Russia; a photo of daughter Nancy at her graduation as he explains how the commencement speeches he gave took longer to write than his plays; photographs of Joe DiMaggio and Ted Williams; an original Herschfeld drawing of Mercedes Ruehl, Kevin Spacey, and Irene Worth in *Lost in Yonkers*; and an autographed picture of Babe Ruth.

Mike Wood: To begin, I've noticed that a number of modern American playwrights had fathers who were salesmen or working class. Tell me about your father.

Neil Simon: Yes, my father was working class. He sold swatches of material to manufacturers, to the companies, and they bought the prints that they wanted which they would ultimately make into dresses. He worked in the garment center in New York. He worked there basically during the Depression, and the only time he made a little money was I think during the war. When the younger men went off to war my father was too old for it, but there weren't enough salesmen around so those were his few good years—but the rest of it was a struggle. He really wasn't much of an avid theatergoer, but it was because of my father and my mother I think that I first got interested in the theater. The first play I went to see was *Native Son* by Richard Wright; I saw that at the local theater in my neighborhood, but then I got bitten by it. The first play that my mother and father took me to in New York was *Oklahoma!* I was going to say if I hadn't grown up in New York I would never have been a playwright, but there was August Wilson being born where he was and William Inge in his place and Tennessee Williams in the other, so that's not a truism at all; but it just felt like it for me, basically because I write about New York.

MW: Another similarity it seems is that many of these fathers who were salesmen in the Depression were not always around. It sounds like your father was in and out because of domestic differences.
NS: Right. My father lived at home but he didn't live at home all of the time. He and my mother broke up six or seven times and they were pretty lengthy stay-aways; you never know how that affects a young boy. I was seven, eight, nine, ten all during those years, never knowing when he was coming back. I had a brother; he was eight years older than I am so that's like having a father in a sense. I wasn't with Danny all that much, so I spent a lot of time by myself. I remember writing bits and pieces of things that had nothing to do with school work—just writing as one might draw. I would write sort of thumbnail sketches of friends and people I knew, making predictions of what I thought their lives would be like in twenty years. In some cases I went to search them out and found out what they were like. In some cases I was right, in a lot of cases wrong.

MW: You had writing, but I also know that you had, and still have from what's around this office, a love of baseball.
NS: Yes, I do. That was another luxury of growing up in New York City because we had not one major league team, but we had three. We had the Brooklyn Dodgers, the New York Giants, and the New York Yankees—and I was basically a Yankees fan because I lived a little closer to Yankee Stadium and then became a Giants fan through the Polo Grounds. Baseball is still a very big part of my life.

MW: I see references to it in the plays; you describe things in baseball terminology.
NS: I do, yes. There's a lot of metaphors about baseball that seem to apply, and I read a lot of literature about baseball too. There's something about

certain sports that attract writers. I mean if you were to talk to Harold Pinter, he could go on and on for ten days about cricket. I've tried watching cricket every time I've been in England which is many, many times and I've lived there for a while. I don't understand one moment of cricket, whereas I think baseball is a basically simple thing. You hit it and you run to a base. But there's something about keeping statistics for a young boy—and I find it true today of my friends who have young children and grandchildren. An eight- or nine-year-old boy can tell you the batting average of a player who's not on a team more than six months. We in America get attracted to that, but maybe in all cultures they feel that way about their sports stars.

MW: From the plays, it looks like your mother was perhaps more support-ive of the theater than your father. Is that true or were they both?
NS: My father wasn't supportive of the theater basically because of his deal-ings with my brother. As I said, Danny was eight years older and I think he thought that Danny wanted to go into the theater simply to meet girls, which was true for a lot of young men —more so of actors than I think play-wrights. My father thought that there was a gamble in it. He didn't know anything about literature. We literally didn't have a book in our house. I had to go to the library every week to get three or four books to read. My mother was more affirmative, not just about the theater but about whatever we wanted to do. Danny and I were writing for comics in the early days, and we would write a monologue. Danny was more the performer than I was, so Danny would read the monologue to my mother, and she would laugh and laugh, and he felt very good. He would say, "Did you understand that joke?" She would say, "Oh, was that a joke?" He would say, "Well, why were you laughing?" And she would say, "Well I don't know. You do it funny, and it makes me happy to watch you do it." So we didn't learn anything from my mother's appreciation of our work, but it was nice to have her support. It took a long time for my father to become supportive, especially with me. It took a long time, because I wrote the first couple of plays when he was ill, and the last play he saw was my third, which was *Barefoot in the Park*.

MW: In your book, you talk about him coming to see *Come Blow Your Horn*.
NS: Yes. It was a very fearful moment for me, because I was really putting my mother and father and brother on the stage—and myself as well. And because I was a beginning playwright, they were more caricatures than really three-dimensional people, but they were quite funny. My mother came on opening night, but she was at that point parted from my father.

She saw the play, and after the play was over I said, "What do you think of it, Mom?" and she said, "Oh, I don't know. I'll have to come another night." I said, "What were you doing." She said, "I was looking at all the celebrities." So she came back night after night and day after day on matinees. My father came about a week later, and I really worried about him, because I was afraid he might have felt that I was poking fun at him. I wasn't. I was pointing out his human and comic foibles, but I never meant to make a joke of what he was like. So he saw the play, and I waited anxiously at the back of the house for him to come out. I saw him; he didn't have a smile on his face, and so with great trepidation I walked over to him and I said, "What'd you think, Dad?" He said, "It's nice. It's good. I liked it." I said, "Well, I'm glad." I said to him, "What did you think of the father?" And he said, "Oh, I know so many men just like him." He never saw himself in the play; but he felt he was responsible for the play's success; he went back to the garment business and said, "You've got to see my son's play; it's hilarious. Wait till you see this father, he's really funny."

MW: There's another version of that I think in *Broadway Bound*. I noticed as they gathered around the radio that there was some realization on several faces that this might be too close to home.

NS: My brother and I wrote a radio show for CBS that was on at six o'clock on Saturday nights when no one would listen, because CBS was just trying out writers, and they invented this show for writers to learn their craft. My father was still very much against my going into the business. He wanted me to go into the post office where he knew I would get one hundred dollars a week for the rest of my life. He listened to the first program—and my brother and I just sat there looking at him. When the program was over, my father said, "I didn't hear many laughs," which was like a knife in both of our hearts. I didn't think he meant it to be cruel. I think he was trying to say, "What do you two know about writing? You know you're never going to make a living at this." He was not very accommodating or encouraging. But, in *Broadway Bound*, I did something much different, which I think was more to the point than what happened in real life. We wrote the show, and the mother and father were funny, but slightly at their own expense. I can't quite remember; I don't think we talked about his dallying with other women or anything, but when the show was over, it was the nightmare part of the dream of what I hoped my father would say, like "That was wonderful and I can't wait to tell other people about it." He was furious that he was being made fun of. What happened was that my brother took him on: when the father started to yell at him: "I'm ashamed of you. Don't you have any shame for what you're doing to your father?" the older brother said, "Don't you have any shame for what you're doing to our mother?" It was much more dramatic. That's why I say that my plays are not autobiographical. You take real incidents in life and put them into a much more pressurized sort of atmosphere. I was glad I never really had to live through a scene like that where my father said, "How dare you write about me that way."

MW: I thought it was interesting that in the play there was tension between the sons and the father, but as the radio play is about to come on the air it's obvious that it's so important that the father be there. They are disappointed that he hasn't shown up yet.

NS: They were disappointed and worried that the father wouldn't show up because there was no way to prove to them that they were good, because the show itself actually was getting big laughs from the radio audience and the mother—to use a Jewish word —was kvelling that her two sons were getting laughs, that the audience had seemed to like it, that the people at CBS would now give them a job. So she was very happy for us. The father was very single-minded. All he could see was that he was being made a joke of.

MW: There's another scene in *Broadway Bound* that's very touching: when the son dances with the mother. Is that autobiographical?

NS: It's a pretty interesting story the way it got into the play. I think that's the most famous scene in that play, when the son gets up and dances with the mother to bring back the memory of when she danced with George Raft. It was not in the original play. We sat down to read the play at the first day's reading. Linda Lavin played the mother, brilliantly, and I listened to her. And there was a scene with another girl that I had brought in and I saw the producer Manny Azenberg sitting next to me with the script, and out of the corner of my eye I saw that he was turning the pages quickly. I knew what that meant: how long does this scene go on? So I quickly wrote a little note and passed it to him and said, "Don't worry, I'll fix it." When we left the reading and went out to lunch, director Gene Saks and Manny and myself, they kept talking about how to fix that scene and what the girl should really be doing. I was half-listening and then I said, "Don't worry about it. She's not in the play anymore." They said, "When did this happen?" I said, "In the walk from the studio to the Chinese restaurant, I got rid of the girl." It wasn't because the actress wasn't right. I said, "What the play is missing is that we don't see one happy moment in the mother's life." From the time the curtain goes up the mother's in trouble with the father. She knows that he's fooling around, and she learns that it's happening again a year later, despite the fact that she's wrong about it. The woman that she sees is actually dying of cancer and he just sees her at lunch to commiserate with her, but some woman—a gossiper—gets back to the mother and says, "Well she's back with him again." And so the mother is willing to gamble and lose the whole marriage by saying to the father, "I don't want you in my bedroom. I don't want to see you." So everything is tumbling—her father having to move to Florida because he's getting old and thought it would be better if he lived with his wife that he was estranged from, and the two boys growing up and about to go to Broadway and actually making their name in radio and television before the lights ever came up on Broadway.

The son, Eugene, who was really my alter ego, wants to draw the mother out of her unhappiness for the moment and he says, "Tell me when you danced with George Raft," and she says, "You never believed that story." He says, "I do. Just tell me again." And so she starts to tell the story, but she tells the story of how she first met George Burns, or George Raft rather, in a dance hall, who used to go around from place to place and pick out the best dancer there. My mother was a terrific ballroom dancer—not a professional, but she would have loved to have been—and he picked her out and that was the greatest night of her life. That was her Academy Award, and she got up and danced with him. As she's telling this story, the boy goes over and turns on the radio and I remember it was a Benny Goodman tune and he says, "Come on, Mom. Get up and dance with me." She says, "No, I can't do that." He gets her up and dances with her and it became the most poignant moment in the entire play. People who saw the play assumed that that was the first scene I thought of and that I built the play around it, whereas it was the very last thing that was put into the play.

There's a great addendum to the story. On my fiftieth birthday my mother came to the party that my wife Marsha had thrown for me in Beverly Hills and George Burns was there (it was actually George Burns in real life that this happened with—that's why I've been making those mistakes a little bit; I thought it was much more romantic to say George Raft in the play, but it actually was George Burns). My mother never believed that we believed the story; she thought that we thought she was making up the story about dancing with George Burns. So George Burns was at the party, having just finished making *The Sunshine Boys*, and he came over to me and put his arm around me and said, "Well, Neil, we have a big hit. I'm very happy. Thank you." And then he looked at my mother and said, "Who's this charming lady?" And I said, "Well, it's my mother, George." And he said, "Would you like to dance, Mrs. Simon?" So she got up, didn't say a word, and danced around the room, and as she came back around to our table she turned her head towards me and said, "What did I tell you?" Like she finally proved it! It was not an epiphany for me I guess, but it fulfilled everything that I wanted my mother to have which she didn't have in her own life.

MW: That's a wonderful story. You mentioned writing for radio, and another commonality I see with so many playwrights is that they had radio and early live television. And the summer camps; several of them participated in summer camps. All three of those things probably aren't as available today as they were then.

NS: Well, I think that commonality of writing for early radio and summer camps and early television is for writers about sixty or over. I don't know where young writers get their chance to break in today. It was very helpful for Danny and myself to get our first job at CBS making twenty dollars a week apiece which was big money back in the late 1940s. We learned, and there were other writers working on the staff; George Axelrod, who wrote *The Seven Year Itch* and some wonderful movies, was on the staff and a number of other writers. Then later on getting to work on all of those television shows—everything from Red Buttons to Tallulah Bankhead, and then eventually doing some specials for NBC where we worked with Tyrone Power, Burt Lahr, Nancy Walker, and a young Tony Randall. Working with Burt Lahr was one of the best experiences I had because to me he was the king of comedy. I thought he was brilliant because he was a man who could do the lowest of vaudeville comedy to *Waiting for Godot*. He was the man that I always wanted to play the lead in *The Sunshine Boys*, but he died before that ever happened. And at Camp Tamiment in the Pocono Mountains in Pennsylvania, we did ten weekly shows running an hour and a half each; we did it on a Saturday night and a Sunday night and on Monday morning we started writing the next show, which is exactly what happened later on *Your Show of Shows* with Sid Caesar and Max Liebman and Mel Brooks and all those writers. Now we were getting a chance to write for a live audiences and getting paid for it.

Not a lot of people get that kind of opportunity today. I see lots of kids sending in scripts, who write to me, "Where do I send this script? How do I get a script done?" The thing that I always tell young writers to do, because there's no way for them to get their work heard—I'm talking specifically about plays, it might work with screenplays also—is to get a bunch of actors together who are your friends. They don't have to be profes-sionals, they just have to be fairly good. Just sit around the table and read it. You find out more about your material when you hear it read for the first time. It's taking your own x-rays. You see the places that need work. Strangely enough, for the first three plays I did, *Come Blow Your Horn*, *Barefoot in the Park*, and *The Odd Couple*, I never had a reading of the play. I just wrote it; Mike Nichols and I worked on it for six months and we got it to a point where we thought it was wonderful and then we'd sit down and read it. I remember with *The Odd Couple*, we sat down and read the play with the actors on the first day of rehearsal—Walter Matthau and Art Carney playing the roles and the other wonderful actors in that group. The first act was hilarious. It was a three-act play as plays were in those days. The second act was even funnier. So I felt, we're home; this is going to be a huge hit. The third act was deadly. There was not a laugh from one of the actors nor from myself nor Mike Nichols, and I knew we were in big trouble with it. Walter was so perturbed that he wanted to quit the play. He said, "This play's not going to work. I thought it was the funniest thing I ever read, but the third act is awful." Mike said, "Be patient. You know Neil will fix it." And so Mike and I walked off into a corner, and I said, "What do we do?" And he said, "Well, I go and direct the first two acts, and you go home and write a new third act."

So I went home, and I spent three days and three nights working on a new third act. I finally got the third act into some kind of shape, which I knew was a lot better than the other one. We sat down at the table again, and Mike said, "Let's sit down and read the new third act." And we did, and it was worse than the first one. That's when the real panic sets in, because you say, "I have no place else to go in my mind. There's no one who's going to call me and say, 'Here's what you do, kid.'" So we took a train to Wilmington, Delaware—it took three and a half hours—and Mike and I spent those three and a half hours talking out the possibilities of a new third act. We hit on some ideas, and I thought, "Maybe I can make them work." Mike went on to rehearse—now we only had three days to set up technically, and then do our first preview. I stayed up that whole day and that whole night, and I wrote a new third act; I knew it was rough, and I brought it in to Mike, and he sat at breakfast and read it. We were in this big dining room in the hotel, and Mike is a wonderful, wonderful audience. The guffaws were heard all around the room. Then he turned to me, and he said, "It's not there yet, but it's better than the other ones." I said, "Well, what do we do? Wait till Boston and I get it right and we'll put it in?" And he said, "I'll tell you at the rehearsal today."

Twenty minutes later at the rehearsal Mike said, "Neil has written a new third act. It's not all there, but it's better than what we have." Then we sat down and read it, and they heard that it was a lot better. They said, "So what do we do, put it in in Boston?" Mike said, "No, we're going to put it in in Wilmington." And they couldn't believe him. They said, "Mike, we have to do three acts. Two of the acts we know fairly well. The third act we won't know at all." He said, "What's the point of doing a bad act well when you can do a good act badly, which will get better?"—which was reasonable enough except to an actor. Walter Matthau said, "No, I'm not doing that." He said, "I'm too professional. I'm not going to go out there and make a fool of myself." Mike said, "Walter, we'll learn nothing about the play if we just go back and do this deadly third act." Walter said he would take the script, and he would try to sleep on it that night, which he literally did. He read it over and over again, and then he put it under his pillow hoping that the words somehow would get past the feathers and through the silk—not silk, they were far from silk in that hotel!—into his head. He came down to rehearsal the next morning, almost with tears in his eyes, and he said, "I can't do it. I can't learn it." Mike, being the brilliant director he is, said, "Okay, Walter, don't worry. The other actors will do the new third act. You can do the old third act." He had to laugh at that, so he said, "Okay, I'll do my best." We did it, and it was surprisingly good. It faltered, and the critics said it faltered, and the act was sagging, but it was the beginning of something.

I stopped going to rehearsals and kept working and working until we got to Boston with the play, and we opened. The critic from the *Boston Globe*, Elliot Norton—a great critic—the headline to his review, which I found out later that critics never write, it's always the editorial staff—said, "Oh, For a Third Act." And I'm saying, "What about 'yay' for the first two acts? Give us a break. Give us a little encouragement." But at any rate, the play was a big enough hit to start off with that we packed the house every night, and then Elliot Norton called me—actually I was on his television show—and he said, "You know I have a suggestion for the third act. Why don't you bring back those Pigeon sisters? They're really good." It was as if a neon light went on over my head, and I said, "Of course, the Pigeon sisters!" So I wrote another scene for the Pigeon sisters, and we laughed so hard at rehearsals that Mike said, "We can't put this on the stage, because we will be accused of manslaughter. People will be carried out of the theater dying from laughter." We did get it on that night, and did not get a single laugh in the Pigeon sisters scene—and the two actresses were wonderful. I walked out dejected again, realizing how difficult this playwriting business is; you think you have it and like quicksilver it's gone. I said, "What went wrong, Mike?" And he said, "They don't like what's happening in the scene. They don't like the turn of the story. If you could find another thing that they can relate to and understand, then maybe the laughs would come easier." Knowing that, I went home, and it took me a couple of days, and I gave it to them. Now we didn't laugh so much at rehearsal, but when we put it in that night, we got huge laughs, even when the lines weren't that funny, because the audiences now were enjoying the sense of the comedy, the progression of the play itself, the characters coming into their own and learning something about themselves. The third act still never lives up to the other two, but the play is the biggest hit I ever had and ever will have. Here it is thirty-five years later, I think, and the play is doing as well as it ever did.

One of the really difficult things about writing a play—I guess it applies to a movie or something else but it does not apply to adaptations, it applies only to originals—all of you, the writer, the director, and the actors are going somewhere where no human being has been before. You're discovering this new piece of work, so none of you knows too much about it including the author. He may have spent two years working on it, but he starts learning more about it. In each day's work he starts to hear the words read. I remember with the first play I wrote, *Come Blow Your Horn*, I wrote it on an old typewriter, not an electric, and with all the errors I would just draw a little line and put in the new words and there were just all of these terrible pen marks all over the papers. And my agent then at the William Morris office read the play as best she could through all that garbage in there and said, "I'm going to send this play to Herman Shumlin."

Herman Shumlin was one of the finest dramatic directors of his day, and he wanted to do a comedy. He read the play and said, "I like the play very much and I want to come out and talk to you about it, but I want you to do something first." I said, "What's that?" He said, "Have it typed." I thought he meant just to clean it up. So I said, "Yeah, I need to do that. It will be easier to read." He said, "No, I'm not saying it because it will be easier to read. I just want you to do it and you'll see what I'm talking about." So I sent it to a typist who would do it professionally and I got it back and I read it and it was like it was a different play. When you're reading the play for the first time it's as though someone else sent it to you and you have a much more objective view. It looks very professional on this well-typed page and you start to see the flaws in the play and you start to make your changes.

The next time you start to learn about the play, as I said before, is when you read it for the first time with the actors. People always ask me, "Are you nervous on opening nights?" I'm not nervous on opening nights, because opening night was months before—or at least weeks before. The very first opening night is the day that you read the play around the table with the actors. Then you know. You don't need reviewers then. They're the reviewers and critics, although they don't say it. Some actors, if they're a star, will say, "It kind of falls apart over here, you know?" The next most important night in the life of a play is the very first preview audience that comes to see it; there's always six or seven previews before the critics come. On that night you find out if you have a healthy baby or not. Is this going to survive? You learn a lot. You have to be careful; you can make mistakes, because that first audience is so excited to see it, at least once you become well known. There's great anticipation and they may laugh much too much. You don't know this, though; you just think every minute of the play is hilarious. Then you have the second act, and they don't laugh quite as much. You say, "Oh, now I have to balance it out." So it takes three or four of these previews to sort it out and say, "Where is it consistently funny or moving and touching, and where is it sort of blah?"

Then you quickly and hastily try to do the work, because now the critics are going to come. They finally come, and then you find out what the play is about. Up until then you never knew what your play was about until they tell you. I'm being slightly facetious about that, but people always ask me, "What's the theme of your play?" And I say, "I never know. I wait until the critics tell me what the theme is." By the time you get to opening night—and in today's world opening night doesn't mean what it used to be when all the critics used to come and that night you got the reviews—now the critics have already come to the previews, so the only ones left are maybe a couple of people from television and a few magazines. But the major critics—I'm talking about a New York opening—have already seen the play, so opening night is for your family and friends and the only thing that has some importance to it is that that's the night that you read what the critics say.

Then there's that divisive thing that happens; you get those split reviews all the time. Once in a while you'll get all good reviews from somebody, but that's generally when they want to discover somebody. Your earliest plays, strangely enough, generally do better. Then as you get better and better as a playwright, they get tougher with you.

They say, "No, no—we want it better." And you say, "Better, how?" "We don't know. Just better." I don't mean that that conversation takes place, but it's written in between the lines of their newspapers. I have plays that I think are some of my best which didn't get as good reviews as, say, *Barefoot in the Park,* which is a nice, light comedy. But then you get the reviews that throw you completely. When *Lost in Yonkers,* which I consider to be the best play I've written, opened in Washington, DC, there was a new critic there, a woman I can't remember—Lloyd something or other. I guess I purposely don't remember her last name! The opening paragraph of her review of *Lost in Yonkers* was: "After thirty years of playwriting, Neil Simon still doesn't know how to construct a play." I was just aghast, because I knew what I had up there. I knew what Mercedes Ruehl and Irene Worth and Kevin Spacey were doing on that stage. That was as good as I could write. The other reviews were all wonderful, but you say, "Who is this person who knows so well that this is a bad play, for which we won the Tony Award and the Pulitzer Prize?" It still jars you, and you're never immune from it. I don't know about those people who say, "I don't read the reviews. I don't pay attention to the reviews." You try not to; but I try to learn from the reviews. The difference is that what you learn from a reviewer of a play that you're doing out of town means you can fix it based upon what he just said, or she said, in the review. When you open in New York you don't learn about what you can fix in the play because it's a matter of opinion at that point. All you might learn is what you might do in the next play if you've gone right or wrong.

We are living in an era now, which is the beginning of maybe worse days to come, when plays are disappearing from the New York theater. As we're talking today there may be two or three plays on Broadway. Maybe a few more will open, but that's not what the theater is about anymore. It's about musicals. It's about events. I think the movies have done that to Broadway. It's the young people that want these sort of showy, bombastic sorts of entertainments. They're trying to do them on Broadway; Andrew Lloyd Webber has been very successful with huge sets and some wonderful scores in his musicals. The audiences now are about only 40 percent from New York; 60 percent come from either out of town or out of the country. It's easier for them to enjoy a musical because they can hear the music, watch the dancing, and look at the sets; plays are something you do basically Off-Broadway now. I did my last play, *London Suite,* Off-Broadway. I think I did it knowing that it really wasn't right for Broadway—not that I think Broadway means quality and Off-Broadway doesn't mean quality. It's probably the opposite in a way. But there is more scope to it.

I still think if Tennessee Williams and Arthur Miller were around today at their best, their plays would belong on Broadway. They have something so large to say that it reaches everyone. And some Off-Broadway plays have a much more—I don't want to say esoteric again, but I'll have to say it—a different point of view. But so many of them are brilliant and that's where we find the David Mamets and Sam Shepards and other wonderful playwrights. I write for Broadway I guess because I was brought up in it. Comedy helps you a lot on Broadway, but less and less have I been writing out and out comedy. Once in a while I'll still go back and do one like *"Rumors,"* which is a farce—or something just for the fun of it. I really miss going to the theater and seeing a good play and it's rare that we do it. Maybe something will turn it around. I'm hoping. But big business in a way prohibits it. In movies you're not a big hit unless you gross $100 million, which is insane, because I've seen some of these wonderful little movies out now that gross $3 million if they're lucky and are brilliant movies. Everyone is looking for *The Phantom of the Opera* or *Cats* to run ten, eleven, or twelve years; *Death of a Salesman* ran a year and a half and it's one of the great American plays. I don't know how long *Streetcar* ran, maybe a little longer because it had a wider appeal to people in some respects, but it would be tough going—I guess maybe I'm contradicting myself a little bit—but maybe it would be tough for Tennessee Williams and Arthur Miller today because that's not what the theater's about now and that sort of frightens me.

MW: It's definitely a TV generation, one that's expecting helicopters to land on the stage. They have a harder time sitting and working at it with the actors and the playwright, getting inside what's going on.

NS: What puzzles me about it is the dichotomy that people are reading more today. At least that's what I read in the newspapers—and having just done a book I've learned more about the book publishing business. When I had a book coming out there were about seventy books coming out around that same week or a period of weeks around it, whereas a play opens once a year, two plays a year, something like that. So people are reading. You see people reading everywhere, but going to the theater is not quite the same thing. A thousand years from now, I can't imagine what kind of entertainment we will have. Maybe there'll be nothing on the stage at all, but just something you stick in your ear or it's a pill you take with water.

MW: Realizing that attention spans and so forth are changing, how have the plays on Broadway adapted to that? I'm thinking about lengths and number of acts and so forth.

NS: You are aware when you write a play today—I'm speaking for myself so I shouldn't use "you"—that there are other considerations. Plays have bigger sets today. I'm trying to think of the play with the rain coming down—*An*

Inspector Calls. An Inspector Calls when it was originally written some fifty years ago was a one-set play that was right down front in front of the audience. It was a big hit in today's world when they pushed that set all the way back and there were twenty young people on stage standing in the rain who never had a word to say. It was an interesting concept because these were the poor people looking in as best they could at a world they never could have. And then the set moved down and unraveled, opened up and showed us how these people lived. The play was the same; the play itself, the content, wasn't changed. But the concept of how we watched it and what was visual was there. More plays have been doing that. There was a revival of I think a Tennessee Williams play that Kathleen Turner did last year, and I met a critic I knew and I asked him—before he had seen the play—"What do you hear about the play?" And he said, "Oh, I hear the sets are great." You take it for granted that the sets are going to be great because those designers have done their homework and almost all of them, the really good ones, are brilliant.

Getting a good play is another matter. It's got to be on the printed page and then up there on the stage. So the set shouldn't be the thing you think about most. *Proposals*, which we will start rehearsing in June, is the first outdoor play I've ever done. It takes place outside of a house, so there's foliage; there's an unseen lake. There are paths going this way and that way. There are cars that are pulling up that you don't see, that you hear. But it gives you the sense you're watching a movie. I didn't think of that first. I thought of the play, and I said, "The reason I can't do the play inside is that there are too many people who have to have conversations that other people should not be hearing. I can't do this in a room. I'd have to keep clearing the room: "Would you please leave the room, because these two people have something important to say?" As I wrote it, it was a one-set play. It was the back of a house. The front of the house was on the other side, and all of these paths lead to it, and there was a porch and all this furniture, and out on the ground the stump of a tree. It actually sounds like a William Inge play to me, like *Picnic*, I suppose. But it gives you greater latitude. What Joe Mantello wants to do, and I hope it works, is that house will sometimes move in this direction, so we can play a scene here, and it can move in the other direction so you get different perspectives. It also raises the cost of the play, so this play will cost about $1.6 million. The cost of everything goes up: the cost of costumes, the cost of building the set, the cost of actors, the cost of advertising —all of it. So that's another thing that inhibits plays from being done. If backers are going to put money into a play, I guess they'd rather go for the home run and get a big hit.

MW: You've talked about doing a play in front of the actors then finally in the theater and on opening night, and how you keep changing it and rewriting, but at some point, the rewriting can't go on forever. How do you know when you're going to leave it?

NS: The question about rewriting and when to know when to stop has two answers. One is the obvious one: it stops when you have to open the play; you have an opening night. But I think something very good happened to me with *Proposals*. We wanted to start the play off at the Ahmanson Theater, because we would get an eight-week run there, and so I would get a lot of time to fix the play. But in order to get into the Ahmanson Theater this year, the bookings were such that we would either have to go in very quickly after I'd finished the play or wait until they had booked other plays, one of them being *Show Boat* which was going to run six or seven months. So we were delayed for a year and four months. Now I had a year and four months with the play. I was doing other things too. I was writing my book *Rewrites*, and I was starting a movie. I did a draft of the play and I put it away and didn't look at it for three months. Then I took it out and read it, and I said, "I can make this better," and I went through it and made it better. I *think* I made it better! Then we had auditions —countless numbers of auditions where I heard the words every day—and I'd say, "Wait a minute. This scene isn't working." So because I had extra time I had more time to work on the play, I saw it improving session after session and draft after draft. Then we went into rehearsal. The first draft was now the seventh draft of the play.

So I think I'm well ahead of the game, which doesn't mean that I won't get up there on the first night with an audience and say, "This scene doesn't really work." The difficult thing of knowing whether a scene works or not is very delicate because sometimes you think you have the right actor and they're not capturing what you want. They convey something to an audience, because an audience rightly assumes that whoever's doing that play was meant to do that play; you picked that person, but it may be the understudy that night, and the play changes enormously. They look different from what you picture. They have a different manner of speaking or something. The audience may say, "Oh I didn't like that girl," or "I didn't like that guy." We got all the right people with *Lost in Yonkers*, probably more than any play I ever did, the three perfect people; I got exactly and Gene Saks got exactly what we all wanted and so it was perfection.

But I like the long writing period. When I said to Joe Mantello, "Joe, you know we're going to have to go to Phoenix, Arizona, for two weeks and two weeks in New Haven and then four weeks I think at the Kennedy Center before we take it New York. How do you feel about that?" He said, "Great! The more time we have the better we have to fix it." It takes the pressure off me. I don't have to do as I did with *The Odd Couple*—go back and stay up all night in the hotel room, although I'm prone to do that. I'm very quick at rewrites, because I can't stand it when I see something up on the stage that isn't working; that's my fault, that's not the actors. I can say, "If I could just rewrite the scene," which I can do; I can't do that in a film. Once they film it, it's goodbye, gone. The set is gone. But with a play I can always say, "Just try this." And then very often the director will say, "You know the earlier version of this scene was better. Can we go back and try that?" So you get all those opportunities, which is what I love about playwriting—which is what I assume someone like August Wilson loves about playwriting. He tinkers all the way through.

MW: But with all your playwriting, you also have worked a lot in film— in fact have done several original film scripts; so I assume you enjoy that too. Perhaps not as much as the playwriting, but you certainly have worked more there than most playwrights.

NS: I've never counted my films. I know how many plays I've done. This will be the thirtieth play; I think I've done twenty-four or twenty-five movies. Maybe nine or ten of them were adaptations. The others were originals, like *The Heartbreak Kid* or *The Goodbye Girl* or *Murder by Death*. I seem to have a better time with those because I'm not trying to preserve what I have on the stage, because if I do I tend to be a little stage-bound with it. I'm reluctant to give up some of the dialogue. I need a really good director to say, "Listen, we can open this up. We can do other things here." So I'm learn-ing to do that now. I'm writing two of them right now. One is *Laughter on the 23rd Floor*. I like the play *Laughter on the 23rd Floor*. I think it was not only a really funny play, but it had a lot of things to say about the McCarthy era and working in that era, about what it was like, not just to write comedy, but to be a family, a group of people who spend more time together than they do with their wives and their children, and the pressure of what it's like to get it out week after week. What was told in this story was the changing times in America in the fifties when television first came out when it was only in the large cities—New York, Chicago, Boston, etc.—but then it began playing in smaller places, maybe at that time less sophisticated places which changed the kinds of sketches we had to do on the Sid Caesar show. We had to stop doing the Japanese movies and the Italian movies. The show got watered down, and consequently, we came to the end of it.

I thought it was an important play for me to write and a fun one to do because I think I sort of captured the characteristics of Sid Caesar and Mel Brooks and the other people. In making the movie I found other dynamics to deal with, more of the personal life of the Sid Caesar character by bringing his brother and his wife and his children into it, to show the pain that he went through at the end of the day which has nothing to do with being funny. He knew he could be funny. He also knew that the networks and the sponsors wanted him to be funny their way, not his way. And that was anathema to him. He really was heartbroken about that, as we all were. What was great about that also though was that it was a spawning ground for some of the most prolific and successful writers in the country. I don't think there's ever been a show that spawned as many terrific writers into all fields of entertainment, and it was because Sid Caesar knew who the best writers were. He didn't know them by reputation. He could just tell after being around them for a little while—the way they talked, the kind of humor they had. If he didn't like it, they didn't stay, they were gone. Some of them were sort of peripheral writers. They hung around and would say a funny thing now and then, and Sid kind of liked having them around, but he knew who the big batters were. So I look forward to doing that movie.

Now I'm writing an original movie also, because I don't want to start another play until I'm finished with the play I'm doing. I can't wear two hats. I can write a play and then write a movie while the play has not yet been put on; but I can't write a play while I'm waiting to see how this is received, because after *Proposals* opens in New York, I may change my mind about what kind of a play I want to do next. Right now I don't have an idea of what kind of play I want to do. I don't write a play because I say, "I have a great idea." I just stare at a wall thinking, looking for that germ that sort of, if it's good, starts to grow a little bit stage by stage as *Lost in Yonkers* did.

The great thing about writing in the theater is that I don't have a studio or a conglomerate to deal with. I don't have Gulf and Western or Viacom to say, "No, no, no, *this* is what you have to do with this play." I only have me, the producer, and the director. And at some point the producer, Manny Azenberg, will even back off and leave it to Joe Mantello and myself to put the play on. Then Manny will come in and make his comments. But it's still our play and even beyond that it's my play, basically. I like that. Working in movies, you not only deal with the head of the studio. There are twenty-seven underlings who all send you notes that contradict each other, so you throw them away because they have no meaning unless there's one really smart kid in the group who makes a point and you say, "That's not bad," so you have to be careful and listen. But it's very hard for me to picture what's going to be up on the screen because I have no idea where the director's going to put the camera or how he wants to shoot the scene or where he wants to shoot it. When I do a play I can see in my mind what the audience is going to see in the theater. We're not going to go beyond that, although a really good director like Joe Mantello and some of the others can add some visual things to it that don't necessarily change the basic play, which is what a film studio might make you do, change a sense of the play.

MW: I want to be sure to talk some about your writing habits. What kind of routine do you have? What would we see if we were in your writing space?
NS: I got a letter from a young man a few years ago and he said, "I'm interested in being a playwright and would it be possible for me to come sit in your office and just watch you write?" I said, "What would you see? You would just see me doing this (*looks up at the wall*) and then typing (*looks down*) and then doing this (*returns gaze to the wall*) and then typing or writing on the pad. What would you learn?" I write longhand. I'm not a computer person; I'm never going to be, because I can type rather quickly. I don't mind making the mistakes that I have to correct, which I usually white out. I guess they look pretty antique by the time they get to the producer. But I don't mind going back over the mistakes because, after I change the mistake, I'll stop to look at the sentence and say, "Oh wait, I can make this sentence better." I think computer users contradict this; they say that you would do it anyway on a computer. But I don't think I would, because I'm looking at it much more carefully and I'm saying, "If I'm going to spend the time to retype this entire page, I want to make sure that every word is right, because I don't want to retype it again." I don't mean spelling it right, but getting the right amount of syllables and words. Sometimes you write a sentence and you say, "I've said everything I want in this sentence, but it needs another word." It has to do with the music of it, with the beats in it. It's not a conscious thought, but I read it and I say, "Something is wrong here." Sometimes it has an extra word in it that I don't need. People like Jack Lemmon—I've seen him say it in print, and he's said it on television a number of times—say, "With Neil Simon's work, because of the rhythm that he works in, you can't leave out a preposition—if, and, but—not just because the word is important, but because it's part of the music." He says, "I've tried taking it out, and it doesn't work, so I put it back in." Where I learned that I don't know. Sometimes people say, "I can tell a Neil Simon play." I can't—maybe only by the subject matter; I guess they think it's mine

if it comes from Brooklyn, where I don't come from. I wrote the plays about Brighton Beach only because I was originally going to write them about Far Rockaway, where these stories happened, but "Far Rockaway Memoirs" has no alliteration to it, and *Brighton Beach Memoirs* does. Then I found myself into the B.B. plays. *Biloxi Blues*, I went in the Army and took basic training in Biloxi, Mississippi; and *Broadway Bound* was exactly where I was going. I stopped writing B.B. plays because it would look a little affected.

MW: I think I've read cookies and peanuts or something on the side are part of your process.

NS: I wrote about it in *Rewrites*. I was doing a number of plays in Boston, from *The Odd Couple* on, *Plaza Suite* and some others, and I began to get nervous, because I was new to the theater, so I started buying peanuts and candy and things and eating them and then found I didn't like them. But they were there, so they assumed I loved them; so every time I came to do another play in Boston there were baskets of cookies and peanuts, which I never ate and I felt so guilty about it. But I did have the honor of being voted the neatest playwright at the Ritz Carlton Hotel in Boston because they had very little cleaning to do in my room. That's what happens when you have a mother who brings up an anal-retentive son!

MW: You were talking there a minute ago about syllables and rhythms within the writing. Several modern American playwrights have had a musical background. Terrence McNally is very interested in opera; Garson Kanin I think started out up in the Poconos playing saxophone. Do you have a musical background of any kind?

NS: I have no musical background. No one in my family plays an instrument, no one sings; we all sing badly, but the words have a music to me. You can certainly find it in Shakespeare. The rhythms of the words—especially when they start to rhyme in the sonnets or at the endings of scenes—are so powerful. You say, "How could he get a rhyme in this incredible speech that he's making that's gets over such an important moment which is always the end of a major scene?" It comes as second nature. I don't look for it first; it's only when I start to read it again or I hear it with an actor. A lot of actors who come to audition for me will say, "It's very easy to learn your plays." I say, "I think it's because I write connective sentences." Some abstract writers write where they jump from thought to thought, but the audience after a while gets the rhythm of it and goes along with it—but I can't. I have to write connective things.

First of all, I don't—and I don't imagine most writers do—know what the next line is going to be. I rarely write a line preparing for the next line I want to say. I just write the line that this character has to say, because that's what he or she has to say at that moment, which then has a reply or answer from someone else. But then suddenly I find the scene starts to go off on a tangent that I had not thought of, and I just let it go, because it leads to such interesting things. I don't plan any of the play. I never know what the ending is going to be. Only in the very beginning did I write an outline of a play, with *Come Blow Your Horn*, and found out that, after I got through the first act, the characters didn't want to stick to the outline at all. They wanted to go their own way, and I just followed them. I never know when the play's going to end. I always think it's going to end at a certain point and I suddenly say, "Wait a minute. I just finished the play. I don't have to go on forever." Other times I have to wrap it up in a different way and go in another direction. In writing *Proposals*, I had an ending in mind, but I didn't know exactly what it was. I said, "There's a picture onstage I want. I want the three women, the three important women in the play, on stage alone"— because I knew what the subject matter was and that they were dealing with somebody's death, and they were all dealing with it differently. There was a mother, there was this black woman who worked for the family, and there was the daughter—and they all had different things on their mind. I said, "They will talk about something." I just loved that image, and it came out that way. But that just comes in a flash. If you get it, fine. If you don't get it, you'll get it when you get to the end.

MW: Where in all of that does the conscious versus unconscious come in?
NS: The conscious and unconscious? Do you mean in terms of writing?

MW: Right. Maybe that's not a fair question.
NS: No, I think I know what you're talking about. There was a problem in my life—if it was a problem at all—in that I always felt like two different people. One was a very normal, fairly even-tempered, average person, who goes about doing his life the way everyone else does, and the other one is the playwright. And the playwright has many more facets to him than the other Neil does. He's smarter. He can deal with things that Neil can't deal with or doesn't want to deal with. He's much more neurotic than Neil the person is. I sometimes felt that the playwright didn't like Neil very much, because Neil wanted to go to the ballgame. The writer wanted to write. And this battle went on. It's not a conscious battle, and there's no conversations

going on between these two people, but it's inside there someplace. Over the years I think they've become more wedded to each other, or else I've moved over to becoming more the playwright. I don't know, to tell you the truth. I think I'm becoming more well-adjusted in my life. I'm in a happy marriage. I have three daughters and three grandchildren. But even when I go to see my daughters, I stay at a hotel, because I don't like to stay in their houses because then I have to do what they want to do. I want to come over, spend the day, go home at night. I'll take the pad with me; I'm always working on something. Besides doing the books and the plays and the movies; I'm writing a column for a magazine which I do just for the fun of it. I'm always writing and I spend most of my life in a room like this. If it's not here it's in New York, it's in a hotel room or it's in an airplane or in a dentist's office. In a way it's an evasion of life, I guess, because it distracts me from the things that I don't want to think about, like talking about going through a bad time physically or some things that are pending. I worry, but when I write I don't think about it—so those three or four hours are devoted to that. When my first wife Joan was very ill and up almost to when she was dying, I still spent at least an hour a day writing, because it was an escape from dealing with things that were too tough to handle. But the escape is a positive thing. It's not just to get away from something. I'm also doing something that's very practical and productive. I get letters from people who say, "Please don't stop writing. We need you to write. We need playwrights to write things that help reaffirm our feelings about life." I've been very lucky. There aren't a lot of people in life who get to do the thing they love to do, but I knew very early on that this was what I wanted to do. I've been doing this since I was fifteen or sixteen years old. I'd come home, as I said earlier, put my school books aside having done my homework, and write something for myself, because I couldn't draw very well; I couldn't do other things.

MW: You have been lucky. You've also, as anyone does, had your personal problems to overcome. But from the lucky standpoint, do you ever imagine yourself in an airplane looking out the window at that sea of people down there—whether it's way out in the Midwest where there aren't very many people, or whether it's flying into a big city—and think about your relationship to all those people?

NS: I really don't know. I really didn't know what contact I had with the people who may or may not have seen my work; but then I went on a book tour and when I was in Houston and St. Louis and Philadelphia and Minneapolis, people came up to me as if they knew me and they said, "I've seen every play that you've done. I'm reading this book. I'm enjoying it and I want you to do more." They'd talk about their favorite characters in the plays. This went on in the hundreds and the thousands sometimes because I'd be speaking in a theater of eighteen hundred people. So then I knew we had been connected all the time; I just didn't see them. They see you through your work. And they see you in a slightly distorted view of your work sometimes, because they don't see an original production. It's some kind of solace to me and a sense of joy to know that there are people, young people, kids in school who are doing *Lost in Yonkers* or *The Odd Couple* or whatever. All of the plays. "*Rumors*" too; they just take out the "F" words in the high schools! They're doing the plays all over the country, and not only all over the country but all over the world. In most countries I've been to they're doing my plays constantly; but I've never dealt with myself as a world figure. I can read about it and say, "Oh, look, he's doing this, he's doing that." I don't disassociate myself from him, but it isn't me. I don't think I'm a famous person at all, though I know that I am. I can walk around this little village where I live, Westwood in Los Angeles, and they see me and they go, "Hi, how are you Mr. Simon?" And I go, "Hi." I know them and I can go have lunch by myself and not be bothered or anything. It doesn't interfere with your life. I would hate to be a movie star—to be Tom Cruise or any of those people. People in those little towns that we see from the airplane say, "I'd give anything to be Tom Cruise or any major star." They don't know what kind of life that is. If you ever read about how Michael Jordan can't go to a movie, can't go anyplace with his family, without being mobbed, you know that fame has its drawbacks—so I try not to deal with it.

MW: On the one hand, you've got to preserve your privacy, but the material that you're dealing with is the human condition. . When you're someplace watching people talk or interact with each other, do you find yourself listening to the dynamics of that and thinking, "Look how people talk, look how they interact, look what happens here?"

NS: I travel all over the country, I hear people talking, and I hear the conversations, but I never say, "Hmm, that would be interesting to use one day." That never happens. First of all, I couldn't write a play about Texas. I mean I wouldn't know how they talk. I don't know how they're brought up. I only learned it through the movies as we all did. That's why Tennessee Williams writes his plays about the South. I still write basically about New York. I've written about London, I've written about California, but I'm still basically a New York playwright. I have no need to change that. By osmosis all of these things that you hear filter in through your mind, so you find yourself coming up with a phrase here and there that's really accurate. In *California Suite*, I wrote about an English couple: the man is bisexual, the woman is heterosexual. They have a loving relationship and people say to me, "How did you know them? How did you know how to write them that well?" And I say, "I never thought of him as being bisexual or homosexual. I thought of him as being heterosexual and he could just as well have been attracted to some other woman, having an affair with this other woman, wanting to be with somebody else. It would be the same problems." The reasons why they were that way are different—what their childhoods were like. When you're dealing with the dynamics of being unfaithful and still loving someone, being in love with your wife or a wife with a husband and still wanting to know what's out there: that doesn't happen to everybody, but it happens a lot. That's what I was basically writing about because I think I knew those people from people I met in the theater. I was able to capture the dialogue.

In *Proposals*, I'm writing about a black couple in 1954 just prior to the civil rights movement, and these are by no means Uncle Tom kind of people. The woman especially is very enlightened; she is very sure of herself because she learned it from her mother. And the mother was very respectful to the people she worked for, but she knew her own position too. So, in a sense, both the mother, whom you don't see in the play, and this woman—the black woman who is now about forty-four years old—feel that they run the family, not with malice but with great love. August Wilson may find fault with it; but the dialogue is from people that I knew and came in contact with in those days. People have come up to me after reading the play and said, "How did you know these people so well?" And I said, "I don't know." There's that osmosis thing again. The woman who was playing the role, Scotty Caldwell—a wonderful black actress who won the Tony Award I think in August Wilson's play *Joe Turner*—first heard that it was a domestic, and she said, "I don't want to play a domestic," and I said, "Read the play." She read it, and she said, "Oh, this isn't really a domestic. This a woman who has a sense of herself." She did the audition, and she was great; and as she was leaving, she said, "You could have gone wrong there, but you didn't." That was the best compliment I ever got. I think she's maybe the most important character in the play.

MW: You mentioned a moment ago that high schools might be doing some of the plays and all they have to do is drop the "F" word. Talk a minute about the changing standards in the theater and how comedy has been affected by that. You probably couldn't have used any kind of profanity in *Come Blow Your Horn* but as time has gone on over three decades, it could be dropped in. When do you feel like you can do that and preserve the longevity of the play? **NS:** I don't really deal too much with the language in terms of what is or is not good taste. In some places you expect it. In a David Mamet play, he hits the words again and again and again until, as we learned in that Lenny Bruce movie, the words no longer have importance; it's just the language of those people, and if you left it out, it would sound like he's writing a play from the 1940s or something. He's a person of today who has captured today's language. Most of my plays were contemporary when I wrote them—*Barefoot in the Park* and *The Odd Couple*. As they went along, *Prisoner of Second Avenue* told you the story of New York in the early seventies. And when I went back in the Brighton Beach trilogy, they spoke the way they spoke, and if there was an "F" word in it, I said it once, and it had so much more impact saying it once. In *Proposals*, it's 1954. There is a little bit more innocence to the people, but still I think in a way they're pretty contemporary because they're very bright, and it's much more interesting to write about bright people than dumb people. You write the language that belongs where it belongs. I have to know where I am geographically. When I wrote *Star-Spangled Girl*, a play that was not a big favorite of mine, I wrote it about San Francisco, a city I had never been in. I can't write about a city I've never been, because I don't know what restaurant they go to, where they go to school, where they buy their groceries. I don't know anything about them. I wrote it, and I couldn't capture it. If I'd written that same play and set it in New York, it would have been a better play. It wouldn't have been a great play, but it would have been much better, because I would've known more about them. So I don't write about places I don't know about.

Max Gordon was the first major producer I met who gave me some advice about the theater after reading *Come Blow Your Horn*; he said, "One day you're going to write a great play. This isn't it." And I said, "What's wrong with it?" He said, "You're not into the characters enough. What you've written is a sand castle. It's very pretty, but it's going to sink, because it doesn't have any real strong foundation to it. Start with the characters. Then get your story"—which I've done almost always, with the exception of a play like *"Rumors."* When you're writing a farce, you've got to write the situation first—what it's all about—and then you can do the characters. The reason that I don't like to do movies today is because they hate the word "character-driven." They're all plot-driven, and I'm not very good at plotting out things. *Proposals* is the most complex play that I've written in terms of the interrelationships between people. Almost everybody has a scene with everybody else, even though they're not dealing in the life problem of that person, but through contact they all have to meet each other. That's quite a step up from writing two-character plays, four-character plays. I really enjoyed writing *Biloxi Blues* because we had ten or eleven people in that play from all different parts of New York, but then they moved down to Biloxi and I had to deal with the South for the first time—and with the girl who played a hooker from Biloxi, Mississippi. But I knew these people. I met these people, so I was able to write about them.

MW: You've been talking about *Biloxi Blues*, which is one of my favorites. What really appeals to me is that community of people. A favorite scene of mine is in the brothel, the boy's first sexual encounter. Was there any hesitation in writing that? Obviously, people are going to say, "This is autobiographical."

NS: That scene is in a sense autobiographical, but I deal with that in *Rewrites*. It didn't happen in Biloxi, Mississippi, at all. It actually happened in a hotel in New York where my brother said, "It's enough. I'm taking you in. You've got to become unvirginized."

It was pretty funny, because it's a rite of passage. I was so fearful. The things that you're afraid of are like, "What is this woman going to think of you?"—like that's the most important thing that should be on your mind! But it fit really well in *Biloxi Blues*. What really amazed me is that I did it for the stage first; that scene's actually played on the stage, and it was very delicately played. The young man was in the bed with the girl, but they had the covers over them, and the dialogue was the same. In the film with the angles that they shot, you got more of a feeling of sexual contact going on. I don't know if it gave anyone the jitters or not. I think people just love that scene because he was innocent. If this was a scene about a man and a woman, no one would care about it. But it's the things that he had to say and how frightened he was that I'm sure goes on for young men and young women. It's a horror, that first time. I remember the line that I said. It's not in the play, but I felt it, "I really don't care if this is a good time or not, I just want to get it over with." It can be a very painful experience for some people as well as the most wonderful. I think it's the most wonderful and the luckiest if you're in love with somebody and that's the first time it happens.

MW: You mentioned your brother Danny setting you up the first time around. He has often said that he inspired several of your plays.

NS: A lot of the plays *were* inspired by Danny. I think I used the character of Danny in at least four plays, and he is completely different in all of them, because there are many facets to his personality. He definitely is Felix. He is very prissy about his house. I don't mean prissy in a feminine way, but he's so clean about everything. He wants to keep his house clean. He does his own cooking for the most part. He's also the playboy in *Come Blow Your Horn*, which is the direct antithesis of what Felix is like. Then I used him in *Brighton Beach Memoirs*, and I used him again in *Broadway Bound*.

Danny has obviously always been a wonderful mentor for me over the years. We broke away from writing together because I knew that I couldn't breathe the air I wanted to breathe and become a playwright with a brother; you can't both have the same take on something in life. After we were able to get back together again, and I started to show him my plays, he's the only one I know who would read them four times before he would call me and say, "Okay, now I know how I feel about the play." He would say, "I love it. It's terrific." But he's a real nitpicker; he'd say, "On page 54, there's a line," and I'd say, "Danny, don't worry about that line. That line's going to go. They're all up for grabs. Tell me what you think of the whole thing." Then he would invariably point to the weak spot. He would say, "I just don't get it when he does this and this. Why does he do that?" And I would say, "I don't know, but let me think about it." And then I'd change it, and he'd be right. So that's why I'm patient enough to let him go through the four readings of them before he comes to a decision. I just recently gave him a screenplay that I finished, and he got right to it. He said, "It's wonderful. I really love it."—and he told me why he loved it. There's a few times that he said, "I don't know about this one." If he really loves it, he says, "Can I invest?" If he doesn't say "Can I invest?" I know he thinks something's wrong with the play!

MW: As I looked back over the plays, it looks like there's the perfect opportunity someday at a UCLA Festival or something when they're doing a Simon Suite to arrange the plays, not in chronological order, but in order of how they tell the story. They would start with *Brighton Beach* and then . . .
NS: No, no, you'd start with *Come Blow Your Horn*.

MW: Would you?
NS: *Come Blow Your Horn* precedes it as a play, but it is about two different things. *Come Blow Your Horn* is about a mother and father living together and they're very different from the people who are living in *Brighton Beach*, so you'd have to eliminate *Come Blow Your Horn*. If you want to chronicle

my life, I guess you would start with *Brighton Beach* and go to *Biloxi* which is the next step and then *Broadway Bound* and then *Barefoot in the Park* which is about meeting Joan, and then, perhaps—maybe I'm skipping something—*Chapter Two*, which would be after the death of Joan, and about the problems I had with being married so soon to Marsha Mason, and how I had to deal with letting go of one person and trying to start a life with somebody else. I knew when I was doing it that I was covering all of the bases of my life, one way or another. Where it would go from there I don't know. Maybe even something in *California Suite*. The scene I did in *London Suite* was a scene where I had a terrible back injury which turned out to be hilarious; that was out of real life, but it doesn't chronicle what my life was about.

MW: I assume *The Prisoner of Second Avenue* was about a period in your life.
NS: Yes, but that wasn't me. *The Prisoner of Second Avenue* was really an uncle of Joan's who, at the age of forty-eight, decided to give up his profitable printing business because all of his life he wanted to own a newspaper. He cashed in everything and bought a small newspaper out of town, and after a year he didn't know how to run it and he went broke—I mean flat broke. So the idea came then of what happened to this man, walking around the four walls of this apartment literally being a prisoner. I was writing about the period rather than myself. That's not me.

MW: But wasn't it also about a time when you were beginning to be fairly disillusioned with New York City?
NS: Yes, a little bit. I noticed that New York was changing the first time I got into a taxi and saw a shield separating me from the driver that I always used to spend so much time talking with: "What do you think the Yankees are going to do? What about politics?" There's no more conversation. And then putting money through a little slot in the window and him putting it back in. In the very beginning, when this first happened in New York, the driver would lock the doors in the back, and you couldn't get out until he let you out, for fear of him being robbed. I said, "Boy, we're living in a strange city now," and that became frightening. But I don't think I would have moved to California had Joan not died. I would still be living there today, I think."

MW: Last question: You said earlier that *Lost in Yonkers* is a favorite of yours. What makes that a favorite?
NS: *Lost in Yonkers* is a favorite of mine, first because I think it's the deepest play. I went very far into why these people became the way they are, why

they are such a dysfunctional family. Yet it's not autobiographical at all. I did not have a grandmother like that. I did not have an Aunt Bella. They come from some place in my psyche way, way back. I remember there was a boy in my neighborhood, when I was twelve or thirteen years old; he was retarded, and his father used to come down and beat him up in the street and say, "I told you to be back upstairs at six o'clock for dinner," and this boy would cry like a six-year-old, and it just broke my heart. Bella is not that extreme, because I don't think she has medical or physical problems. I think she's been held back by an overly dominant mother who learned because of the problems she went through in Germany and coming to America as a Jew, that your aim in life is to survive, not to live. And that's all these kids learned, to survive. So they all became dysfunctional. The other daughter couldn't speak properly. The one son became a small time gangster, and the boy's father was a weakling. It just kept writing itself. I never had any problems. Once I hit on all of the four characters, scene after scene played itself out for me. That's when you think you're the middle man, which most writers feel anyway—that someone else is writing the play and you're saying, "And then what do you want me to write? Okay." And you type it out. But I saw the surprise on many of the New York critics when they saw *Lost in Yonkers* and said, "Wow, what a breakthrough. Where did this one come from?" Not too oddly enough, it won the Pulitzer Prize. To me it was a great surprise only because I never thought I would win it, because I thought they always considered me a light comedy playwright. I knew I wasn't as I was progressing; but I was sure the Pulitzer Prize was going to go to *Six Degrees of Separation*, which was a terrific play—as Frank Rich called it, "John Guare's masterpiece"—so it really surprised me that we won.

MW: The grandmother character is wonderful; she'll be a staple of theater history forever.

NS: Writing the grandmother in *Lost in Yonkers* was a challenge for me, because I knew I could not relent and make her nice. There's a moment when she realizes that she may have crushed this girl's life when the girl walks off the stage, and Irene Worth did it herself. I just left that there's an emotion there that is so powerful that she doesn't know how to express it. What she did was she opened up her mouth to scream like the famous painting, *The Scream*, and she stuffed a handkerchief into her mouth, and it was as scary as hell. Incredible. She never relented. You knew that at the end she liked the boys, they were nice, but at the age of eighty-two or something, she was not going to change her life around.

The Unlikely Couple

Sean Mitchell / 1997

From the *Los Angeles Times*, July 13, 1997, *Calendar*, pp. 3, 86. Reprinted with the permission of Sean Mitchell.

It is often said that politics makes strange bedfellows, but can show business be far behind? Not this month at the Ahmanson Theatre, where Neil Simon's newest play, *Proposals*, is being directed in its world premiere by thirty-four-year-old Joe Mantello, who helped make Terrence McNally's *Love! Valour! Compassion!* one of the most celebrated gay plays in recent years.

A director fluent in frontal male nudity joins forces with America's most conventional playwright for an evening of . . . what? Neil Simon Undressed? We'll find out Wednesday night, when the curtain goes up on this, Simon's thirtieth play and the seventh to have its premiere in his adopted home of Los Angeles.

Proposals is set in the 1950s at a summer cottage in a resort area of eastern Pennsylvania, where a man is visited on a fateful afternoon by his ex-wife, his grown daughter, and his housekeeper's wandering husband. It's an ensemble piece, with a cast of nine that includes Ron Rifkin and Suzanne Cryer. After its Ahmanson engagement, the play will travel to Phoenix, New Haven, Connecticut, and Washington before reaching Broadway in November.

Apart from his last-minute work on *Proposals*, Simon is also looking in on Paramount Pictures' *The Odd Couple II*, which is currently shooting here, reuniting Jack Lemmon and Walter Matthau in their original roles as Oscar and Felix thirty years later.

Mantello, who received a Tony nomination as an actor for his part in *Angels in America*, is scheduled to direct McNally's next play, *Corpus Christi*, at the Manhattan Theatre Club after the first of the year. He lives in New York with playwright Jon Robin Baitz, author of, among other plays, *Three Hotels*, which Mantello directed.

Before this current association, Simon, who turned seventy on July 4, and Mantello had never met. They agreed to discuss their collaboration and the new play in a second-floor conference room at the Center Theatre Group offices on Temple Street.

Question: Whose idea was it to bring the two of you together?
Neil Simon: My wife's. When I finished writing the first draft of the play, I said to her, who do I get to direct this? And we had seen *Love! Valour! Compassion!* in New York together. And she said, "Joe. Joe Mantello." I said, "Great idea. Absolutely."

Q: And Joe, how did you greet this offer?
Joe Mantello: My boyfriend came home one night and said, "Are you directing the new Neil Simon play?" And I said, "Excuse me, what?" He said, "I was just out with my agent and he says you're directing the new Neil Simon play." I sort of fell on the floor, and I was, like, there's not a world in which I'm going to direct the Neil Simon play, that's just not going to happen. He doesn't even know who I am. And I put it out of my head. A couple days later I got a call from Bill Evans, the press rep who has worked with Neil for years and is a friend of mine, and he said, "There's going to be this reading of this play and I'd like you to come and see it."

Q: Can it be said that Joe Mantello has always wanted to work with Neil Simon?
Mantello: I don't know that I would say that, just because I never thought it was a possibility. There are plays of Neil's that I would have no natural affinity for, like, for example, *Laughter on the 23rd Floor*, which I think is a wonderful play, but if that had been the play, I don't think I could have done it. I don't know that I understand that world in a way that would bring anything new and fresh to it or even any innate understanding. But when this play began, I started smiling, thinking, "Oh, I can do this; I understand this." There's a kind of Chekhovian quality to it. [Laughter] It may make you nervous for me to say that . . .
Simon: Well, if you didn't, I was going to mention it.

Q: How did it go at that first reading?
Simon: Joe made about ten points about the play that he thought needed addressing. And I thought every single one was a good suggestion. So I thought, "We're going to hit it off." I mean, you never know until you start to work together.

Q: And you felt this play needed a young director?

Simon: It's a young play basically. There are five young people out of nine and they pretty much dominate the story, although there are other stories that are very important. I needed somebody who was not of the older theater—not to put anybody I've worked with down because I've worked with some really terrific people. But the two plays I've seen that Joe directed, in terms of just the set and the physical side of it, were so fresh and it seemed like today's theater.

Q: You say you admired *Love! Valour! Compassion!*, which got a lot of attention for its sexual candor and male nudity. Did seeing a play like that make you want to do something different?

Simon: Well, this play *is* a lot different than a lot of the plays I've done. I've never written such a complex play. It's like a spider's web, where everything crosses each other. So the play would have gone that way anyway. But when I saw *Love! Valour!*, despite the fact that our lifestyles may be different, I saw nothing foreign in that play to me. These were all people I could relate to, problems I could relate to and the way he handled it, both in the humor and the drama.

Q: So, is it safe to say audiences should be prepared for something not entirely familiar from Neil Simon this time?

Simon: The form is new to me. I always felt that if you want to get deeply into the characters, you could only just use a few characters—four or five—and then really tell their story. But because you can tell a lot more with less now—in film and [it's] starting to happen on the stage . . .

Mantello: People are going to bring whatever agenda or perspective they have to Neil's work, and, to a much lesser extent, to my work; and then they will also have a preconceived notion of what the collaboration between the two of us is going to be like, based on whatever we've done separately. This will be viewed as these two sort of . . .

Q: An odd couple.

Mantello: Maybe.

Simon: But we're really not.

Mantello: No, not at all.

Simon: Joe has the same attributes as the best directors I've worked with, in that he is so open to everything and also contributes so much to what I should be thinking. Maybe the closest comparison is Mike Nichols. I've worked with other directors who are great with the actors but don't get into the play as much, kind of leave it to me to do it.

Q: Let me ask each of you if you feel confident saying, especially about a new play you've seen, that it's been well-directed or not well-directed?
Simon: When I go to the theater, I hope that when I come out I don't say, "This was well-directed," or "It was a good play," either one. I just want to say, "What a great night." I don't want to know what the director directed or what the writer wrote. It should be seamless, a meeting of the minds, including what the actors contribute.
Mantello: I think it happens with me more in the reverse, where I've seen a play that hasn't been well received, and I thought the play was much more interesting than the production, that somehow the production diminished the play. I think that's unfortunate when that happens. I've also seen direction that takes a mediocre play and makes it thrilling.

Q: Neil, there have often been parallels drawn between your life and your work. Is there something in particular that suggested this play?
Simon: Yeah, it goes back to a place, a resort that was the first place I ever wrote with my brother, where we were found by the producer Max Liebman and brought to work on *Your Show of Shows*. There was a place outside of this resort called Sandyville and that's where people had these cottages. If there's any of me in this play, it's only one character, one small part of the play, nothing major. It's far from my story. It's really a story about this girl and her parents and then all of the other people.

Q: Back in 1980, you and the Center Theatre Group were criticized in this newspaper for "trying out" a new play, *"I Ought to Be in Pictures,"* at the Mark Taper Forum. The question was whether the city's leading nonprofit art theater should be spending its resources on aiding America's most commercial playwright.
Simon: Yeah, but it made a lot of money for them, you must remember. For a long time, they got a percentage of the play's profits. I mean, my name is on one of those [benefactor] blocks out there. It happened, too, when my plays were done in regional theater. "Why are we doing him, he's so commercial?"

Q: Has that criticism softened at all in recent years since you won the Pulitzer Prize?

Simon: It may have softened. But you know, "commercial" comes after the fact. When you see *Chorus Line* in the first week of previews down at the Public Theater, you say, "Wow, breakthrough, a new kind of theater." Fifteen years later, "I'm sick and tired of that thing." It happens all the time. You can't win for trying, sometimes. You do a play and it becomes an enormous hit and runs for two years and then the critics start to take potshots and call it "commercial." If the same play didn't run very long, then it's a "flop," not very good. The same play.

Q: Let's go back to what you said about getting by onstage today by saying less.
Simon: I don't want to be held to that. I don't want to imply that we don't dig deep enough into the characters. I think we do. But look at commercials on television—there must be 180 cuts in a thirty-second commercial. You go to the movies and it's bang-bang-bang. I think the same in the theater: the more you can have in it and say with fewer words seems to be the way things are going now. I myself like that. I like the plays that move along.

Take *Love! Valour!* That kept moving—a lot of quick scenes. But I got to know a great deal about those people. As opposed to—to take the same subject matter—*The Boys in the Band*, which was in one set and the story went all one way. That was a great way, the only way to do that kind of play at that time. In today's world, you might have done it differently.

Q: Joe, as a director, do you think about how styles have changed?
Mantello: I try not to be a slave to fashion in that sense. You know, I feel like my job is to interpret the play to the best of my ability and to not impose anything on it. I don't know that I would do it that well and it's not very interesting to me to have a signature style, to get locked into something like that. My job is to serve the play, period.
Simon: I don't think he has taken the style of *Love! Valour!* and imposed it on this, not at all. This play was this way when we gave it to Joe. We've just worked on the innards of the play—what the characters are about, what the story is about.
Mantello: I have a sensibility, but not a style, maybe. Whatever my innate sensibility is about the world, you can filter a play through that. I think it would be a disaster if people walked away from this play saying, "Wow, that was really brilliantly directed." If you can see my hand in this play, I've failed. I'm serious. It's just not that kind of play.

Q: It sounds like you're going against the grain. Haven't we seen the rise of the director as auteur, onstage as well as in films? As in "Joe Mantello's *Henry IV?*"

Mantello: I don't think I'd be very good at it. It's not interesting to me. If you can do a play and a house falls over at the end [slaps table], you're [considered] a good director. I thought when that play, *An Inspector Calls*, was on Broadway a few years ago, it was one of the most ridiculous things I've ever seen. Utterly ridiculous. If you ask any person what the play was about, they'd say, "I have no idea." But when it rained and that house fell over, *Damn!* Now what is that about?

Q: What's the hardest part of directing? Is it working with actors?

Mantello: For me lately it's been having a kind of patience. I used to have more patience. And I forgot what it's like to be on the other end.

Simon: And yet he's more patient than I am. I mean, I watch things sometimes and I think, "If I had a gun now . . ." But then you come in the next day and go, "Oh, that's good."

Mantello: I'm not troubled when anyone in the room is wrong. I'm troubled by no ideas, when I feel like we're treading water.

Simon: No ideas from the actors?

Mantello: Or me. Some days you'd rather be by the pool.

Q: So, it sounds like directing must be a subtle skill as you have defined it, getting out of the way of the play and yet leading at the same time.

Mantello: It can be. It's always different. It really depends on the play.

Simon: The mystique for me is what a good director can do that I could never, ever do, is to know how to communicate with the actors—without stepping on their toes, without diminishing them and making them feel secure, knowing how far to go. I just watch it, I have always watched it. And I have worked with a few who didn't know *at all*. Those are the plays where the actors start looking at me instead of the director, and I know, God, am I in trouble.

Q: So you have never directed your own work?

Simon: I redirected *Plaza Suite* in London, but to direct from the beginning? I would not know how to block a play in a million years. I can visualize the entire play but I never know where they're standing. I put down [stage] direction which I don't really mean to be used.

Q: In thirty plays, you never ever filled in?

Simon: It happened to me one time, when we were doing *Sweet Charity* and Bob Fosse was sick for the day and he said, "Neil, would you direct the scene?" and I freaked out. I did it. I had them say the lines and had them cross and move over. And I said, "When is Bob getting back?"

In Conversation with . . . Neil Simon

Joel Hirschhorn / 2003

From *The Dramatist* 5 (January/February 2003): 4, 6–8, 10–11. © 2003 The Dramatists Guild of America, Inc. Reprinted with permission from The Dramatists Guild of America, Inc., www. dramatistsguild.com.

Neil Simon's new play, *Rose and Walsh*, is set for a January 2003 opening at Los Angeles's Geffen Playhouse. The Geffen Playhouse holds happy associations for Simon, since it presented his highly successful *Oscar and Felix* (a sequel to *The Odd Couple*) in June 2002.

"With *Rose and Walsh* I had the same feeling I've had so often," says Simon, "particularly with *Lost in Yonkers*—a feeling that the words came from someone else. When I finished it, I wondered, 'Where did this come from?' Ideas spring to mind that you have to eliminate because you know very soon they're not going to get past five pages. Others, as with *Rose and Walsh*, you think, 'This has the possibilities of a good play,' so you move ahead. I don't try to work the whole play out in advance. I never think it out until I write it."

Unlike many playwrights, who prefer to have an ending in mind and work backward, Simon feels exactly the opposite. "Sometimes there's a natural ending—with *The Sunshine Boys*, you do know they'll end up in the old actors' home—but most of the time when I write a play, I just do eight pages or so and say, 'If this is flowing well, then I have the confidence to go all the way with it.'"

I asked him if he was always sure that good ideas would come. "At this stage of my life, yes, because they've come already," says the soft-spoken recipient of four Tony Awards, two Emmys, a Writers Guild Award, and the Pulitzer Prize. "I tried other jobs when I was kid—in the garment center, advertising agencies—just menial jobs, and I said, 'I don't want to be doing this. Writing is so much fun.'"

Recalling his literary beginnings, he credits his mother with giving him a sense of confidence. "My mother would have given me confidence if I said I wanted to open a candy store. She was very much for me. My father wasn't so easy about it. He thought my brother Danny and I were crazy for wanting to be writers, that we'd never make a living. He felt writers came from another planet and I'd be better off working at the post office. As a matter of fact, I did work there."

His brother Danny, nine years older, was his mentor. "I saw him watching plays and TV, and he wrote a lot. It influenced me strongly, and then I found other mentors, people I worked with." The Simon brothers first broke through on radio, writing material for Tallulah Bankhead, then hit their stride on TV providing material for Sid Caesar, Imogene Coca, Jackie Gleason, Red Buttons, Garry Moore, and Phil Silvers.

"Danny wrote one play, but he didn't follow through with others," recalls Simon. The younger brother stepped out on his own, resulting in a solo Broadway hit in 1961, *Come Blow Your Horn*, which later evolved into a Frank Sinatra film. "I was so nervous standing in the back of the theater and having them judge what my career would be. I was petrified. What the success of *Come Blow Your Horn* did was to give me a sense of security that I could write plays, that I could hold an audience . . . but nervous? Yes! I get even more nervous today."

Directors can do a great deal to alleviate panic. According to Simon, many of them can tell you where to fix a play—but rarely how. Mike Nichols is an exception to this rule. "He saved me so much time and aggravation," Simon remembers. "We'd be in the midst of a show and during rehearsal he'd say, 'That's not going to work.' I'd say, 'Really? I'm surprised. We'll know tomorrow night, when the audience comes.' Mike would say to me, 'Audience? Why wait till then? Fix it now?' He had me writing at two o'clock in the morning, and it was fixed. He just knew, and he helped me enormously."

Despite all the pre-thought involved, playwrights can't always anticipate audience reactions. "More often than not, I won't know how they'll react. They surprise me. You watch with the director, hear a big laugh, and say, 'I had no idea that would happen.' When I wrote *The Odd Couple*, I actually didn't think I was writing a comedy. Maybe I was naïve enough to think I was writing a semiserious play. The man in the beginning [Felix] is about to commit suicide; his wife has left him. Oscar is down and out; he has nothing in his life except that poker game." The first person that Simon showed *The Odd Couple* to was director Bob Fosse, who said, "Very sad play." "So, it surprised me the way it went."

Another unexpected, delightful twist of fate occurred with the casting of *The Odd Couple*. "I was invited to a party," says Simon, "and met Walter Matthau for the first time. I'd finished the first act and was in the middle of doing the second. Something clicked. I said, 'This is the guy for Oscar!' He didn't know me, but I told him I was sending him a play. He stared at me as though I was crazy. That was that."

Sometimes humor is so ingrained in a script that—as directors like to say—you can't kill the baby. "You're told that the great, hilarious lines that have nothing to do with the play should be taken out. In *Plaza Suite*, the first scene of the three stories was serious, but the audience, used to me writing comedies, laughed all the way through it, so we cut out a chunk, all the things that were funny, and left in just the serious stuff. They laughed anyway, because they wanted to."

At the outset of a production, Simon clearly visualizes all the specifics onstage. "I draw the set, not literally, but I do draw it in my head. I need to know where there's a door, where there's a window, or a chair. I know they're going to move to these places, and sometimes I'll put it in the directions. The director will probably never use it, but it's like a blueprint of where they should be. I saw somebody recently who wrote a play with no directions at all, but I don't go along with that. I don't want to do the director's work, but I need to give them clues."

Pre-work, however, rarely includes writing bios for his characters. "Once in a while, I'll sketch out who they are, what they are, but if I have to do that, then I figure I don't know them well enough. I see all these books that say, 'Outline your play.' I read a book [*Playwright at Work*] by John Van Druten, the only book I ever read on playwriting. Van Druten wrote *Voice of the Turtle*, *I Am a Camera*, and *I Remember Mama*. His advice was, 'Never write your play all the way through to the end. Never think out your play to the end, because you'll know what's coming, and then the audience is going to know what's coming too.' So, if you don't know what's coming—just keep your characters going, deal with the problems they're facing—at some point, you'll discover the finish of the play."

The wisdom of Van Druten's approach was brought home when Simon recently attended an uninspired, predictable show. "I said to myself, right away, 'I know where this is going,' so there were no surprises for me, and it took some joy out of the experience. I like when you get to the end and something new happens."

When he first began writing, during the era of three-act plays, a producer gave Simon another valuable nugget of advice to sustain the climactic sense of surprise: "When you write the end of the third act, have the fourth act in mind. That way, there's a feeling that the story goes on, and the audience can talk about it when they leave."

Surprise always creates drama. In the words of Joan Crawford, so does "confrontation, baby, confrontation." Simon laughs at the definition. "Yes, but I don't put the word 'baby' in. A play without confrontation wouldn't work. What would the characters talk about? Would you say, 'Sunday, I visited my mother?' You've got to have confrontations."

Many of Simon's plays and movies stem from his memories, because he doesn't keep journals, diaries, or date books. "I used to. I'd write a page and then get bored with it, because I was so busy writing my plays, which were diaries for me—but I was glad I wrote the two autobiographies [*Rewrites: A Memoir* and *The Play Goes On*]. They became my diaries, and I remembered all the incidents I wanted to talk about."

One particular theme that has surfaced repeatedly in Simon's work is abandonment—from *Broadway Bound* and *Chapter Two* to *Jake's Women*. I wondered if he planned to continue exploring this emotional problem in his work. "No, I've worked it out in my life. Actually, because I'm getting older, it's more likely I'll be doing the abandoning. What creeps into my mind when I think of abandonment is *Lost in Yonkers*. I set that up as a Charles Dickens story: two kids, father leaving, mother dead, and a tyrannical old grandmother. I used Dickens in my mind constantly."

A misconception exists that the remarkably prolific Simon churns out plays by the dozens, and via some magical instantaneous process, they leap fully formed onto the stage. Simon is quick to correct that impression. "With my new play, *Rose and Walsh*, I wrote the first twenty pages in London, liked what I did, then forgot about it. Just this year, I thought of it again and still felt it was good, so I completed it, but it took time."

In the case of the 1983 *Brighton Beach Memoirs*, Simon completed thirty pages and initially didn't know where to go with it. "I gave it to a few people to read," he says, "first to Gordon Davidson, who told me, 'This is wonderful, finish it,' then to Manny Azenberg, but I still put it in a drawer and didn't take it out for nine years. One day, I was in my office saying, 'What am I going to do now?' and started searching through ideas I'd written. I found it, read it again, and that was the test. If you read those twenty or thirty pages years later and they still sound good to you, you know you're in terrific shape."

Brighton Beach Memoirs is one of Simon's most personal works, and the naked honesty of its plot and characters resonated powerfully with audiences.

"I wrote it as a familial play about my brother and myself and the breakup of our parents, but I didn't know what the reactions would be. We sent the script to well-known theater owners, and they said it was too episodic and turned it down, so we brought it over to the Nederlanders, and they loved it. Of course, what Matthew Broderick contributed was pure magic. He helped to make the play. An amazing thing: the actors asked if we would change the bows and make Matthew the last one at the end, because they didn't want to come onstage after him, knowing the applause would diminish."

Once in a while, as in the case of *Broadway Bound*, extra and unnecessary characters interfere with the overall impact of a production, and Simon reluctantly has to do what he calls "firing a character." "It usually isn't about the actor or actress," he points out. "When we were reading *Broadway Bound*, I had a character—a girl—coming into the second act to do one scene. The director, producer, and I walked into a restaurant, and they said, 'This scene has to be fixed up.' I told them, 'No, it doesn't. It has to be cut, taken out of the play, because we don't need it. You can't introduce a character that late in the play that doesn't bring some major news.'"

Situations like these can have bittersweet repercussions. Simon was walking down the street a year ago, and he ran into a girl he didn't recognize. "'I was so and so,' she explained, 'who never appeared in the play again.' That's the way it is sometimes. If you look to save somebody, you get in trouble with the play itself."

Trouble can take the form of personal discord during rehearsal, although Simon discounts Bette Davis's statement, "If people love each other while doing a play or movie, it won't be good. You need tension." Shaking his head, he states, "You can love each other and still have tension. Some of the best plays have starred actors who loved each other. When they're acting, they bring tension to their roles."

Along with tension that stems from the play, rather than offstage conflict, reality remains a number one priority for Simon, and he refused to compromise this reality during *Plaza Suite*. "The general manager of the show said to me, 'You can't do this play.' It was about a married man who comes to New York and has a fling with a woman, but tries to hide it. He told me, 'There are a lot of out-of-town men in the audience, men who have come here to pick up a girl and take a girl to the theater.' I said, 'I'm not going to protect these men and not do a good piece of work.' I didn't change anything."

To protect the integrity of his work, a playwright must be a fighter. Simon learned about fighting, in general, from his mother, who always reminded him, "Don't worry. I'm a fighter," as she aged and grew ill. "She would

238 CONVERSATIONS WITH NEIL SIMON

recover—then recover—and keep telling me, 'I told you, I'm a fighter.' She fought tirelessly until her eightieth birthday. When I drove her home from my house, she started toward her door and said, 'I think I've had enough,' and I knew she wasn't going to fight anymore. She died that week." He adds, "My father was also a fighter."

Simon's artistic fight for quality has extended beyond plays into a series of superb musicals, including *Sweet Charity*, *They're Playing Our Song*, and *Promises, Promises*. "Musicals are tough," Simon acknowledges, "You get to write what leads up to a song, but you don't get to write the song itself—which is the explosion of what the sentence is about, what the subject is about. It doesn't bother me, though, since I work closely with composers."

This closeness was strikingly evident when he wrote the libretto for *They're Playing Our Song*, a show that dealt with the turbulent real-life romance of songwriters Marvin Hamlisch and Carole Bayer Sager. "Marvin and Carole wanted to write a musical based on a play of mine, *The Gingerbread Lady*. Marvin would always tell me about his relationship with Carole and how they worked with each other. I finally said to both of them, 'This musical should be about you.' Carole said, 'What do you mean?' I told her, 'The two of you, how you write,' and she laughed. I came back with thirty pages about the battles between composer and lyricist, and they said, 'This is good!' Even in the best of relationships, like Rodgers and Hammerstein, you'll find conflict. It's hard but wonderful when it comes out right."

An example of a musical that worked in every respect was *Promises, Promises*, Simon's 1968 collaboration with Burt Bacharach and Hal David, which was based on the 1960 Oscar-winning film *The Apartment*. "I also wrote a few songs with Burt Bacharach, just to try my hand in it. This was after *Promises*. The process is like a giant jigsaw puzzle, because you have to find the rhymes that also tell the story—and it was so restraining. I had fun doing it, though I wouldn't want to do it again. I also don't like doing anything where I think people can do it better than I can. I know there are lyricists out there who are better than I. I did a couple of songs for *The Good Doctor*, and we lost two of them only because the actor had a difficult time. I liked the songs, but they weren't blockbusters."

Jule Styne, composer of *Gypsy*, once protested that the line "I'm a woman with children" from "Small World" killed the tune commercially. Collaborator Stephen Sondheim argued that it was right for the character, whatever it might cost in terms of a chart hit, and Simon sees the validity of that viewpoint. Simon is well aware of the mistake some songwriters make, composing numbers for the pop charts rather than tailoring them to the character needs of the show. He also has an instinctive knack for know-ing when a song should be removed. "I've been critical, working on shows, when I hear a song and say, 'I don't think that makes it.' The melody could be good, the lyrics could be fine, but as a song it doesn't tell the story. The show shouldn't stop, everything should be pushing it forward."

"We had something in *Little Me* that was terrible. The producer approached the actors and said, 'We're cutting the song,' and they said 'Why?' He explained, 'If you listen carefully at the end of the number, there's no one applauding. No one!' So, the song was cut, but the actors continued to say, 'Why?' From their point of view, being onstage singing, they certainly couldn't see that the song was rotten. They couldn't see the overall show."

On a practical level, Simon has mixed feelings about the tendency to hold musicals in theaters for fifteen years, tying up theaters and making it impossible for new plays to open. "It's difficult—not unfair but difficult—when a show runs as long as let's say *Cats* or *Les Mis*. It stops people from working, because those theaters aren't available." This is in sharp contrast to former hit musicals, which traditionally ran in the neighborhood of two years. "*Gypsy*—the most brilliant of them all—ran even less than two years," Simon comments with shock. "I couldn't believe it, because the show was so brilliant."

Whether in musicals, comedies, or dramas, Simon has generally been happy with the casting of his work. "It gets harder, though. You always find a couple of people that you love—and they hold up the play. Sometimes, you have to make compromises, because actors are working more than ever. There's more work in TV and movies and you can't get the performers you want, so you move to the second people—who may, after all, turn out to be better casting. That depends a lot on the director."

Simon's reactions about film adaptations of his work are less positive than his viewpoints about casting. "Occasionally, they've captured the origi-nal spirit of what was intended. First of all, when you're writing for the stage, invariably you're writing one-set pieces. The minute you take them out of those sets and put them in other places, they become arbitrary. They're play-ing a scene that ought to be playing there, but because the director needs to open it up to make a film, they shoot it someplace else. *The Odd Couple* was very successful, because we didn't go out that much—there were a couple of sequences outside but basically it was in the apartment. That's what it was about: two guys living together in an apartment."

Since film and theater are generally based on different coasts, Simon has shuttled back and forth from New York to Los Angeles. "I've been living in LA for the past twenty-five years, but I keep my place in New York and return constantly. I find both places tough, though. New York can be overbearing, and Los Angeles can be monotonous—neither is the ideal place, but if I had to choose, it would be New York."

No matter what the environment, though, Simon claims in *The Play Goes On* that "discipline is a game I play with myself, and I almost always win." He says firmly, "I have that discipline. I did from the very beginning. I wrote that statement to help other writers, to emphasize that if they don't sit down and put in the time and effort and do the rewrites, they're in trouble. I meet kids in school who say, 'I wrote a play. Could you tell me where I can send it—which producer or director?' I answer, 'If you wrote one version and didn't do another version, I don't think it's ready yet.'"

The playwright practices what he preaches. There were twenty-two versions of *Come Blow Your Horn* before it was produced, and John Larroquette, who starred in the Geffen Playhouse production of *Oscar and Felix*, joked that "with Neil, you don't get a finished script until a couple of days after you close."

Simon has a history of being reluctant to discuss plays publicly before they're produced, but of *Rose and Walsh* he comments: "I always hate to say what the critics are going to speculate about. They may not agree with me, and it changes their opinion of the play. *Rose and Walsh* is a love story, but it's a love story with such major problems between people that it becomes a drama. The relationships between characters are serious."

I asked if he felt that critics, in general, offered useful observations to a playwright. "The only useful ones are out of town; critics on opening night aren't. I like showing a play to my wife [Elaine Joyce]. Wives are generally very helpful. They want it to be good—but they can be honest. They say, 'It's okay,' and then you redo it again. That part is fun, and if you don't have fun, what's the point?"

"However, the last play I did—which was not taken to Broadway—was an unhappy experience, because we went into rehearsal on September 10 [2001]. I had to take a lot of things out of the play that reminded people of the Holocaust, but when I removed them what I had was this bare, funny play, which wasn't enough. I needed the drama, and I had to remove it."

In Simon's view, though, the wonderful upside of creativity is not always a professional production of his work but regional presentations that underline how meaningful his plays are to the great majority. "I was doing a book tour," he reminisces, "where they took me to a high school in Chicago and said, 'A dramatic class is going to present a scene from *Lost in Yonkers.*' I thought, 'How will I get through this?'—because they had a fifteen-year-old girl playing the grandmother. But I watched her and was deeply touched. She believed in what she was doing—what the whole cast was doing—and that's a tribute to the director. Throughout the production, there were tears in my eyes."

That emotional response demonstrates the intensity of Simon's love for playwriting, a commitment so total that it has guided him through many a voyage in his career. "Once I was writing this movie on a boat. The water was so rough that my wife, who loves sailing, got seasick and stayed in bed. But I stayed on deck and wrote. I kept looking at the page, only the page, and not at the horizon."

Neil Simon Keeps On Writing

John Nathan / 2010

From the *Jewish Advocate*, April 28, 2010, pp. 38–39. Reprinted with permission.

You do not need to read newspaper articles to learn about the life and times of Neil Simon. You could just watch his plays. His early, Depression-era childhood was the inspiration for *Brighton Beach Memoirs* (recently revived on Broadway and at Watford's Palace Theatre). His time billeted in the Deep South with the US Army became *Biloxi Blues*; his struggle to escape the treadmill of television provided the motive and material for his first play *Come Blow Your Horn*. That is only three, and Simon has written over thirty plays and musical scripts. And he is still writing, on and off. He is eighty-two, so a lot of the time he does his second favorite thing, which is watching baseball. But those plays . . .

The idea for *The Odd Couple* came about when a theater agent called Roy Gerber and Simon's older brother Danny shacked up together after they each split up with their wives. Danny cooked and kept the apartment ship-shape while Roy was the more genial half. The two ended up having the same arguments they had with their wives. Then one day Simon said to his brother that this would make a brilliant comedy.

If you want to know what life was like for Simon and his first wife Joan when they were newlyweds, watch *Barefoot in the Park* in which Corie (Jane Fonda in the 1967 movie) and Paul (Robert Redford, who was also in the first production of the play) move into an apartment on the top floor of a Greenwich Village house, just like Neil and Joan did. And just like Neil's and Joan's place, it had a hole in the skylight, which in the New York winter allowed both fictional and real-life couples to be the first in the city to know that it was snowing.

Of course, Simon's output is not all about him. The script he wrote for Bob Fosse's musical *Sweet Charity*, which returns to the West End next week with Tamzin Outhwaite in the title role, was based on the Fellini film

Nights of Cabiria. And *"Rumors,"* which begins with a dinner party whose guests discover their host lying in a pool of blood, is pure French farce.

And nor is Simon's output all about laughs.

"The comedy writing reputation is from the beginning of my career," says Simon, speaking from his New York apartment. "But apart from the first couple of plays, I don't sit down and say I'm going to write a comedy. I sit down to write a play."

But for all that, it is fair to say that Simon has taken to the limit the maxim "write what you know." He writes about himself and the people around him, including his wives. His first, Joan Baim, with whom he had two daughters, died of cancer in 1973, a trauma that led to *Chapter Two*, a play about emergence from grief and falling in love again. Simon's second wife Marsha Mason starred opposite Richard Dreyfuss in *The Goodbye Girl* (for which Dreyfuss won an Oscar), and nine years ago Simon married for the fifth time to his fourth wife Elaine Joyce. The extra wedding is because he married his third wife, Diane Lander, twice.

Simon will not be traveling to London for the opening of *Sweet Charity.* His health is less than tip top, and he is busy reworking the book he wrote for the musical *Promises, Promises,* based on the Billy Wilder film *The Apartment. Promises, Promises* opens in New York just before *Sweet Charity* opens in London. It must feel like old times for the writer once known as the King of Broadway. But it is not.

Last year a tremor shook up New York's theater landscape when one of Simon's most bankable plays, *Brighton Beach Memoirs,* closed soon after it opened.

"Things are changing," says Simon who puts the failure down to more than one factor. "It was a terrible thing that happened. We closed the next day after the *New York Times* review. We were put in 41st Street. Broadway stops at 42nd Street, so that was another reason we didn't do well. And we didn't have any stars. On Broadway, if you don't have stars, you're not going to get the people to come."

It was not always that way. Time was when there was no star name in the theater bigger than Neil Simon's. In terms of popularity, he leaves Arthur Miller, Eugene O'Neill, and Tennessee Williams in his wake.

The *New York Times* review was less than gushing, but it could be argued that it was part of a reassessment of Simon's work that questions the personality of the plays and asks if the Simonesque moral—"it doesn't matter how much pain you go through as long as you grow and learn by the experience"—has become dated.

Yet the best of the plays—*Barefoot, Lost in Yonkers,* which won him a Pulitzer, and what is known as the Eugene trilogy of *Brighton Beach, Biloxi Blues,* and his third explicitly autobiographical work *Broadway Bound*—will always be constantly revived.

Simon has not a single chip on his shoulder about theater critics. "I don't pay any attention to what people say. I write what I write. But you can't avoid critics. It's rare they're going to say that something is really great. And then you leave it up to the audience to have the final say. As for the critics who are out to kill you, I don't care about them. What are you going to say to them? 'Give me a break?'"

The big break came for Simon when he decided to escape the treadmill of writing TV comedy. He learned his trade writing material with his older brother and mentor Danny for stand-up comedians in the Catskills. Many of the performers were fading talents living on past glories. It was this world that Simon had in mind when he wrote *The Sunshine Boys.* The comedians he would soon be feeding lines to in TV were the kind of performers most comedy writers would give their writing hand to work for—Sid Caesar, Jerry Lewis, and Phil Silvers, the star of *Sergeant Bilko.* For the three years the nineteen-year-old Simon worked on Caesar's *Show of Shows* he had to battle with a bunch of fellow unknowns. One was called Mel Brooks, another Carl Reiner. For a year or so, the team was joined by Woody Allen.

"In the writers' room you fought for your life and your laughs," remembers Simon. "Sid Caesar would sit in the middle. He would come in the morning, take his pants off, and sit on a stool in his shorts. We would have to get his attention to be heard, only instead of raising your hands like schoolchildren, we were screaming. I sat next to Carl Reiner because I knew I could talk to him and, through him, I could get my lines through. And Carl would say: 'Neil's got it! Neil's got it!' That's how I learned, and after a while it was time to move and start on a play." The play was *Come Blow Your Horn* which later got made into a movie with Frank Sinatra.

"It wasn't much of a play," says Simon. "But it gave me enough money to get through to the next one."

Does he see many of his colleagues from the old writer's room? "Only Carl Reiner when I get to California." Not Mel Brooks? There is a pause. "The thing about Mel is that he would make you laugh more than anyone in the world. But he was also someone you wanted to kill more than anyone in the world," he says. It probably means no, not Mel Brooks.

There might be another reason why Simon is not coming to the opening of *Sweet Charity.* It was a project which the show's director/choreographer

Bob Fosse brought to Simon. Fosse's script was tinder dry. He asked Simon to give it a lift with some humor, which he did brilliantly. But the book is still considered to be the show's weak point, and Simon himself has said that he never considered the script as his own.

In many ways, it is a series of great one-liners. And despite great one-liners being a signature of Simon's work it comes as a surprise to hear that he resists the association. "The comedy writing reputation is from the early plays," he says. "I'm not denigrating them. If the show is funny, it's funny."

But is not great to be known as the king of the one-liner? "I don't like to think that that's me. These last forty years I've written plays mostly. I don't even know what a one-liner is," he says.

And you can see what he means. Neil Simon fans sit down to Neil Simon plays and films and wait for Neil Simon lines. In the film of *Sweet Charity* starring Shirley MacLaine, they wait to see the lovelorn Charity sit in that nightclub full of celebrities, look around and say: "I'm the only one I never heard of." And they wait for one of her fellow dance hostesses to describe Charity perfectly as running "her heart like a hotel," with guys checking in and out. But the lines would mean nothing without a context—called plays. "I'm still working on plays," says Simon. "And I never think in terms of jokes. I hate jokes. Jokes are a ridiculous thing."

With Simon, playwriting is a process undertaken with pen and paper. There is no computer. Not even a typewriter, other than the one used by his assistant for typing up his long-hand. "I get an idea for a play and sometimes I don't know where it's going. I just go line by line or word by word. But then you see it. The people in the play, they're the ones who control it. And then suddenly it's not about showbiz, it's about real life, at that stage."

"After I give it to someone to type, I read it and then I say: 'Okay, I have to make a lot of changes here. So I do it over, and over and over. Then I get to rehearsal and start making changes every day. It just goes on and on and on." And then after some thought, he adds, "But I'm slowly pulling away from it. I just write what I can every day. And when I get tired of it, I watch baseball."

Index

Abbott, George, 95
Absurd Person Singular, 51
Academy Awards, 162, 243
Ace, Goodman, xii, 32, 56, 94
Act, The, 65
Act One, 133
Actors and Actresses, ix, 87
Adventures of Marco Polo, The, 119
After the Fox, 13
Ah, Wilderness!, 81, 132, 139, 147
Albee, Edward, 135, 138
Alda, Alan, 172, 177
Aleichem, Sholem, 134
Alexander, Jason, 173
Allen, Woody, xii, 23, 38, 74–75, 96–97,
    145, 168, 244
All in the Family, 29
Amadeus, 124, 136, 167, 195
American Buffalo, 137
Anderson, Robert, 186
Angels in America, 226
Apartment, The, 8, 62, 238, 243
Arkin, Alan, 27–28, 33
Arthur, Robert Alan, 96
Axelrod, George, 8, 21, 204
Ayckbourn, Alan, 51
Azenberg, Emanuel (Manny), 105, 110,
    124, 128, 144, 176–77, 202, 214, 236

Bacharach, Burt, 8, 33, 238
Baitz, Jon Robin, 226
Baldwin, Alec, 137
Bananas, 23

Bankhead, Tallulah, 234
Barefoot in the Park, ix–xi, xiv, 4–5, 6–8,
    14, 17, 23, 25, 29, 32, 34, 36–38, 40–41,
    43, 46, 49–50, 55–56, 58, 60–61, 78,
    84, 88, 91, 99–100, 108, 110, 113–16,
    119, 123, 126–27, 134, 141, 147, 150–51,
    156, 158–59, 163, 165–66, 169, 173, 184,
    186, 197, 200, 205, 208–9, 221, 224,
    242, 244
Barnes, Clive, 72, 109
Barrie, Barbara, 74
Barthel, Joan, x–xii, xiv, xvi
Basinger, Kim, 137
Beckett, Samuel, 159
Benchley, Robert, xi, 45, 94
Benjamin, Richard, 102
Bennett, Michael, 105, 128
Benny, Jack, 150
Berlin, Jeannie, 62
Best Foot Forward, 67, 99, 119
Biloxi Blues, ix, xi, xiii–xv, 91, 103, 105,
    108–13, 115–17, 123, 129, 132, 139–40,
    141–42, 144–48, 150, 156, 159,
    164–65, 167, 170, 173–74, 176, 180–81,
    216, 221–22, 224, 242, 244
Black Comedy, 124, 195
Blazing Saddles, 65, 74
Bogart, Humphrey, xi, 42, 127
Bogart, Paul, 97
Bogart Slept Here, 34, 38, 71
Born Yesterday, 121
Boston, MA, 4, 32, 35, 101, 130, 137, 161,
    165, 193, 205–6, 213, 216

Boys in the Band, The, 230

Bryer, Jackson R., x, xiii, xv, xvi

Brighton Beach Memoirs, xi, xiii–xv, 80–84, 86–88, 90–91, 103, 105, 107, 108–16, 122–24, 129, 132, 138–40, 141, 143–48, 156, 159, 164, 174, 176, 179, 190, 216, 221, 223–24, 236–37, 242–44

Broadway, ix, xiii–xiv, 7–8, 11, 22–23, 25, 30, 34, 48–51, 55, 62, 67–68, 80, 87, 91, 96, 106, 108, 114–16, 118, 120–21, 134–36, 158, 172, 174–75, 187–90, 194, 196–97, 208–10, 226, 231, 242–43

Broadway Bound, xi, xv, 122–23, 125, 129, 132–33, 139, 141, 143–48, 152, 156, 158–59, 164, 169, 173–75, 198, 201–3, 216, 221, 223–24, 236–37, 244

Broadway Open House, 94

Broderick, Matthew, 83, 237

Brooks, Mel, xii, 5, 26, 38, 66–67, 74–75, 94, 145, 148, 168–69, 204, 214, 244

Bruce, Lenny, 167, 221

Brustein, Robert, 103

Burns, George, 60, 102, 203–4

Burton, Kate, 175

Buttons, Red, xii, 14, 234

Caesar, Sid, xi–xii, 9, 14, 16, 25–26, 32, 66–67, 89, 94, 96–97, 99, 110, 118, 144–45, 185, 204, 213–14, 234, 244. See also *Your Show of Shows*

Caesar's Hour, xii

Caldwell, Scotty, 220

California, 4, 34, 44, 46, 53, 56–57, 85, 119, 136, 141–42, 158, 176, 186, 219, 224. *See also* Hollywood, CA; Los Angeles, CA

California Suite, 48, 57, 61, 73–74, 78, 220, 224

Camino Real, 138

Campanella, Joe, 28

Capote, Truman, 34

Carney, Art, 27, 70, 149, 205

Carnival, 66

Carol Burnett Show, The, 66

Carson, Johnny, 94, 157

Cat on a Hot Tin Roof, 136

Cats, 136, 210, 239

censorship, xiii, 25, 28, 121

Center Theatre Group, 227, 229

"Change of Plan, A," 62

Channing, Stockard, 175

Chaplin, Charlie, xi, 18, 23, 45–46, 56, 89, 111, 150, 167–68

Chapter Two, xi, 40, 47, 55–57, 59, 65, 69, 72–73, 75, 78–79, 81, 91, 108, 111, 113–14, 123, 131–32, 158, 163, 169, 173, 224, 236, 243

Chase, Chevy, 198

Chayefsky, Paddy, 96, 162

Cheap Detective, The, 47, 75, 81

Chekhov, Anton, 17, 48, 104, 108, 135, 159, 188, 227

Chorus Line, A, 105–6, 128, 230

Christian Science Monitor, 101, 161

Coca, Imogene, 234

Coco, James (Jimmy), 27–28, 33, 104

Coe, Richard L., x, xvi

Cohan, George M., 93

Come Blow Your Horn, ix–xi, xv, 4, 14, 16–17, 21, 31–32, 46, 50, 55, 68–69, 76, 78, 87, 91, 95–99, 108, 112, 113, 115, 118–20, 124, 141, 146–47, 149–50, 153, 155–56, 158, 163, 168, 177, 186, 200, 205, 207, 217, 221, 223, 234, 240, 242, 244

Connecticut Yankee, A, 99

Corpus Christi, 226

Cosby, Bill, 27, 74

Counterfeiters, The, 146

Courtenay, Tom, 51

Coyote, Peter, 175

Crawford, Joan, 32, 236

Crimes of the Heart, 129

critics, ix–x, xiii–xiv, xvii, 4, 9, 17, 31, 37, 52–54, 55, 61, 69, 72, 80–81, 84, 96, 98, 102–5, 107, 109, 111–12, 116–17, 128–29, 134–35, 138–39, 143–44, 147, 149–51, 158–66, 174, 176–77, 188, 193–96, 206, 208–9, 211, 225, 240, 244
Cryer, Suzanne, 226

Damn Yankees, 192
Dancing at Lughnasa, 189–90
Danner, Blythe, 122
David, Hal, 8, 238
Davidson, Gordon, 144, 236
Davis, Bette, 237
Dearest Enemy, 67, 99
Death and the Maiden, 190, 196
Death of a Civil Servant, 104
Death of a Salesman, 121, 210
Dial M for Murder, 60
Dickens, Charles, 170, 236
Dreyfuss, Richard, 71, 74, 175, 243
Driving Miss Daisy, 188

Ellis, Michael, 97–98
Emmy Awards, 233
Ephron, Nora, 136
Equus, 51
Ernie Kovacs Show, The, 68
Eugene O'Neill Theater, 10, 30
Evans, Bill, 227

Falk, Peter, 27, 30, 34, 149, 165
Fellini, Federico, 242–43
Fences, 195
Fiddler on the Roof, 145
Five Finger Exercise, 17, 136, 195
Fonda, Jane, 242
Fools, xvi, 106–7, 115–16, 134–35, 158–59
Foote, Horton, 96
Ford, John, 141
Fosse, Bob, 8, 100, 128, 166, 232, 234, 242, 245

Fried, Wally, 98
Friedberg, Billy, 67
Friedman, Bruce Jay, 62
Furth, George, 23

Gardner, Herb, 182, 187
Geffen Playhouse, 233, 240
Gelbart, Larry, xii, 8, 26, 66–67, 94, 145, 148
Gerber, Roy, 242
Gide, André, 146–47
Gingerbread Lady, The, xvi, 22, 24, 32, 37, 50–51, 53, 66, 75, 101–2, 161, 164, 186, 188, 238
Glass Menagerie, The, 121, 138
Gleason, Jackie, xii, 14, 32, 89, 234
God's Favorite, xvi, 36, 46, 48–49, 51, 53–54, 64–65, 75, 134, 158–59, 188, 194
Goodbye Girl, The, 47, 55–58, 63, 69, 71, 73–74, 76, 81, 127, 175, 186, 190, 213, 243
Good Doctor, The, xvi, 17, 48–49, 53, 104, 116, 135, 158–59, 188, 238
Gordon, Max, 221
Grand Hotel, 61
Grant, Cary, 127
Grant, Lee, 27, 30
Gray, Simon, 51
Greenburg, Dan, 23
Grimes, Tammy, 74
Grizzard, George, 74
Guare, John, 129, 225
Guinness, Alec, 34
Gwenn, Edmund, 141
Gypsy, 238–39

Hackett, Buddy, 5
Hallmark Hall of Fame, 66
Hamlet, 21, 68, 165
Hamlisch, Marvin, 175, 238
Hammerstein, William, 97–98
Hammett, Dashiell, 126

Hart, Moss, 45, 106, 121, 133
Heartbreak Kid, The, 24, 33, 56, 62–63, 65, 73, 127, 213
Heidi Chronicles, The, 136, 195
Hellman, Lillian, x, 102, 130, 142, 150
Hello, Dolly!, 66, 145
Hemingway, Ernest, 195
Henley, Beth, 129
High Anxiety, 168
Hiken, Nat, 68
Hiller, Arthur, 13
Hirsch, Judd, 123
Hirschhorn, Clive, xiv, xvi–xvii
Hirschhorn, Joel, xi
Hitchcock, Alfred, 60, 69
Hoffman, Dustin, 27, 74
Hollywood, CA, 10, 34–35, 55, 87, 99, 127
homosexuality, xv, 112, 140, 146, 220
How to Seduce Another Man's Wife, 104

I Am a Camera, 235
I'm Not Rappaport, 195
Inge, William, 199, 211
Inspector Calls, An, 210–11, 231
Invisible Man, The, 156
"*I Ought to be in Pictures,*" 84, 229
I Remember Mama, 235
Ivey, Judith, 122

Jacoby, Coleman, 67
Jake's Women, 124, 144–45, 161, 164, 172–77, 187, 191, 197, 236
J.B., 65, 159
Jerry Lewis Show, The, 68–69
Joe Turner's Come and Gone, 220
Joe Versus the Volcano, 136
Joyce, Elaine, 240–41, 243
Jumpers, 167

Kael, Pauline, 174
Kanin, Garson, 121, 216

Kaufman, David, x, xiii–xv
Kaufman, George S., xi, 3, 45, 121, 135
Keaton, Buster, 45–46, 167–68
Keller, Shelley, 67
Kerr, Jean, 136
Kerr, Walter, 4, 53, 56, 109, 134, 149, 159, 165, 193–94
Klugman, Jack, 29
Knickerbocker Holiday, 119

Lahr, Burt, 204
Lander, Diane, 141, 151, 169, 174, 227, 243
Larroquette, John, 240
Last of the Red Hot Lovers, The, 14, 23, 25, 33, 34, 61, 79, 91, 103–4, 108, 137–38, 164
Laughter on the 23rd Floor, xi, 16, 145, 190–91, 197, 213–14, 227
Laurel and Hardy, 45–46, 150
Lavin, Linda, 103, 122, 137–38, 202
Lazar, Irving, 98
Leacock, Stephen, xi, 94
Lemmon, Jack, 18–19, 122, 215, 226
Lerner, Alan Jay, 33
Les Misérables, 239
Lester, Jerry, xii, 32, 94
Lettice and Lovage, 196
Levene, Sam, 33
Lewis, Jerry, 9, 119, 244
Liebman, Max, 66, 99, 119, 204, 229
Lindsay, John, 20
Little Foxes, The, 150
Little Me, xvi, 14, 33, 50, 99, 119, 166, 239
Lipton, James, x–xiii, xv–xvi
Logan, Joshua, 95
London, England, 46, 49–51, 78, 136–37, 192, 196, 219, 231, 236, 243
London Suite, 209, 224
Loney, Glenn, x–xiv
Long, Sumner Arthur, 23
Long Day's Journey into Night, 121–22, 131–32

Los Angeles, CA, xiii, 53, 68, 74, 107, 174, 196, 219, 226, 233, 239–40
Los Angeles Times, 65, 175
Lost in Yonkers, ix, xv–xvi, 118, 122–25, 128–29, 131, 137–38, 140, 141–42, 148–50, 155, 157–60, 163–64, 172, 175–76, 181–83, 190–91, 197, 198, 209, 212, 214, 219, 224–25, 233, 236, 240–41, 244
Love! Valour! Compassion!, 226–28, 230
Luv, 14

MacLaine, Shirley, 245
MacLeish, Archibald, 65, 159
Mamet, David, 135, 137, 210, 221
Mantello, Joe, 211–15, 226–32
Man Who Came to Dinner, The, 45
Marrying Man, The, 127, 137
Martin, Steve, 198
Marx, Groucho, 98
Mason, Marsha, xi, 44, 47, 55, 57, 71–72, 74, 79, 80–81, 83–85, 91, 104, 113, 144, 162–63, 169, 174, 203, 224, 243
Matthau, Walter, 5, 20, 27, 59, 61, 70, 73–74, 102, 104, 123, 149, 205–6, 226, 235
Max Dugan Returns, 80, 83
Max Liebman Presents, 67
May, Elaine, 7, 24, 33, 63
McNally, Terrence, x, xii, xiv, 216, 226
Medea, 150
Merrick, David, 95
Miller, Arthur, 135, 137, 177, 189, 209–10, 243
Minnelli, Liza, 65
Miss Saigon, 136–37
Modern Times, xi, 9, 89
Moonstruck, 136
Moore, Garry, xii, 9, 234
Moore, Robert, 72
Moreno, Rick, 91
Morgan, Al, xiii

Morris, Howard, 66
Mosel, Tad, 96
Mother's Kisses, A, 62
Mr. Roberts, 121
Murder by Death, 34, 63, 75, 127, 213
musicals, ix, xiv, xvi, 7–8, 15, 25, 33, 48, 50–51, 57, 62, 67–68, 99, 119–20, 127–30, 136, 140, 160, 163, 167–68, 175, 178, 189–90, 194, 197, 209, 216, 238–39, 242–43
My Fair Lady, 33

Nathan, John, xvii
Native Son, 120, 199
Natwick, Mildred, 5
networks, xiii, 28, 66, 96, 123, 214
Never Too Late, 23
Newman, Paul, 7
New York City, NY, ix, xii–xiii, xv, 9, 19, 33, 34–35, 46, 52–53, 56–57, 65, 68, 70, 72, 79, 93, 98, 102, 112, 120, 161–62, 174–75, 187, 190, 196–97, 198–99, 208–9, 213–14, 218–19, 221–22, 224, 237, 239–40, 243
New York Times, 4, 52, 58, 73, 111, 113, 135, 139, 146, 186–88, 194, 243
Nichols, Mike, 7–8, 13–14, 19–21, 38, 52, 57–59, 70, 72, 91, 100–101, 105–6, 111, 130, 134–35, 144, 151, 164–65, 180, 185, 205–6, 228, 234
Nights of Cabiria, 242–43
Niven, David, 34
Norman Conquests, The, 51
Norton, Elliot, 165–66, 193, 206

Odd Couple, The, ix–x, xiv, 3–5, 7–9, 14–18, 21, 24, 25, 29, 32, 34, 36, 41–42, 46, 48, 50, 52, 56, 58–61, 65, 69–73, 76–77, 87, 90–91, 100–101, 104–5, 108, 114–16, 126, 130, 133–34, 139, 141, 144, 147, 149, 153, 157–59, 163, 165–66, 169, 184, 186–87, 193, 197,

205–7, 213, 216, 219, 221, 223, 234–35, 239, 242

Odd Couple, The (television series), 38, 123

Odd Couple II, The, 226

Off-Broadway, xvi, 22, 48, 121, 134, 136, 188, 190, 209–10

Oklahoma!, 120, 199

Old Man and the Sea, The, 195

Old Times, 22

O'Neill, Eugene, 9, 81, 114, 121–22, 131–32, 243

Only When I Laugh, 81, 102, 164

Orton, Joe, 167

Oscar and Felix, ix, 233, 240

Otherwise Engaged, 51

Outhwaite, Tamzin, 242

Out-of-Towners, The, 11, 14, 18–20, 92

Paramount Pictures, 12–13, 99, 186, 226

Parker, Dorothy, 163

Phantom of the Opera, The, 136, 210

Phil Silvers Show, The, 14, 67–68. See also *Sergeant Bilko*; Silvers, Phil

Piano Lesson, The, 195

Picnic, 211

Pinter, Harold, 22, 200

Play Goes On, The, 236, 240

Playwright at Work, 235

Plaza Suite, 6–8, 18–19, 25, 34, 43, 48, 56, 60–61, 65, 69, 79, 101, 103, 108, 111, 116, 124, 130, 138, 141, 152, 165, 168, 180, 193, 216, 231, 235, 237

Poitier, Sidney, 7

Polan, Tracy, 175

Power, Tyrone, 204

Powers, James, ix–x, xii–xiii, xvi

Prisoner of Second Avenue, The, 22–23, 25, 30, 34, 42, 48, 51, 61, 70, 79, 84, 92, 108, 130, 141, 149, 163–65, 192, 221, 224

producers, 50, 72, 84, 95, 97, 104, 123, 166

Producers, The, 74

Promises, Promises, xvi, 25, 33, 50, 62, 105, 108, 163, 238, 243

Proposals, 211–14, 217, 220–22, 226

Pryor, Richard, 74

Pulitzer Prize, ix, 142, 158, 172, 195, 209, 225, 229, 233

radio, 9, 14, 32, 45–46, 52, 68, 82, 94, 110, 118–19, 156, 201, 204, 234

Raft, George, 202–3

Rains, Claude, 156

Randall, Tony, 29, 204

Redford, Robert, 5, 242

Reiner, Carl, xii, 26, 66, 94, 145, 198, 244

reviews, 4, 6, 9, 17, 30–31, 50–54, 80, 98–105, 109, 114, 116, 134, 138–39, 146, 161, 165–66, 174–77, 186–87, 193–95, 206–9, 243

Rewrites, 200, 210, 212, 216, 222, 236

Rich, Frank, 114, 138–39, 146, 193–94, 225

Richards, David, xii, 31, 135

Rifkin, Ron, 226

Rimsky-Korsakov, Nikolai, 119

Robards, Jason, 80

Rodgers and Hart, 67, 99

Rose and Walsh, 233, 236, 240

Rosen, Arnie, 67

Rose's Dilemma, ix

Ross, Herbert, 38, 55, 57, 59–61, 64, 72, 100

Rousuck, J. Wynn, ix, xi–xii, xv, xvi

Royal Hunt of the Sun, The, 17, 136, 195

Ruehl, Mercedes, 175, 198, 209

"*Rumors*," 123–26, 130–31, 133–34, 137, 152–53, 158, 166–67, 184, 195, 210, 219, 221, 243

Sager, Carole Bayer, 238

Saint-Subber, Arnold (Saint Subber), 8, 58, 100–101, 105, 123

Saks, Gene, 100, 164, 185, 202, 212

Scherick, Ed, 62

Scoring, 23

Scott, George C., 7, 19–20, 27–28, 33, 122, 164–65

Seagull, The, 104

Sellers, Peter, 34

Sergeant Bilko, 15, 25–26, 96–97, 110, 118–19, 155, 191, 244. See also *Phil Silvers Show, The*; Silvers, Phil

Seven Year Itch, The, 204

Shadow, The, 156

Shaffer, Peter, 17, 124, 136, 167, 195–96

Shakespeare, William, 30, 37, 68, 87, 109–10, 165, 187, 216

Shanley, John Patrick, 136

Shaver, Helen, 175

Shaw, George Bernard, 109, 192

Shepard, Sam, 135, 192, 210

Show Boat, 212

Shumlin, Herman, 150, 207

Silvers, Phil, xii, 9, 25, 32, 56, 67, 89, 234, 244. See also *Phil Silvers Show, The*; *Sergeant Bilko*

Simenon, Georges, 126

Simon, Danny, xii, 9, 16, 25, 27, 32, 45, 50, 69, 76–78, 82, 86, 90–91, 93–95, 120, 143, 151, 157, 160, 173, 175, 184, 199–201, 204, 222–23, 229, 234, 237, 242, 244

Simon, Joan Baim, xi, 9–10, 32, 37–38, 40, 42–44, 47, 67, 78–79, 81, 83–84, 91, 99, 113, 119, 121, 126, 134–35, 142, 145, 158–59, 163, 169, 173, 175, 188, 192, 218, 224, 242–43

Simon, John, 109, 194

Simon, Neil: daughters, 5, 10, 32, 43, 57, 75, 83, 99, 105, 119, 131, 141, 143–44, 151, 173–75, 198, 218, 243; on directors and directing, 12–14, 21, 35, 38, 53, 59–60, 62–64, 70, 72, 98, 100, 107, 127–29, 136, 151, 160–61, 164–65, 170, 175, 179–80, 189, 191, 196, 207, 213–15, 227–32, 234–35, 237, 239, 241, 244–45; on fame and success, xiv, xvi, 3, 8–10, 14, 29–31, 33, 36, 40, 48, 53–54, 88, 116, 138, 145, 158–59, 189, 219; and family, xi, 10, 41, 78, 155–56, 159, 218; father, xi–xii, xv–xvi, 41–42, 82–84, 90, 119–20, 132, 137, 148, 155–56, 159–60, 173–75, 198–202, 234, 237–38; and money, xvi, 9, 10, 31, 48–49, 55, 65, 81, 85, 92, 110, 117, 119, 135, 138, 174, 186, 192, 211, 229; mother, xi–xii, xv–xvi, 41–42, 45, 82–83, 90, 112, 119–20, 132–33, 137, 148, 156, 159–60, 199–201, 203–4, 216, 234, 237–38; on profanity, 137, 167, 219–21; on psychoanalysis, 106, 147, 151; on race, 195, 220; and religion, xv, 42, 65, 82, 112, 122–23, 134, 140, 181; and rewrites, 3–4, 13–14, 24, 32, 52, 58, 63–64, 67, 70–71, 73–76, 96, 100–102, 114–15, 124, 128–29, 160–62, 164, 176, 187, 196, 212–13, 240; and sports, 5, 23, 28, 31, 83, 87, 90, 135, 142, 156, 163, 192, 198–200, 217, 242, 245

Sinatra, Frank, 16, 94, 234, 244

Six Degrees of Separation, 136, 225

60 Minutes, 174

Slater, Jack, xi–xii, xvi

Smith and Dale, 31, 125, 183–84

"Sneeze, The," 135

Some Like It Hot, 166

Sondheim, Stephen, 238

Spaceballs, 168

Spacey, Kevin, 198, 209

Spielberg, Steven, 146

Spinetti, Victor, 50

sponsors, xiii, 28, 66, 96, 214

Stapleton, Maureen, 7, 20, 27, 101–2, 122, 161–62, 188

Stark, Ray, 69, 127

Star-Spangled Girl, The, ix, xvi, 8, 21, 24, 49, 53, 58, 108, 164–65, 186, 193, 221

Stein, Joe, 145

Sterritt, David, xiii

Stewart, Jimmy, 127

Stewart, Michael, xii, 66–67, 145

Stone, Harvey, 3, 5

Stoppard, Tom, 167

Streetcar Named Desire, A, 22, 121, 138, 163, 167, 210

Stritch, Elaine, 50

Struthers, Sally, 91

studios, 53, 61, 74–75, 127–28, 214–15

Styne, Jule, 238

Sunset Boulevard, 166

Sunshine Boys, The, xv, 30–31, 33, 34–36, 38, 50, 57–58, 60–61, 63, 69, 76, 102, 106, 108, 110, 112, 125, 133, 153, 158, 166, 169, 183–85, 203–4, 233, 244

Sweet Charity, ix, xvi, 8, 25, 33, 50, 108, 232, 238, 242–45

Table Manners, 51

Talbot, Lyle, 3, 5

Taubman, Howard, 52, 73

Tea and Sympathy, 186

television, 4, 9, 14–15, 25–29, 33, 45, 52, 55, 66–69, 73, 82, 89, 94–99, 110, 118–19, 123, 135, 158, 167–68, 170, 186, 191, 204, 210, 213–14, 234, 239, 242, 244

They're Playing Our Song, 108, 238

Thin Man, The, 126

Three Hotels, 226

Time magazine, 142, 174

Tony Awards, ix, 36, 53, 102, 139, 162, 172, 188–89, 209, 220, 226, 233

"Too Late for Happiness," 104

Travesties, 167

Trouble with People, The, 25

Tucker, Sophie, 164

Turner, Kathleen, 211

Twain, Mark, xi, 45, 94

Twigs, 23

van Druten, John, 147, 235

Variety, 55, 177

Voice of the Turtle, 235

Walker, Nancy, 34, 204

Wallis, Hal, 60

Wasserstein, Wendy, 187

Webber, Andrew Lloyd, 209

Weston, Jack, 74

Who's Afraid of Virginia Woolf?, 8

Wilder, Billy, 125, 166, 243

Wilder, Gene, 27–28

Williams, Tennessee, 135–38, 166, 192, 199, 209–11, 219, 243

Wilson, August, 122, 195–96, 199, 213, 220

Wilson, Earl, 93

Wilson, Flip, 26–27

Wilson, Lanford, 114

Winters, Jonathan, 5

Wood, Mike, xi

Worth, Irene, 198, 209, 225

Wright, Richard, 120, 199

You Can't Take It with You, 45–46, 73

Young Frankenstein, 74, 169

Your Show of Shows, xii, 25, 55–56, 66–68, 94, 96, 99, 118–19, 144–45, 148, 185, 191, 204, 213, 229, 244. *See also* Caesar, Sid

About the Editors

Jackson R. Bryer is professor emeritus of English at the University of Maryland, College Park. He is editor of *Conversations with Lillian Hellman* (1986) and *Conversations with Thornton Wilder* (1992), published by University Press of Mississippi, and author or editor of many more volumes. **Ben Siegel** (1925–2010) was professor of English at California State Polytechnic University in Pomona and author of *The Puritan Heritage: America's Roots in the Bible* (1964). With Gloria Cronin, he edited *Conversations with Robert Penn Warren* (2005) and *Conversations with Saul Bellow* (1994), published by University Press of Mississippi.

CPSIA information can be obtained
at www.ICGtesting.com
Printed in the USA
BVHW072057241019
562001BV00001B/2/P

9 781496 822901